DISCIPLINES OF A GODLY WOMAN

DISCIPLINES
of a
GODLY WOMAN

BARBARA HUGHES

CROSSWAY BOOKS
WHEATON, ILLINOIS

Library of Congress Cataloging-in-Publication Data
Hughes, Barbara.
   Disciplines of a godly woman / Barbara Hughes.
     p. cm.
   Includes bibliographical references and index.
   ISBN 13: 978-1-58134-759-3 (alk. paper)
   ISBN 10: 1-58134-759-6
   1. Women—Religious life. 2. Discipline—Religious aspects—
Christianity. I. Title.
BV4527.H844   2001
248.8'43—dc21   2001004135

LB		17	16	15	14	13	12	11
16	15	14	13	12	11	10	9	8

For my daughters,
Holly, Heather, Tricia, Kristin,
and my granddaughters

JESUS CHRIST IS LORD

CONTENTS

ACKNOWLEDGMENTS

I would like to thank the women of College Church, whose faith and practice of the Gospel have been my inspiration for over twenty years; our Australian friends Lois Hagger, Peter and Christine Jensen, Phillip and Helen Jensen, John and Moya Woodhouse, and John Chapman, whose teaching has had a profound influence in my life—they are faithful and valiant for the Gospel; Annette LaPlaca and Lila Bishop, my editors, whose good humor and patience made this book a reality; my brother Wil and his dear wife, Lorraine, who persistently encouraged me to "keep typing"; Lane and Ebeth Dennis, for their long-term commitment to Christian publishing and their loving friendship; my husband Kent. Chapters 4, 5, 6, 10, 15 and 16 are adapted from his book *Disciplines of a Godly Man,* and beyond that, his words of instruction and teaching are interwoven throughout the pages of this book. His life validates the truth of his teaching.

1

Discipline for Godliness

Train yourself to be godly.

1 TIMOTHY 4:7

I had been married barely two years when I came across my husband's prayer list. As I dusted his ever-tidy desk, my own name caught my attention—right at the top of his list. Next to my name were the letters *D* and *O*. I was instantly curious. What did the letters stand for? Delightful and openhearted? Darling and optimistic? Distinguished and outstanding?

I had no idea what he was thinking—and what he was praying for me. After several days, I drummed up the courage to ask him. Without hesitation, he replied, "Disciplined and organized, of course!"

My mouth fell open, my face reddened, and I cried out involuntarily. My husband was puzzled at my astonished response. He was thinking, *Doesn't she know she needs help in these areas? Doesn't she want help to be disciplined and organized?*

The truth? At the time I wasn't aware that these were difficult areas for me. More truth? After thirty-seven years—even though I've made a lot of progress—Kent is still praying for *D* and *O* for his wife!

Discipline for me and discipline for Kent are not exactly the same thing, we've discovered. Our personalities are different, for starters. My husband is a morning person, and I wake up with the evening news. He finds sanity in structure—a well-ordered calendar with no unexpected interruptions. I welcome interruptions and love the surprise of a drop-in visitor.

But I've found that while a spontaneous personality may cause me to adopt a more flexible schedule, spontaneity isn't an excuse for me to ignore the importance of discipline. And discipline *is* important for my spiritual life. In fact, it is the path by which the good news of Christ gives meaningful shape to all the days of my life.

Maybe *discipline* seems like a hard word to you now—one full of challenge and perhaps of duty. But be prepared to discover that discipline is your lifeline, something that you learn to embrace and thank God for as you grow in him.

THE GODLINESS WORKOUT

Years ago when I was in my early thirties and the busy, flabby mother of four, a friend and I made up our minds to get in shape and exercise a little physical discipline. We donned ratty old tennis shoes and weather-beaten T-shirts and shorts and set out to run around the block. To our dismay, we made it only as far as the first corner, nearly fainting with that much exertion. But we didn't give up. Every morning we tried again. The day we made it to the half-mile marker, we were so happy we celebrated with donuts! That morning workout eventually lengthened to three miles, then to five—always ending with the prize, a donut! We got fit, but we didn't take it too seriously. We understood that some disciplines are more important than others.

The apostle Paul links this idea of necessary training or discipline with the spiritual life. First Timothy 4:7 says, "Train yourself to be godly." That word *train* is derived from the very ancient Greek word from which we get the English word *gymnasium*. By New Testament times it referred to exercise and training in general. In a sense, Paul is saying, "Gymnasticize yourself for the purpose of godliness." He's calling for a spiritual workout.

It's this spiritual workout that Paul deems so much more important than a morning jog around town. He goes on to say, "For physical training is of some value, but godliness has value for all things, holding promise for both the present life and the life to come."

I'm nearly sixty now—a soft grandmother of sixteen youngsters. I don't jog anymore, though I regularly make the most of my occasional bursts of energy by using the few pieces of high-tech exercise equipment stashed in our basement. The older I get, the more I understand Paul's exercise priorities: "Therefore we do not lose heart. Though outwardly we are wasting away, yet inwardly we are being renewed day by day" (2 Corinthians 4:16).

Like the Greek athletes who lay aside even their clothing to avoid encumbrances, we Christian women need to get rid of every association, habit, and tendency that impedes godliness. The writer of Hebrews talks about this shedding of hindrances: "Therefore, since we are surrounded by such a great cloud of witnesses, let us throw off everything that hinders and the sin that so easily entangles, and let us run with perseverance the race marked out for us" (Hebrews 12:1).

There have been habits and pastimes I've had to shed over the years. For example, I used to be unable to begin my day before I read the morning news. I finally noticed that I consistently headed for the front porch for the newspaper before I reached for God's Word. It seems like a simple thing, a newspaper, but I found I had to cancel my subscription in order to pursue a better habit. I have also had wrong ideas that have had to be altered or replaced by truth based in God's Word and in His character. I've had to dump lots of dead weight.

What is weighing you down today? Those things will have to go. Once you've removed obstacles and hindrances, your call to training also demands that you direct your energy toward godliness. "But I discipline my body and bring it into subjection, lest, when I have preached to others, I myself should become disqualified," writes Paul (1 Corinthians 9:27 NKJV). Remember Paul's instruction to "train" for godliness? Just a few sentences later he comments on this command, saying, "for this we labor and strive" (1 Timothy 4:9). In the Greek *labor* means "strenuous toil," and *strive* is the word that gives us "agonize" in English.

In other words, Paul isn't promising us a cushy, low-impact workout. Spiritual disciplines call for serious commitment and "no-pain, no-gain" effort. Athletes in serious training willingly undergo hours of discipline and pain—in order to meet the goal, to win the prize. Many women will understand this easily in physical terms, having already made a commitment to train their bodies, spending long hours at the gym for the outward prize of a trim figure. But even those women may be neglecting to bring that same discipline to a flabby soul.

DO WE HAVE TO?

Why should we Christian women turn our attention to the disciplines that will train us for godliness? First of all, because in today's world and in today's church, disciplined Christian lives are the exception, not the rule. Some people might like to find an excuse by saying, "Oh, but that's always been true." Actually it hasn't. Many periods of church history have been characterized by the amazing discipline of believers. We can come up with plenty of reasons why Christians today avoid the disciplines that lead to godliness. Maybe teaching has been poor. Maybe it's the laziness of individual believers. But one reason that stands out in our current culture is fear of legalism.

Let's face it: Many of us think of spiritual discipline in terms of "living the letter of the Law" or as a series of draconian rules that no one could possibly live up to. Such legalism seems to us a path to frustration and spiritual death.

But true discipline is a far cry from legalism—thank God! The difference lies in motivation: Legalism is self-centered; discipline is God-centered. The legalistic heart says, "I will do this thing to gain merit with God." The disciplined heart says, "I will do this because I love God and want to please Him." The true heart of discipline is relationship—a relationship with God. John Wesley's words express this relationship beautifully:

> O God, fill my soul with so entire a love of Thee that I may love nothing but for Thy sake and in subordination to Thy love. Give me grace to study Thy knowledge daily that the more I know Thee, the more I may love Thee. Create in me a zealous obedience to all Thy commands, a cheerful patience under all Thy chastisements, and a thankful resignation to all Thy disposals. Let it be the one business of my life to glorify Thee by every word of my tongue, by every work of my hand, by professing Thy truth, and by engaging all men, so far as in me lies, to glorify and love Thee.[1]

Paul knew the difference between the motivations of legalism and discipline, and he fought the legalists all the way across Asia Minor, never giving an inch. Now he shouts to us, "Train yourselves to be godly!"

What's another reason why Christian women need to turn their attention to the disciplines discussed in this book? Because we need to embrace a concept that is key to living a godly life authentically—a concept we stumble over and stumble hard. A Christian's life is about bringing the will under submission to God's will, and submission is an idea that has fallen on hard times. Confusion abounds about rights and boundaries, roles and authority. This confusion muddies our thinking about God and creates roadblocks to our spiritual growth. The only cure is a proper theology about God in order to bring every area of our lives under submission to His will. So each topic we touch on in this book is framed in terms of this surrender.

With the Word of God taking my measure, God has sometimes gently and sometimes brutally chiseled away at my life to make it one of substance. God is still at work on me. With each day that passes I am more aware that the time is short, and there remains so much to be done in me. I open my heart and thoughts to you with the hope that they will help you choose to train arduously in your pursuit of God and godliness and that you will submit to His plan for your life.

RENEW YOUR MIND

What is spiritual discipline, and why is it so important? What usually prevents you from exercising spiritual discipline (see Romans 3:9-18)? What can a lack of spiritual discipline do to your life?

Reflect on 1 Timothy 4:7-8 ("Train yourself to be godly"). What is the literal meaning of *train?* What does this definition tell you about the way to approach spiritual discipline?

What does Hebrews 12:1 say about running the Christian race? What things are holding you back in your walk with God? What makes you hang on to them?

Is there a cost to spiritual discipline? Check out 1 Corinthians 9:25-27. What could greater discipline cost you? Are you prepared to pay the price?

How does the motivation in legalism differ from the motivation in discipline?

SOUL

2

Discipline of the Gospel

The Source of Godliness

By this gospel you are saved. . . . Christ died
for our sins according to the Scriptures.

1 Corinthians 15:2-3

I'm an evangelist at heart. I love interacting with people who haven't a clue about the Bible's message. It's incredible to watch the light dawn in the eyes of an unbeliever who suddenly begins to grasp the truth, and I'm disappointed if the person closes the door to discussion or debate. Why do I get so excited about the Gospel? Because it reveals God's loving plan for this world and for humanity—men, women, and children. It's good news—the best news anyone can ever receive. When a person understands God's love in Christ Jesus, life finally makes sense.

Do you remember the moment when you first understood the Gospel? Every day the good news of the Gospel is being revealed to someone around you. Seven years ago God was making His good news known to the young woman who regularly served Kent and me coffee at Starbucks. My husband and I enjoyed walking into the shop—not only because of the grande skim cappuccino, but because Stacey was behind the counter. She's a red-headed, perky Meg Ryan type who made buying a cup of coffee an experience. Even before the caffeine, you felt better because Stacey took your order.

Because she always appeared so cheerful, we would never have guessed that she was involved in a devastating divorce and child-custody battle. But someone knew—a former neighbor, a Christian, who now lived in a distant city. Concerned for Stacey, she encouraged her to visit our church.

A few weeks later Stacey, alone and uncertain, came to College Church for the first time. When the pastoral staff walked onto the platform at the start of the service, Stacey did a double take. What was that "nice man" who comes into Starbucks with his wife doing on the platform? When that "nice man" stood to pray and preach, she listened as she had never listened before.

The following morning, Stacey greeted us with even greater energy than usual. She told us about her surprise at discovering that my husband is a pastor. She asked if I could meet with her because she had questions about the Bible. We were overjoyed.

Stacey's former neighbor called to tell us that she would be praying for us. Long before we met Stacey, God had been at work in her life preparing her. She was ready to hear the good news of the Gospel and receive Christ as her Savior. And she did.

With her conversion, Stacey began a new way of life. Her belief in the Gospel's good news has become the center of her life. She is a devoted student of God's Word. Her skill in parenting reflects her desire to help her children grow in godliness. After her commitment to her family, Stacey prizes most her ministry to junior high students. In the Gospel she found life itself!

But not every person who professes to be a Christian treasures the Gospel with this same enthusiasm and tenacity. For some Christianity is just one part of their busy lives. They've got work, their Tuesday morning self-help group at the YMCA, their workout schedule—oh, and their spiritual life, too. Others see their Christian experience as something to look back on—"the day I said 'the' prayer" or "walked the aisle" or "joined the church."

For many Christianity is a ticket to heaven. They want the assurance that everything will be okay when they die, but they don't want to get too serious about it today.

Many families fit Christianity in as part of their lifestyle package. They enjoy the wholesome atmosphere the church provides, good moral teaching for the kids, potluck suppers, and women's meetings.

Not one of these last few views of the Gospel is the real deal; none of them sees the Gospel as the Bible reveals it. The Gospel of Jesus Christ is unrelenting in seeking to convert every area of our hearts and lives. The Gospel is all-encompassing. It is in fact the only source of godliness. Search anywhere else, and you have nothing more than self-reform at best and idolatry at its worst.

Do you want to be a godly woman? Since we intend to discuss the many, many areas of a woman's life that are shaped and informed by the Gospel, we must know what this Gospel is and believe it! Then, like our friend Stacey, we must be prepared to make it the center of our lives.

WHAT IS THE GOSPEL?

Recently, a diverse group of women from our church (young and old, married and single, widowed and divorced) came together to study how faith in the Gospel impacts the way we live. At the first session, I asked each to write down a clear answer to the question, "What is the Gospel?"

Easy, right? The answer should fall from our lips like the ABCs. Wrong! All these born-again, godly women found it difficult to compose a clearly stated, succinct definition of the Gospel. We were humbled! Some women wrote pages describing how to become a Christian. Others laid out witnessing techniques. Some listed the Gospel's benefits. The Gospel itself got lost in that fog of words.

When asked how they know they are Christians, people often answer with "Because I accepted" or "I prayed" or "I went forward." Notice the *"I"*? All of these answers give prominence to what the person has done. This is the root of the general confusion about the Gospel. The Gospel is about what *God* has done!

Christianity is the only religion in which salvation cannot be earned. Christians know our salvation has been accomplished by what God alone has done, not by what we have done. This is the truth that Jesus shouted from the cross: "It is finished!" (John 19:30).

God's Gospel

The Gospel belongs to God. It is His Gospel.[1] From cover to cover the Bible is about God's Gospel. It was His idea and His plan: "The Scripture foresaw that God would justify the Gentiles by faith, and announced *the gospel in advance* to Abraham: 'All nations will be blessed through you'" (Galatians 3:8).

The Bible, beginning in Genesis, reveals God's plan to restore us to what we were created to be—people made in His image, joyfully living under His loving rule and blessing. But while it saves us, "the Gospel is not primarily about man and his needs, although these are not unimportant nor are they unrelated."[2] As good as it may sound, a man-centered gospel is not God's Gospel. A gospel that primarily focuses on man's needs or guilt or feelings or wants or ambitions is not God's Gospel. God's Gospel is amazing news about what His son Jesus Christ accomplished on the cross. It is about what God has done.

Christ Crucified . . . According to the Scriptures

Jesus Christ is the central figure of God's Gospel. Our study group concluded that Paul's explanation of the Gospel in 1 Corinthians 15:1-4 is the foundational text: "I want to remind you of the gospel I preached to you, which you received and on which you have taken your stand. By this gospel you are saved, if you hold firmly to the word I preached to you. Otherwise, you have believed in vain. For what I received I passed on to you as of first importance: that *Christ died for our sins according to the Scriptures, that he was buried, that he was raised on the third day according to the Scriptures*" (emphasis mine).

Paul keeps it simple: Jesus Christ died for our sins and was resurrected from the dead. Then he adds—twice!—an all-important but often overlooked phrase: "according to the Scriptures." In other words, the Old Testament is the source and validation of this Gospel and this Christ.

By pointing us to the Old Testament Scriptures, Paul is telling us that Jesus Christ didn't come in a vacuum—an event unrelated to past or future. He came as the culmination and fulfillment of God's great plan in history as revealed in the Old Testament. That is why Paul declared, "For no matter how many promises God has made, they are 'Yes' in Christ" (2 Corinthians 1:20). Jesus Christ is the prophetic "yes" to every gospel promise in the Bible from Genesis to Revelation! The first hint of this truth was revealed in the Garden of Eden where God promised that a descendant of the woman would crush Satan's head (Genesis 3:15).

Christ Himself also referred to the Old Testament Scriptures in order to explain the Gospel to the dejected disciples along the Emmaus road following His resurrection. He chided them with the words: "'How slow of heart [you are] to believe all that the prophets have spoken! Did not the Christ have to suffer these things and then enter his glory?' And beginning with Moses and all the Prophets, he explained to them what was said in all the Scriptures concerning himself" (Luke 24:24-27).

What a "Bible study" that must have been! Christ systematically walked them through the entire Old Testament, explaining His death and resurrection as fulfillment of its prophetic promises.

Peter makes the same significant point about Christ's place at the center of scriptural truth: "Concerning this salvation, the prophets, who spoke of the grace that was to come to you, searched intently and with the greatest care, trying to find out the time and circumstances to which the Spirit of Christ in them was pointing when he predicted the sufferings of Christ and the glories that would follow. It was revealed to them that they were not serving themselves *but you*, when they spoke of the things that have now been told you by those who have preached the gospel to you by the Holy Spirit sent from heaven. Even angels long to look into these things" (1 Peter 1:10-12, emphasis mine). Did you see it? The Old Testament prophets were serving us. You and me!

Isaiah, Jeremiah, Daniel, David, and all of the rest of the prophets wrote their books in order that we who live on this side of the cross might recognize Jesus as the Christ, the one true Messiah who alone holds the words of life—the Gospel. They wrote for our benefit! So hear this: "For everything that was written in the past was written *to teach us*, so that through endurance and the encouragement of the Scriptures we might have hope" (Romans 15:4, emphasis mine).

Why so much emphasis on this? Because as Paul said, if we believe any other Gospel, *we have believed in vain*. In a day when everything (including theology) is decided by popular opinion, how easy it is to believe another gospel. How easy it is to shape our god according to what we think he should be like and not allow the whole of Scripture to explain Him.

Some men came to Jesus and asked Him this question: "'What must we do to do the works God requires?' Jesus answered, 'The work of God is this: *to believe* in the one he has sent'" (John 6:28-29, emphasis mine).

Our part is to believe. But we must believe in *this* Jesus—the Christ God has revealed in the holy Scriptures and not one of our own imagination. Here I must ask: In what gospel do you believe? Is your Jesus a messiah defined by your own imaginings or the promised Messiah defined by the Scriptures? The Jesus of the Bible is utterly wonderful! And His Gospel is the only path to godliness.

> *That if you confess with your mouth, "Jesus is Lord," and believe in your heart that God raised him from the dead, you will be saved. For it is with your heart that you believe and are justified, and it is with your mouth that you confess and are saved. As the Scripture says, "Anyone who trusts in him will never be put to shame." (Romans 10:9-11)*

It is possible that you may not have fully understood the Gospel. To make sure that you do, I have included "Two Ways to Live" at the end of this chapter. It is the clearest explanation of the Gospel available today. If you're not certain of your spiritual status, read and work through it now—before you go on.

GOOD NEWS

William Tyndale, the martyr who gave us the English Bible, wrote that *gospel* comes from a word that "signifieth good, merry, glad and joyful tidings, that maketh a man's heart glad, and maketh him sing, dance and leap for joy."[3]

A young woman in our singles' group at church discovered the joy that comes from seeing Christ in light of the Old Testament. Michelle grew up attending church. She knew "the Sunday school answers." She'd been taught that Jesus died for her sins, but she felt she was a pretty good person who only sinned once in a while. As an adult, Michelle became more and more aware of her sinfulness. She wasn't the good person she thought she was.

One Sunday evening, as the pastor traced the history of Israel, he told how God made a covenant with Israel, gave them His Law, and established animal sacrifice to atone for sin when the people disobeyed. The pastor posed the question: "How is a holy God to dwell with a sinful people?"

Michelle recalls, "I began to realize that because of my sin I could not approach a holy God on my own." At that point the pastor explained that

Jesus Christ came to fulfill the Law and the prophets and quoted 2 Corinthians 5:21: "God made him [Jesus] who had no sin to be sin for us, so that in him we might become the righteousness of God."

That night Michelle understood for the first time that "I was not a passive onlooker at the death of Jesus. I was an active participant in His death. My sins were the nails pounded through His hands and feet and the thorns pressed into His brow. Only in Jesus can I be made righteous. That Sunday I wanted to climb up to the rooftop and shout, 'I'm forgiven!'"

"According to the Scriptures," Michelle understood the Gospel as she never had before—and now it could hold a central place in her heart, her relationships, and her choices.

THE GOSPEL IS EVERYTHING

So you see, the Gospel is not just one more thing you schedule into your day planner or kitchen calendar. The Gospel shapes everything about you. The discipline of the Gospel is coming to God on His terms. That is what this book is all about. As women who understand and embrace the Gospel, we find God's Word so dynamic that it at once defines us, satisfies us, and motivates us.

The Gospel Defines Us

When we are born again, life starts to make sense. Within the pages of Scripture, we find the blessed answer to the age-old question, "Who am I?" Beginning in the opening pages of the Bible, we learn that we are *made in the image of God*. We learn also that as women, we are made distinctly female as opposed to male. Most importantly, we discover that we are of great value to God, as demonstrated by Christ's death on the cross. The Gospel, therefore, not only brings dignity and value to our humanity, but it brings purpose and meaning to gender distinctions.

We learn further that we are sinners. Genesis 3 records the decision of Adam and Eve together to rebel against God's good plan, bringing sin and death to mankind (Genesis 3; Isaiah 53:6; Romans 3:23). We find that we can be saved from God's wrath against all ungodliness (Romans 6:23; Ephesians 2:3-9). We see that we can become children of God and members of His family, the church (John 1:12; 3:5-8; Mark 3:31-35). Finally, we are partners with all the saints for the sake of the Gospel (Philippians 1:1-6; 2:14-15). The disciplines that we will address in this book are informed by these realities.

Apart from the angels, who were not created in God's image, we are the only beings in the universe who can hear God's Word and respond to it. Genesis reveals that the first thing God did after creating Adam and Eve was to speak to them. You and I can hear the Word of God! Because we were created in His image, our souls have a moral sense that can respond to His Word in obedience, by God's grace. Women, you bear the image of God and are complex spiritual beings who can hear God speak and, through His grace, respond!

Sisters in Christ, think of it! In the Gospel we need have no identity crisis. We know who we are!

The Gospel Motivates Us

The Gospel is motivating; it gives us purpose in life: "Whatever you do, whether in word or deed, do it all in the name of the Lord Jesus, giving thanks to God the Father through him" (Colossians 3:17).

The Scriptures show us where we fit into God's plan for the world and detail what we are to do with our lives. The Bible is the "how-to" manual for bringing our lives under the discipline of the Gospel. As we go on, we'll look at the work we have been given in spreading the good news, in being part of the family of God, in responsibilities to nurture others and to serve the poor and helpless. The Gospel informs every aspect of our lives as single or married women. The Gospel gives meaning to whatever we do, because as gospel women, we are doing it all in the name of the Lord Jesus. If you don't remember anything else about this book, remember that the Gospel is the foundation for every single thing you *are* and *do*.

The Gospel Satisfies Us

Marie Antoinette is famous for her heartless statement to the starving people of France who had no bread: "Let them eat cake." This same queen, surrounded by lavish furnishings, extravagant clothing, abundant and exotic food, and servants to provide for her every wish, also despairingly said, "Nothing tastes." It is not surprising that she could find no satisfaction in material possessions, but it is tragic indeed for those who claim faith in the Gospel to search anywhere else for satisfaction. As a pastor's wife, I have often had Christian women express to me their longing for something they do not possess. In their search to find what is lacking, they casually diminish and even dismiss what they have taken for granted—the knowledge of God and His gracious provisions for us discovered in the pages of Scripture.

Here's the gospel truth: "His divine power has given us everything we need for life and godliness *through our knowledge of him* who called us by his own glory and goodness" (2 Peter 1:3, emphasis mine). God's provision for His children is astonishing! We have everything we need! Do you believe this?

Do not doubt that the simple Gospel has everything you need and more. Jesus told the woman at the well, "Everyone who drinks this water will be thirsty again, but whoever drinks the water I give him will never thirst" (John 4:13). And again on the last day of the Feast of Tabernacles, He declared that He is the source of all satisfaction: "On the last and greatest day of the Feast, Jesus stood and said in a loud voice, 'If anyone is thirsty, let him come to me and drink. Whoever believes in me, as the Scripture has said, streams of living water will flow from within him'" (John 7:37-38).

THE BEST NEWS

Though we all bear the noble image of God, we find that we constantly fall to self-centeredness, envy, greed, rebellion, lust, or exploitation of others, and worse. But that's exactly why the Gospel is such good news. Right now, today, each of us can hear God's Word and respond through His grace. We can think the thoughts of God as He has revealed them. We can do the works of God. We can be pleasing to Him—and pleased with Him. We can be satisfied, in the same way Christ was, by living in obedience to God's Word and will.

I will never forget the day fifteen years ago when a young woman named Carol who had received Christ as Savior only a few weeks earlier came to Bible study for the second time. She sat, with her borrowed Bible in her hand, in a circle of women who were well-versed in the Scriptures. Carol quietly listened as the study questions were answered.

When there was a lull in the conversation, Carol said with great enthusiasm, "I found the most wonderful verse last night!" All those Christian women turned their attention to this baby believer. Slowly and reverently she began to read: "For God . . . so loved . . . the world . . . that He . . . gave . . . His one . . . and only . . . Son . . . that whoever . . . believes . . . in him . . . shall not perish . . . but have eternal life."

The quiet in the room was palpable. She was reading John 3:16—a verse many believers memorize from childhood and can prattle off in seconds—as it should be read, as if each word were a holy treasure. Around the circle eyes began to glisten as Carol's awe of the Gospel laid bare the shame of those of us whose senses had been dulled to its wonder.

Never lose the wonder of the Gospel! Never imagine that you have outgrown it. John 3:16 is not only the beautiful summary of what God has done, but it is the basis for a way of life. It ought to be the true center of our living—defining, motivating, and satisfying us. The Gospel is a woman's first and most important discipline, for it is the source of godliness.

RENEW YOUR MIND

When did you first understand and accept the Gospel of Christ? What immediate effects did it have on your life and choices?

Why must the Gospel take center stage in your life? Has the Gospel slipped from the top of your list of priorities? How will you make it foremost in your thinking again?

How is the Christian defined by the Gospel (see Genesis 1-3; Romans 3:23; Romans 6:23; John 1:12; Ephesians 4-5)?

How is the Christian motivated by the Gospel (Colossians 3:17)?

What is the wonderful, satisfying gospel truth found in 2 Peter 1:3? What do you currently think you "need" for "life and godliness"? How can you claim this promise for yourself?

TWO WAYS TO LIVE: A BRIEF LOOK AT THE MESSAGE OF CHRISTIANITY[4]

What is Christianity about? What does it mean to be a Christian? Most people have their own ideas about these questions, but in the end, God's ideas are the important ones. What does He say Christianity is really about?

That's what we'll be looking at in this short study: God's definition of Christianity as He spells it out in the Bible. There are six basic points.

1. God—the Loving Ruler and Creator

God is the loving ruler of the world. He made it, and He made us to rule and care for the world—under His authority.

Find Revelation 4:11 in a Bible (Revelation is right near the back). Read it and then try to write answers to the following questions from what you've read.

a. Why should we honor and praise God?

b. Is there anything in creation that does not depend on God's will? Explain.

c. What attitude should we have toward a God like this?

2. Humanity in Rebellion

When we look at the world, however, we can see that things are not the way they should be. This is because we reject God as our ruler by trying to run our lives without Him. Have we done a good job of running ourselves, our society, and our world? Support your answer with examples.

Now Read Romans 3:10-13 from the Bible.

a. According to this passage, how many righteous people are there?

b. How many people really seek God?

c. How many people have turned away from God's loving rule?

Note this carefully: Some people rebel quietly by just ignoring God. Others rebel more visibly by doing things that everyone recognizes as sinful. But either way, it's rebellion against God. The real question is: What will God do about it? Let's find out.

3. God Won't Let People Keep on Rebelling Forever.

God cares enough about us to take our rebellion seriously and to call us to account.

Read Hebrews 9:27.

a. What does the future hold for everyone?

b. What must everyone face after death?

God's punishment for rebellion is death and judgment. This might sound hard, and many people don't like to believe that God could feel so strongly about our rebellion. But justice isn't justice unless it brings sin to account. It's simply wrong to turn a blind eye.

The bad news is very bad, but the good news is wonderful. God has provided a remedy for the disastrous position in which we find ourselves.

4. Jesus—the Man Who Dies for Rebels

God loved the world so much that He sent His Son into the world—Jesus Christ. Jesus obeyed God completely. He was the one person who deserved no punishment. He lived a wonderful life of selfless giving, truth, and integrity, but He was executed as a common criminal. By dying on the cross, He, the perfect Man, took our punishment and brought us free forgiveness.

Read 1 Peter 3:18.

a. Why did Christ die?

b. Who is the righteous person mentioned here? Who are the unrighteous?

c. Which of the two terms describes you?

d. What can Christ's death do for you?

The death of Jesus is not the end of the story. Before He died, Jesus said He would come back from the grave after three days. At the time nobody believed Him. But then . . .

5. Jesus—the Risen Ruler

God accepted Jesus' death as payment in full for our sins and raised Him from the dead. The risen Jesus is now what humanity was always meant to be: God's ruler of the world. Jesus has conquered death and now gives new life to us. One day He will return to judge the world.

Read Philippians 2:9-11.
    a. What place has God given to Jesus?

    b. What attitude should we have toward Jesus?

    c. Whether by choice or otherwise, who will eventually bow down
       to the authority of Jesus?

By rising from the dead, Jesus proved once and for all that He did indeed have all the power and authority He claimed to have as the Son of God. That leaves us with only two options . . .

6. The Two Ways to Live
Our Way

    Reject God as ruler
    Try to run our own lives our own way
    Result   • Condemned by God
                   • Facing death and judgment

God's New Way

> Submit to Jesus as Lord
> Rely on Jesus' death and resurrection
> **Result**   • Forgiven by God
>   • Given eternal life

Read John 3:36.

a. What two types of people are described here?

b. What must you do to have eternal life?

c. Why would God's anger (wrath) remain on certain people?

d. Which of these two options is the way you want to live?

What Should I Do Next?

You may want to think more about the truths covered in this brief study. You can get to know Jesus better by reading Mark's Gospel.

If, however, you know that you're ready to give your life to God by submitting to Jesus' rule, you should pray a simple prayer in your own words. Ask God to forgive you for ignoring Him and rebelling. Ask Him to help you let Jesus run your life and to rely on His death for forgiveness and eternal life.

From that point on, it's a matter of living out your new way of life day by day—but you won't be on your own. God will be with you all the way. He'll keep speaking to you (as you read the Bible); He'll keep listening to you and helping you (as you pray to Him); He'll help you to change and live His way (by His Spirit who lives within you); and He'll provide brothers and sisters to encourage you along the way (as you meet with other Christians).

3

THE DISCIPLINE OF SUBMISSION:

The Posture of Godliness

At the name of Jesus every knee should bow, in heaven
and on earth and under the earth,
and every tongue confess that Jesus Christ is Lord.

PHILIPPIANS 2:10-11

It's a great sadness to me that "the S-word" has been eliminated so thoroughly from our cultural vocabulary. It's not surprising that, say, feminists prefer to avoid the idea of submission, but the term is just as conspicuously absent in conversations at church potlucks and Sunday school classes as in the professional marketplace.

What was once a treasured Christian virtue has been turned into something offensive, something to be trashed, virtually overnight. During the sixties, when Betty Friedan introduced the world to *The Feminine Mystique*, a movement began that shook this country and the world. Friedan said, "It has barely begun, the search of women for themselves. But the time is at hand when the voices of the feminine mystique can no longer drown out the inner voice that is driving women on to become complete."[1] Several other books published during the seventies pigeonholed the word *submission* as connoting a woman's acquiescence to male dominance. Then as feminism began infiltrating the evangelical church, the idea of submission became offensive to Christian women instead of central to their identity as children of God.

This presents a serious problem for women who desire to live godly lives. Feminist ideology cannot hold the central place in our lives. Dr. Kirsten Birkett points out the reasons why in her book *The Essence of Feminism*: "Feminism is a selfish movement, with no sustainable philosophy, a fabricated history, and an incoherent morality. It does not bring freedom and fulfillment for women, and it will not right injustices."[2]

All believers, men and women, are called to willingly and cheerfully submit to what we know and trust about God—that He wants us to live a life of blessing. That life of blessing is found in submitting to God's loving rule and God's order in this world. So submission is the path to blessing.

WHAT IS SUBMISSION?

What do you think submission is? Some people correctly believe that submitting involves acting in a kind and considerate way toward another person, but far more often submission is regarded to be degrading or belittling.

Many Christians have a foggy understanding, thinking submission has something to do with marriage and a woman's relation to her husband (which it does), or perhaps a woman's role in the church (which it also does). But the call to submission is much more extensive than these narrow applications.

Submission is yielding to the authority of another. Puritan preacher Jeremiah Burroughs wrote: "To keep under, that is to submit. The Soul can submit to God at the time when it can send itself under the power and authority and dominion that God has over it."[3]

Submission to God's Loving Rule

Of course the authority to which we must yield is God's authority. The Gospel reveals the truth that Jesus is Lord. Christians know this. This phrase even served as a popular bumper sticker for many of us. But far from being trite, these words express the very essence of the Gospel. The archbishop of Sydney, Peter Jensen, puts it this way in his *At the Heart of the Universe*:

There was a monumental difference between Jesus and the other prophets of the Bible. Not only did Jesus bring a message from God; he himself was the chief content of the message he brought. He announced the kingdom and he revealed that he was its King. The prophets pointed to Christ; he accepted their witness. He was in himself the light of the world, the bread of life, the giver of living water, the perfect revelation of God, unsurpassed and unsurpassable. "He who has seen me," said Jesus to his astonished disciples, "has seen the Father" (John 14:9). Not surprisingly, when these disciples began to preach after the death and resurrection of Jesus, their message was summarized as: "Jesus Christ is Lord."[4]

Peter preached the lordship of Christ before a crowd in Jerusalem following Pentecost: "Therefore let all Israel be assured of this: God has made this Jesus, whom you crucified, both Lord and Christ" (Acts 2:36). Paul wrote about Christ's lordship in his letters to the churches:

And being found in appearance as a man, he humbled himself and became obedient to death—even death on a cross! Therefore God exalted him to the highest place and gave him the name that is above every name, that at the name of Jesus every knee should bow, in heaven and on earth and under the earth, and every tongue confess that Jesus Christ is Lord, to the glory of God the Father. (Philippians 2:8-11)

And he made known to us the mystery of his will according to his good pleasure, which he purposed in Christ, to be put into effect when the times will have reached their fulfillment—to bring all things in heaven and on earth together under one head, even Christ. (Ephesians 1:9-10)

The message of the Bible is clear: Jesus Christ *is* Lord! It's a fact. Bringing our lives into submission to His will in everything is the key to being a godly woman. It is also the path to joy.

Jesus, our Lord, is a different kind of king, and we submit to Him, in part, by patterning our lives after His example. As Lord, Jesus behaved in a way that was different from any king the world has ever known. Rather than assume a prideful position of dominance, Jesus humbled Himself. In the Upper Room shortly before His crucifixion, Jesus silenced an argument among His disciples about which of them was the greatest by doing a most amazing thing: "Jesus knew that the Father had put all things under his power and that he had come from God and was returning to God; so he got up from the meal, took off his outer clothing, and wrapped a towel around his waist. . . and began to wash his disciples' feet" (John 13:3-5).

We see from this passage that Jesus Christ had no identity crisis. He knew exactly who He was. He knew that all power belonged to Him. He knew where He came from and where He was going, and He knew His purpose on earth. His humility on that day and throughout His life was born of this confidence.

The Gospel gives us this same confidence. As children of God, we also know from where we have come and where we are going. Like Christ, we also know what we possess. It is the love of God that motivates us to follow Christ's example and enables us to loosen our grip on our plans for our lives, placing ourselves squarely under God's loving rule each day. John Wesley knew this truth and prayed:

> Take Thou the full possession of my heart. Raise there Thy throne, and command there as Thou dost in heaven. Being created by Thee, let me live to Thee. Being created for Thee, let me ever act for Thy glory. Being redeemed by Thee, let me render unto Thee what is Thine, and let my spirit ever cleave to Thee alone.[5]

We can fully entrust ourselves to our Father's beautiful plan for us. As we submit to the rule of our King, we also submit to God's order.

Submitting to God's Order

Part of our rebellion against God is the desire to ignore God's plan for order in creation. But living in submission to God's order is essential to living under His rule. Author Mary Kassian makes the case with these penetrating words:

> Submission is the key concept to understand, for everyone is called upon to submit to God (James 4:7-10; Hebrews 12:9), and all at one time or another must submit to human authority. Believers who cannot submit to human authority do not know

how to submit to God, for it is God who demands submission within human relationships. Conversely, believers will be ineffective leaders, incapable of fulfilling human authority roles, until they learn to submit to others. Submission is for everyone.[6]

Once again Jesus is our prime example. He lived His life in submission to God's order. John 8:27-30 says, "So Jesus said, 'When you have lifted up the Son of Man, then you will know that I am the one I claim to be and that I do nothing on my own but speak just what the Father has taught me. The one who sent me is with me; he has not left me alone, for I always do what pleases him.'"

The two phrases "I do nothing on my own" and "I always do what pleases him" are revealing. Jesus was speaking about all of life, beginning with His childhood. As the years passed, and Jesus matured from childhood to adulthood, the Bible says He "grew in wisdom and stature, and in favor with God and men" (Luke 2:52). We know that Jesus experienced life as a child, a single man, a laboring man, and a citizen. He faced the difficulties that living within the boundaries of these relationships presents if one lives according to God's plan. And we know that in the midst of His everyday life, He pleased His heavenly Father in everything.

Our instinct is to please ourselves. We naturally wish to define our own boundaries, rebelling against any outside authority. So submission is something we have to learn.

When we teach our children to obey us, we are actually giving them their first lesson in submission to God's order for the family. They are learning to align their stubborn wills with their parents' will and, ultimately, with God's will.

Noted child psychiatrist Dr. Robert Coles tells how, during his training at Children's Hospital in Boston, he discovered the importance of training a child in obedience. He was assigned to a ten-year-old boy who had been described to him as having a "learning problem." The boy's behavior was rude, impatient, demanding, and without self-control during their sessions together. Dr. Coles tried reasoning with him, hoping to discover why he was behaving as he was, but each session only increased his own feelings of helplessness. Weeks passed in the same fashion—the boy having his way in the doctor's office and the doctor without a clue how to help.

One snowy day when the boy arrived, he casually took off his galoshes and threw them, dripping slush, onto the doctor's chair. Dr. Coles recalls that he instinctively felt rage welling up inside him, but at the same time he heard an inner voice telling him to discover why the boy had done it. Fighting to control himself, he walked to the chair, picked up the wet galoshes, put them in the hall outside his office, and slammed the door hard. When the boy responded that he wanted them inside the office, the doctor shouted, "Nothing doing!"

They were words his own parents had used during his childhood when their patience had worn thin with his behavior. An astonishing thing happened. The boy sat down, looking as close to repentant as the doctor had ever seen him and asked if there was something he could use to clean up the mess he had made. Finally, the doctor was able to help this boy. Dr. Coles writes: "We are afraid to impose the obvious limits children need, in many cases because we think some psychological theory requires such an attitude. Ironically, if modern psychiatry has learned anything, it is a healthy respect for the darker side of our mental life and awareness of how important it is for all of us to have a sensible kind of authority over our impulses lest they rule us and, yes, ruin us, not to mention others we know."[7]

Dr. Coles discovered what the Bible taught long ago: We do children no favor if we don't teach them to be respectful of boundaries and God-given authority.

As Christians we understand that we must also teach our children what that "darker side of our mental life" is—nothing less than rebellion against our Creator God. How blessed is the child who receives such training, for it gives her a great advantage in bringing her life into submission to God's will.

HOW TO SUBMIT TO GOD

Submission applies to every area of our lives, and we begin by restoring the Gospel to its rightful place at the center of our thoughts and deeds in everyday life. This submitting is an ongoing, daily choosing of God's ways over our own ways. We'll go on having to choose all our lives.

I was humbled by this discipline in my grown daughter Holly as the two of us stood in frustration at a customer service counter. Holly's in-laws were due to arrive in a week for Christmas, and the wallpaper she'd ordered three months earlier had still not arrived—entirely due to the store's inefficiency.

I was disappointed for Holly and disgusted that she'd been given the run-around. As we stood waiting for the clerk to return with yet another lame excuse, I fumed that I was going to give the clerk a piece of my mind. Holly stopped me in mid-sentence, gently putting her hand on my arm. "Mom," she said, "let's be different. Let's act like Christians."

I was so ashamed—and so pleased! My daughter was acting in a way I had worked for years to train her to do—to bring those darker impulses into submission to God's will in everyday experience. She was practicing the discipline of submission to the Gospel—and she was doing it better than I did that day!

Look at all the roles we fulfill that require us to submit in a godly way to authority: child, employee, citizen, wives, church members, and children of God. And the Bible addresses each of these areas with teaching to help us submit.

Look to Jesus

Jesus' prayer in the Garden of Gethsemane is a beautiful model for how we should submit to God's will: "During the days of Jesus' life on earth, he offered up prayers and petitions with loud cries and tears to the one who could save him from death, and he was heard because of his reverent submission" (Hebrews 5:7).

We learn two things from Christ's example. First, that even the sinless Son of God had to pray in order to obey! How much more must sinful people need to depend on prayer to come into obedience.

Second, the Father heard His prayer *because* of His reverent submission. Isn't this stunning? Even within the Godhead, submission was essential.

Matthew references the garden prayer as well: "Going a little farther, he fell with his face to the ground and prayed, 'My Father, if it is possible, may this cup be taken from me. Yet not as I will, but as you will'" (Matthew 26:39). This prayer reveals Jesus' intense desire to submit to God's will no matter what it cost Him. He shows us that the will of God is more important than life itself. Do we understand this truth? Do we believe it?

Is the will of God more important than our lives? It's so natural to get caught up in the ways of the world. We want so desperately to hang on to control of our lives that we forget Jesus' warning in Luke 9:24: "For whoever wants to save his life will lose it, but whoever loses his life for me will save it."

In reality most of us will not physically lose our lives for our faith in the Gospel. But we will be faced again and again with the choice between God's will and our own will. What we "lose" is getting our own way! So we must understand that practicing the discipline of submission will not happen without fervent prayer.

Does the word *submission* feel uncomfortable to you? Put it back into your vocabulary. All the disciplines of a godly woman are about submitting your will to God's loving rule in daily life. Reject the popular voices that entice you to put your needs first, to protect your self-interest and rights, to push at God-given boundaries. Search the Scriptures to understand how Jesus did it—and then follow His example—because Jesus Christ is Lord!

Sisters, we have to discipline ourselves to submit to God's loving rule and order—for this is God's will in the Gospel.

Renew Your Mind

How does a feminist's definition of "submission" miss the mark in respect to Christianity?

To whom must all believers submit (John 14:9; Acts 2:36; Philippians 2:8-11; Ephesians 1:9-10; James 4:7-10; Hebrews 12:9)? What does it mean to you personally to have accepted Jesus as *Lord*?

How is Christ Jesus a different ruler from every kind of earthly king? Check out John 13:3-4. What other times in Jesus' life did He fulfill His servant role?

How did Jesus submit to God while He was here on earth (see John 8:27-30)? How can Jesus serve as your role model for submitting to God's authority?

Jesus found that obeying God's will required fervent prayer (Matthew 26:39). In what ways should you be praying for God's help in this area? If you have a prayer list, add a petition for God's help in giving you a spirit of submission.

4

Discipline of Prayer:

Submission's Lifeline

*And pray in the Spirit on all occasions with all kind
of prayers and requests. With this in mind, be alert
and always keep on praying for all the saints.*

EPHESIANS 6:18

Why must we pray? Apart from the well-known scriptural calls to
prayer, there are two great human reasons why we ought to pray.
The first is found in the fact that prayer is the source of power for growth
and perseverance in our spiritual lives. Just as newly planted seeds need
exposure to the sun in order to grow to maturity, we need exposure to
the Son of Righteousness, or our growth may be stunted; we are left with
pygmy souls.

The second reason is that prayer bends our wills to God's will, which
is what submitting our lives is all about. I never fully understood this
until I heard an explanation by E. Stanley Jones, a missionary and man
of prayer: "If I throw out a boathook from the boat and catch hold of the
shore and pull, do I pull the shore to me, or do I pull myself to the shore?
Prayer is not pulling God to my will, but the aligning of my will to the
will of God."[1] Prayer then is not about getting God to do my bidding,
but the shaping and bending of my will until it aligns with His.

What tantalizing benefits! Yet how few of us capitalize on this opportunity to draw from "home base" the power we need to press on or to have our wills bent to God's. Why do so many women fail in personal devotions and prayer? Primarily because they do not know how to go about cultivating the disciplines of the interior spiritual life. But these disciplines will be welcome ones to women of the Gospel.

Before we go deeper, let's understand up front that the prayer life cannot be reduced to a few simple rules. These areas of spiritual experience are far too dynamic and personal for simplistic reduction. What is good for one person may not be right for another.

Also, though we will discuss five aspects of interaction with God in devotion and prayer (meditation, confession, adoration, submission, petition), there is no prescribed order. Life's rhythms sometimes demand that we launch directly into petition with "Lord, help me!" (which so often is how I begin). Other times will be spent almost entirely in confession, meditation, or adoration.

MEDITATION

Christian meditation isn't the "transcendental" type associated with mantras muttered in the lotus position. Christians aren't instructed to empty their minds! Meditation begins with the devotional exercise of listening to the Word. The words of Scripture are not merely to be read but to be heard. They are meant to go to the heart. Psalm 40:8 reads, "I desire to do your will, O my God; your law is within my heart."

Meditation is also verbal. When the psalmist speaks of meditating on the law of God day and night (1:2), he uses a word that means "to mutter." Muttering God's Word back to Him in prayer involves committing it to memory or praying with an open Bible. So, along with systematic reading of the Bible, we ought to select meaningful segments to reverently verbalize.

When my children were young, I memorized Philippians 4:6 for this purpose: "Do not be anxious about anything, but in everything, by prayer and petition, with thanksgiving, present your requests to God. And the peace of God, which transcends all understanding, will guard your hearts and your minds in Christ Jesus."

Because I did this, I found myself continually rehearsing the much-needed phrases, "Do not be anxious about anything;" "Thank You, Lord, for Your promised peace." I would "make my requests known to God."

You might start with a single verse or pair of verses. There are longer, classic passages that seem tailor-made for meditation, such as the Ten Commandments, the eight Beatitudes, and the Lord's Prayer. Slowly and prayerfully turning over Scripture in this manner engages the eyes, the ears, and the mouth, and drills through to the heart. The effects of meditation bring:

Revival—"The law of the LORD is perfect, reviving the soul" (Psalm 19:7).

Wisdom—"The statutes of the LORD are trustworthy, making wise the simple" (Psalm 19:8); "Oh, how I love your law! I meditate on it all day long. Your commands make me wiser than my enemies, for they are ever with me" (Psalm 119:97-98).

Increased Faith—"Consequently, faith comes from hearing the message, and the message is heard through the word of Christ" (Romans 10:17).

So how do we meditate? The Bible says meditation should be continual, "day and night" (Psalm 1:2; 119:97, 148; Psalm 63:6). Ideally, you could make meditation part of your devotions, your quiet time apart with God. But even your busy schedule can be punctuated with scriptural meditation—in the car, at lunch break, while waiting for a bus. Write a text on a card and slip it in your pocket or purse. Pull it out in a spare moment. Murmur it. Memorize it. Pray it. Say it. Share it.

CONFESSION

Confession can take place anytime. Ideally, it ought to take place whenever we sin. But most often we are too proud and emotionally charged to acknowledge our sin at the time we commit it—say, when we lose our temper in an argument. But devotion becomes impossible if we are overloaded with guilt.

If you've put off admitting your sins to God, confession may need to come first in your devotional time. It is rare indeed for me to begin prayer with anything other than confession. I'm so adept at sinning and so inept at "fessing up" until it is necessary. Coming to God in prayer necessitates confession of sin.

As you meditate on Scripture, hidden sins may come to light, so your moments of devotion may be filled with repeated confession. Psalm 139, which sets out to contemplate God's omnipotence and omniscience, ends with a prayer for divine investigation of the psalmist's soul: "Search me, O God, and know my heart; test me and know my anxious thoughts. See if there is any offensive way in me, and lead me in the way everlasting" (139:23-24).

These are spontaneous confessions offered to God as your wrongdoing comes to mind. But your discipline of prayer ought to involve some systematic confession as well. We must regularly examine ourselves in view of Romans 3:9-20, which reveals that every area of our lives is tainted by sin. Directing our congregation in confession of sin, my husband often draws our attention to this truth by leading us to confess that we are sinners in thought and word and deed.

Thought: "There is no one righteous, not even one; there is no one who understands, no one who seeks God. All have turned away, they have together become worthless; there is no one who does good, not even one" (vv. 10-12).

Word: "Their throats are open graves; their tongues practice deceit. The poison of vipers is on their lips. Their mouths are full of cursing and bitterness" (vv. 13-14).

Deed: "Their feet are swift to shed blood; ruin and misery mark their ways, and the way of peace they do not know" (vv. 15-17).

I am not saying that we simply fail God, but rather that our sin profoundly affects every part of us. Pondering this understanding of sin can then help us confess specific sins in each of these areas, sins either of commission or omission through our own fault.

The importance of confession cannot be overstated. "If I had cherished sin in my heart, the LORD would not have listened" (Psalm 66:18; see also Proverbs 28:13). Unconfessed sin makes us avoid prayer because God seems distant, but confession restores our relationship with Him and brings us back into His favor.

ADORATION

The devotional aspects of our prayer time result in adoration—that is, telling God what we treasure about Him. Reverence—which is often missing—must always characterize our time with God. And along with reverence we need concentration. That means our minds must be fully engaged. This is the best reason for giving your freshest, most attentive time of day to your devotions.

Reverence for God makes us aware of our own humble state. Humility leads to praise. When I praise a friend or a grandchild, I acknowledge something I appreciate about the person. "Well done!" I say, if he or she has reached a goal or done a good job in some area. Or "You are always so kind," or "Wow—that was really generous!" That's how it is with God: I tell Him what I appreciate about Him. Praise is what we will do in eternity, saying things such as: "You are worthy, our Lord and God, to receive glory and honor and power, for you created all things, and by your will they were created and have their being" (Revelation 4:11).

At the heart of adoration is contemplation, especially in considering God as seen in His creation. The Psalms don't ever suggest that God is in His creation, but they tell us that His excellencies can be seen in His created works. Psalm 29 ascribes glory to God through the visual medium of a great thunderstorm. Psalm 19 begins: "The heavens declare the glory of God; the skies proclaim the work of his hands. Day after day they pour forth speech; night after night they display knowledge" (19:1-2). Listen to God speak through creation, says the psalmist. In contrast, Psalm 139 celebrates God's omniscience (vv. 1-6), omnipresence (vv. 7-12), and omnipotence (vv. 13-16) in the creation of the human mind and body.

Have you ever been "knocked breathless" by nature?[2] At such times nature radiates the glory of God. If you have witnessed the power of a Midwest thunderstorm, you'll know what I'm talking about. While weeding the summer garden on Wisconsin's Door County Peninsula, I watched ominous black clouds surge in from the west like a great wave engulfing everything in its way. The storm came with such fierce suddenness that my eighty-year-old mother and young granddaughters and I ran for the house. We stood on the porch watching the storm envelop the blue sky to the east, lightning flashing from horizon to horizon. Mother was so in awe that she grabbed her camera and has pictures to verify the event that caused us to cry out in praise of God's awesome power in creation.

Through the Scriptures, theologians have discerned about twenty attributes of God. Contemplation of these attributes has been a time-honored avenue to adoration. Spending twenty consecutive days with a book such as J. I. Packer's *Knowing God*—a book on God's attributes—can give you insights that lift both mind and soul.[3]

You will express your fervent adoration with spoken words. Sometimes I find myself singing—even my off-pitch melodies express praise of God. Pray or read or sing God's Word back to Him. The Psalms are perfect for this because they are a worship manual, but there are some fabulous New Testament hymns as well, such as Mary's Magnificat (Luke 1:46-55). Her song is among my favorites.

The traditional hymns of the church and the beautiful Scripture songs that are more recent are a source of poetic praise set to music. I have included in the appendix a list of songs for you to enjoy. Don't make the mistake of neglecting this rich source of theology and adoration. They are your heritage!

SUBMISSION

Adoration quite naturally leads to the presentation of our bodies—of our entire lives—in an ultimate act of worship. This is how Isaiah spoke of his great experience with God: "Here am I. Send me!" (Isaiah 6:8). Similarly, after the apostle Paul says, "For from him and through him and to him are all things. To him be the glory forever! Amen" (Romans 11:36), he immediately calls us to submission: "Therefore, I urge you, brothers, in view of God's mercy, to offer your bodies as living sacrifices, holy and pleasing to God—this is your spiritual act of worship" (Romans 12:1).

Our devotion results in a conscious yielding of every part of our personality, every ambition, every relationship, and every hope to Him. Submission to God's will is the true heart of worship.

PETITION

Meditation, confession, adoration, and submission prepare us for petition—the offering of our requests to God. Five elements are necessary to experience fully the power of petitionary prayer.

In the Spirit

The first is to "pray in the spirit." In Romans Paul explains, "In the same way, the Spirit helps us in our weakness. We do not know what we ought to pray for, but the Spirit himself intercedes for us with groans that words cannot express. And he who searches our hearts knows the mind of the Spirit, because the Spirit intercedes for the saints in accordance with God's will" (Romans 8:26-27).

The indwelling Holy Spirit both prays for us and joins us in our praying, infusing His prayers into ours so that we can "pray in the Spirit." Jude 20 offers a further challenge to experience this phenomenon: "But you, dear friends, build yourselves up in your most holy faith and pray in the Holy Spirit." Praying in the Spirit is the will of God, and what God wills, He empowers as we let Him.

Two supernatural things happen when we pray in the Spirit. First, the Holy Spirit tells us what we ought to pray for, and He does this through the Scriptures. As He shows us what needs prayer, He gives us the absolute conviction that certain things are in God's will.

I experienced this while praying for my teenaged daughter. I was concerned that she was not on the right track spiritually, fearful that she might make a decision with lifelong consequences. Down on my knees, open Bible before me, I was reading and praying. In 1 John I read these words: "Everyone born of God overcomes the world. This is the victory that has overcome the world, even our faith" (1 John 5:4). I knew immediately that this was not my present experience, for I was fearful and fretting—hardly "overcoming" or "victorious." Confessing my sin, I continued reading: "This is the confidence we have in approaching God: that if we ask anything according to his will, he hears us. And if we know that he hears us—whatever we ask—we know that we have what we asked of him. If anyone sees his brother commit a sin that does not lead to death, he should pray and *God will give him life*" (1 John 5:14-16, emphasis mine).

I didn't know what a sin that leads to death was, but I was quite certain my daughter was not committing it. This passage revealed to me that I could pray with confidence for what is most important for my daughter—God's will and her spiritual life. The passage provided a promise that my prayers would bring her "life." How and when God would bring about His will was His business; it was my choice whether I would trust Him to do what He promised. And did I pray! The Spirit of God, through the Scripture, informed my prayers.

The other benefit of praying in the Spirit is that it supplies the energizing of the Holy Spirit for prayer, giving tired, even infirm, bodies strength and lifting the depressed to pray with power and conviction for God's work. And that most certainly happened to me; I rose from that prayer time with a peace and confidence I hadn't experienced in months.

Continual Prayer

The second ingredient of petitionary prayer is that it is continuous—"on all occasions" (see Acts 1:14; 2:42; 1 Thessalonians 5:17; Philippians 4:6).

Is continual prayer even possible? Yes and no. It is impossible to carry on a running dialogue while we are working or at other times, but the prayer called for here is not so much the articulation of words as the posture of the heart.

The irrepressible medieval monk Brother Lawrence recorded his experience of continual prayer in the classic *The Practice of the Presence of God*: "In the noise and clatter of my kitchen, while several persons are at the same time calling for different things, I possess God in as great tranquility as if I were on my knees."[4]

Susannah Wesley, mother of nineteen children (including theologian Charles Wesley and hymn writer John Wesley), used to enjoy the Lord's presence right in the middle of her noisy kitchen, just by sitting down and throwing her apron over her head. She created a quiet space, however small, to be with the Lord.

Her son John wrote of the prayerful person: "His heart is ever lifted up to God at all times and in all places. In this he is never hindered, much less interrupted, by any person or thing. . . . His heart is ever with the Lord. Whether he lie down or rise up, God is in all his thoughts; he walks with God continually."[5]

This life of continual prayer isn't meant for just the spiritual elite but for all of us. Continual prayer is God's will for every Christian—no exceptions. We must always be looking up, even when driving to work or cleaning the house.

Varied Prayer

The third aspect of the prayer life is that it is varied—"with all kinds of prayers and requests." Paul wrote to Timothy, "I urge, then, first of all, that requests, prayers, intercession and thanksgiving be made for everyone" (1 Timothy 2:1). Varied prayer grows out of continual prayer because, as we pray continually, the various situations we encounter demand a variety of prayers—prayers to resist temptation, prayer for wisdom, for power, for self-restraint, for protection of others, for growth, for conviction.

Persistent Prayer

The fourth aspect of effective prayer is persistence. "With this in mind, be alert and always keep on praying for all the saints" (Ephesians 6:18). In one of His prayer parables, the Lord dramatized what He wants from all believers:

> *Then Jesus told his disciples a parable to show them that they should always pray and not give up. He said: "In a certain town there was a judge who neither feared God nor cared about men. And there was a widow in that town who kept coming to him with the plea, 'Grant me justice against my adversary.' For some time he refused. But finally he said to himself, 'Even though I don't fear God or care about men, yet because this widow keeps bothering me, I will see that she gets justice, so that she won't eventually wear me out with her coming!'" (Luke 18:1-5).*

At the end of the Sermon on the Mount, Jesus charged His followers to prayerful tenacity: "Ask and it will be given to you; seek and you will find; knock and the door will be opened to you" (Matthew 7:7). Jesus' words actually read: "Keep on asking, and it shall be given to you; keep on seeking, and you will find; keep on knocking, and it shall be opened to you." Such tenacity is what Paul had in mind when he said to "be alert and always keep on praying." God answers persistent prayer.

Intercessory Prayer

The fifth aspect of prayer is intercessory prayer—"for all the saints," that is, for believers in Jesus Christ. My favorite way to pray is to use the prayers in Scripture. They allow me to pray for others in a way I couldn't on my own. Some of these are Ephesians 1:17-19 and 3:16-19, Philippians 1:9-11, and Colossians 1:9-10.

Petitionary prayers for others bring grace to their lives. Few people know, for instance, that the stupendous achievement of William Carey in India was fueled by his bedridden sister who prayed for him for over fifty years.

MAKING PRAYER HAPPEN

The fivefold guide to petitionary prayer is beautiful—prayer in the *Spirit, continual, varied, persistent,* and *intercessory.* It's easy to feel challenged and motivated, but to make it happen in our lives, we have to get practical.

One thing I do that keeps me praying for people outside my immediate family is to make use of the church bulletin. Every week it lists the sick, the grieving, the weekly featured missionaries, and budgetary needs for the church. The bulletin serves as a great up-to-date ready-made prayer list.

Laura Klenk was a most devoted "pray-er." Her daughter-in-law tells me that her method was simple. As she became aware of a prayer need, she would write it down on her prayer list. This list consisted of a number of long, narrow pieces of paper (about three by twelve inches) that would easily fit into her purse. She was continually adding pages, paper clipping them to the existing list. She seldom removed a page. Over time, her sheaf of pages became dog-eared and well worn.

She regularly spent many hours in quiet prayer at home, thumbing through the list. Often when her daughter-in-law visited, Laura would be sitting, Bible and prayer list in hand. She kept the list in her purse so that it was always handy, making the most of time spent waiting in various places (such as a doctor's office). If you asked her to pray, you could be certain that she *would* pray. And she never failed to follow up, asking what the results of her prayers might be. She really looked for God's answers and actions and was delighted when she saw His work that many of us might have overlooked.

Every Christian woman's prayers should include her family. Making a list of her concerns for her family members is a necessity. Otherwise it is so easy to neglect to pray for details, praying general prayers: "Lord, please bless Susie."

My prayer list tames my wandering mind, and it also helps me pray not only for what is important to me, but also for what is important to those who have asked for my prayers.

Besides your prayer list, the next gift you can give your prayer life is some peace and quiet—a challenge in these media-infested times. Choose a situation that works for you. Pick a place where you won't be disturbed. This is much easier for me (now that I have an empty nest) than it is for my daughters who have several young children under foot. But it is possible even for them. Sometimes the best praying is done when you are up regularly in the night with little ones. You are definitely sleep deprived, but the house is always quiet! The point is—where there is a will, there is a way.

Try to give your best time to prayer. If you are a night owl, pray before bedtime. You may find you need some preparation—a shower and a cup of coffee, for example. Just make sure that your mind is fully engaged.

Don't kill your prayer life with some legalistic commitment to pray for a lengthy, set amount of time. Often the best prayers are short and passionate. Make your prayers frequent and fervent, as Martin Luther has suggested.[6]

WORK FOR IT

St. Augustine's *Confessions* reveals that his early life provided little hint of the great Christian he would one day be. From all indications, the brilliant young man would become a dissolute professional, probably in law or academia. As a seventeen-year-old student, he acquired a live-in girlfriend who shared his bed for a decade and bore him an illegitimate son. Intellectually, Augustine embraced not Christianity, but heresy popular during his day, which smugly claimed to reconcile philosophy and religion. At the age of twenty-three, while teaching rhetoric, Augustine wrote a book with a title that today sounds very much twenty-first century: *On the Beautiful and the Fit*. Augustine was hardly a candidate for the church, much less sainthood.

But Augustine had something special going for him—his mother,

Monica, a woman of immense faith and persistent prayer. Her prayers pursued him from North Africa to Rome and then to Milan, where he was soundly converted. Augustine became the greatest theologian of the early church.

When Monica died, he expressed his grief: "I wept [for] my mother . . . the mother who for the time was dead to mine eyes, who had for many years wept for me, that I might live in Thine eyes."[7]

A member of our church, Marilee Melvin, wrote in our church newsletter about her mother's dependence on prayer:

> I remember a night when I was asked to help get dinner on the table. Dad was out of town, and Mom, seven months pregnant and caring for five children ages two to nine, was serving my most-hated meal—black-eyed peas and Spam. . . . I complained loudly about the dinner, and soon Mom disappeared from the kitchen. I called to find her and got no answer. . . . Something drew me to the basement, and I found her at last in the furnace room. It was completely dark, and she was crying. Seeing her seven-year-old standing there in fear, she wiped her eyes and told me she needed to come pray for more strength. That early image of Mom as intercessor and supplicant fills my mind and memory now with its poignancy and truth. Instead of shouting in anger at my childish insensitivity, she withdrew to call on more reserves from her heavenly Father, abundantly available to her for the asking (2 Corinthians 9:8).[8]

This discipline is a call to work! Prayer is work, not a sport. It is not something that you do if you like it or only if you're good at it.[9] It will not come easy. But don't give up trying if you have failed in the past. Confess your failure to God and then discipline yourself to begin something new. For this is God's will in the Gospel!

RENEW YOUR MIND

How much time do you generally spend in conversation with God? In your view (without using evangelical clichés), why is prayer an important part of the Christian walk?

What is the biblical meaning of the word *meditation*? Why should you meditate on the Lord and His Word and will (compare Psalm 1:2; Revelation 2:7, 11, 17, 29; 3:6, 13, 22)?

Why is the image of warfare appropriate for considering the discipline of prayer (see the preceding context of Ephesians 6:18)? Apply this to your own victories and defeats regarding prayer.

What do Romans 8:26-27 and Jude 20 say about the Holy Spirit and prayer? Why are the truths here important to you personally?

Do you find it difficult to find enough time and a quiet place away from interruptions for your prayer time? Why? Are there ways you can minimize conflicting loyalties that you need to ignore or adjust your busy schedule?

Where is the best place for you to pray, and what is the best time?

Make a list of individuals for whom you want to pray regularly. Then establish a time when you will pray for several people on the list (a few times a week). When you pray, ask for specific answers that you will recognize when they come.

5

DISCIPLINE OF WORSHIP

Submission's Celebration

*Therefore, I urge you, brethren, by the mercies of God,
to present your bodies a living and holy sacrifice, acceptable
to God, which is your spiritual service of worship.*

ROMANS 12:1 NASB

M y earliest memories of Sunday morning worship extend back to
1950 when Mrs. White, who led the local Good News Club, took
me to church with her each week. The Christian and Missionary Alliance
church on Lime Avenue in Long Beach, California, was a congregation
of people like Mrs. White—sincere, Bible-centered believers. And they
were missions-minded! The building walls were lined with glass cases
filled with missionary relics from Africa, China, India, and other distant
lands. The displays were at my eye level—and I was entranced. My memories of the actual worship service, however, are not so clear. Try as I may,
I cannot recall one thing about that weekly hour spent in worship. My
mind draws a blank.

Most of my childhood years were spent at Garfield Baptist Church,
and those memories are decidedly more vivid. The services were like
those of most Baptist churches of the time—a warm blend of gospel
songs, choruses, and perhaps a hymn, a choir number, and a sermon. I've
searched my memories of those years, and I don't remember ever think-

ing reflectively about corporate worship. I never gave consideration to the purpose of our Lord's Day gatherings except as a place for preaching.

During the sixties and seventies great changes swept evangelical churches. Every aspect of worship was questioned and subjected to painful tests of authenticity and relevance. In an effort to improve worship services, gospel songs were dropped and replaced with mantra-like music; preachers were replaced by "communicators."

In the last twenty years or so, both of these early models have been set aside for the more popular seeker-sensitive approach to corporate worship. Why all the changes? Is one way of "doing church" better than another? Is the way we think about worship really something serious enough to be considered a discipline?

The answer to these questions lies in an understanding of biblical worship—both individual and corporate. It is crucial that we think about these matters as gospel women, lest we give away the very heart of true worship.

MORE THAN A SUNDAY ACTIVITY

New Testament worship encompasses all of life. Worship is not something we relegate to Sunday mornings or any other single hour of the week—no matter how innovative your church may be in choosing the time. The biblical evidence is conclusive. Jesus' coming fulfilled the Scripture's promise of a new covenant (cf. Jeremiah 31:31-34). It is most significant that the entire text of this prophecy is recorded in Hebrews 8:7-13 in the midst of a section (Hebrews 7—11) that asserts that there is no longer sacrifice, priesthood, or temple because all have been fulfilled in Christ.

The worship language of the Old Testament is changed in the New Testament so that worship is broader, encompassing all of life. There are no longer sacred times or sacred spaces. By that I mean, we need not go to the temple (the holy place) to worship God. Christians are to worship God all the time under the new covenant. That is essentially the message of this book—worshiping God through reverent submission in all of life. Corporate worship, what we do Sunday morning, is simply a particular expression of a life of continual worship.

The best expression of the broad view of worship is found in Romans 12:1: "Therefore, I urge you, brethren, by the mercies of God, to present your bodies a living and holy sacrifice, acceptable to God, which is your spiritual service of worship" (NASB). Remembering the Old Testament sacrificial rituals of worship helps us grasp the significance of this verse. Every single time I confess my self-reliance and submit my life to God's will in a particular area, I am worshiping God—as surely as any sincere Israelite offering a lamb in obedience to God's plan. Before Christ came, Samuel, the priest, proclaimed the superiority of this kind of worship when he instructed King Saul that "to obey is better than sacrifice" (1 Samuel 15:22).

But what about Sunday morning? How are we to understand what the worship service is all about?

SUNDAY MORNING WORSHIP

The confusion lies in the *why* of worship. Why do we worship—for God or for ourselves? The unspoken but increasingly common assumption of today's average churchgoer is that worship is primarily for us—to meet our needs.

Here's a telltale sign that this kind of thinking is prevalent. After the service, everyone asks, "What did you think of the service today?" or they slip out the door as quickly as possible. The real question should be, "What did God think of it—and of us?" We ought to ask, "What did I give to God?" It is easy to forget that our main concern should be to gather with other believers and "worship in spirit and in truth" (John 4:24). Everything in our corporate worship should begin from this understanding—that our holy, transcendent God be pleased and glorified by what we do. This is, after all, our goal the other six days of the week.

And what about our needs? When we worship and adore God as the "church gathered" in our singing and prayer and listening to and submitting to God's Word, unity and fellowship naturally follow—the by-product and evidence of the generous grace of God. Proper worship, individually and corporately, results in meeting every need we could possibly have—a right relationship with God and with people.

Prepare to Worship

Preparing for worship isn't just something that ministers are supposed to do. It's important for each person coming to worship to prepare. I know this isn't easy. Sunday morning can be the toughest morning of the week. Many couples, especially those with young children, have more arguments on Sunday morning than any other day. Sometimes by the time we make it to church, worship seems an impossibility.

The answer begins with Saturday preparation. If possible, get the Sunday morning clothes clean and ready on Saturday night. Even have your breakfast plan in mind by then. Lay out the Bibles and lessons and other Sunday morning necessities. Agree with your spouse and older children about what time you're all going to get up in the morning in order to leave plenty of time to get ready for church. Then get to bed at a reasonable hour!

Pray about the Lord's Day—for the service, the music, the pastors, your own family, and yourself. Ideally, you'll be able to share a quick time of family prayer before you leave the house on Sunday morning. Ask that the Lord be glorified and that He speak to each family member. If you can make these changes in your weekend pattern, your Sunday worship will undoubtedly improve.

Expectant

We must come with great expectation—for we will experience just what we expect. My friend Diane, whose life is filled with many difficulties, has a great sense of expectancy when she attends church. She once told me that every Sunday morning is just like Christmas for her. Her excitement mounts as the sermon approaches, eager to hear and receive the new gift of understanding of God and His will that the pastor will unwrap that morning for the congregation. How beautiful!

THE DISCIPLINE OF WORSHIP

It is the Lord's Day. We've gathered to worship together with God's people. We've prepared, we're expectant. Now how do we "do worship" that pleases God?

God-Centered

God-centered worship begins with a focus on the awesome revelation of God. This God of holy Scripture is the omnipotent (all powerful)

Creator who spoke everything into existence! This is God, who is omnipresent (present everywhere), above everything, below everything, but not contained in anything. God is omniscient (knowing everything), even numbering the hairs on our heads. He knows our thoughts before we think them or make them known. God is *holy* and dwells in the unapproachable light of His own glory.

As we gather to meet in worship, we must consciously begin with this huge picture of God before us and ask ourselves the question: How must we conduct our lives each day and shape our meeting together to glorify this God? This is so important for this present generation because keeping this scriptural vision of God in mind as we worship will help us avoid idolatry. Don't make the mistake of thinking that you are not guilty of idolatry simply because you don't bow down to idols. We are guilty of idolatry every time we think about God in any way other than the way Scripture portrays Him.

Certainly the church must be culturally tuned in and sensitive. It had better be. The preacher should hold the Bible in one hand and the newspaper in the other. Christians must "understand the times" (cf. 1 Chronicles 12:32). The church must be creative and relevant, appealing to the hearts of men and women (both the saved and the lost). But true worship must begin with God.

Jesus tells us in John 4:24 that we must "worship in spirit and in truth." Worshiping "in truth" means that we come informed by the objective revelation of God's Word about the great God we serve and the precepts He has spoken. In this sense our worship is governed by what we know and believe about God. The better informed we are, the better we can worship. We should be familiar with, and take to heart, passages such as Genesis 1, Psalm 139, the book of Job, Isaiah 6 and 45, John 7, John 17, Romans 1—3, Revelation 19, and others in order to prepare for God-centered worship.

This knowledge of God through His Word ought to heighten our expectations and instill healthy fear and reverence. As Annie Dillard wrote:

> On the whole, I do not find Christians, outside of the Catacombs, sufficiently sensible of conditions. Does anyone have the foggiest idea what sort of power we so blithely invoke?

Or as I suspect, does no one believe a word of it? . . . It is madness to wear ladies' straw hats and velvet hats to church; we should all be wearing crash helmets. Ushers should issue life preservers and signal flares; they should lash us to our pews. For the sleeping god may wake someday and take offense, or the waking god may draw us out to where we can never return.[1]

Besides worshiping in truth, we worship "in spirit." Notice the small "s," referring to our human spirits, the inner person. True worship flows from the inside out. Worship is not an external activity, but is of necessity first internal. Jesus warned hypocrites with the words of Isaiah: "'These people honor me with their lips, but their hearts are far from me. They worship me in vain'" (Mark 7:6-7, quoting Isaiah 29:13).

True worship springs from within our spirit, from the spontaneous affections of the heart—as it did from the heart of David when he wrote Psalm 130: "I wait for the LORD, my soul waits, and in his word I put my hope. My soul waits for the LORD more than watchmen wait for the morning" (vv. 5-6).

Christ-Centered

The New Testament does not reveal a greater God than we see in the Old Testament, but it gives us a greater revelation of God. So we could say that Jesus Christ explains God for us (John 1:1, 18). He makes the invisible God visible—God in the flesh.

The teaching of Colossians 1:15-18 provides a mind-boggling revelation of God in Christ. We see Him as the:

Creator: "For by him all things were created: things in heaven and on earth, visible and invisible, whether thrones or powers or rulers or authorities; all things were created by him and for him" (v. 16).

Sustainer: "He is before all things, and in him all things hold together" (v. 17).

Goal: "All things were created . . . for him" (v. 16).

This is an astonishing statement about Jesus Christ. It tells us that He is both the starting point of the universe and its consummation. He is the beginning, and He is the end—Alpha and Omega. Everything in creation, history, and spiritual reality is for Him and moving toward Him!

And not only that, but this statement reveals that Jesus is the reconciler: "For God was pleased to have all his fullness dwell in him, and through him to reconcile to himself all things, whether things on earth or things in heaven, by making peace through his blood, shed on the cross" (vv. 19-20).

Because Christ is the ultimate revelation of God, He must be the central focus of our worship. E. V. Hill, pastor of Mount Zion Missionary Baptist Church, tells a story about an old woman in his church whom they all called "1800" because no one knew how old she was. This elderly woman was hard on visiting preachers because she understood very well that Jesus Christ was to be central in Christian worship. If the preacher was slow about honoring Christ, she would say, "Get Him up!" After a few minutes, if she didn't think it was happening, she would again shout, "Get Him up!" It could be a very long hour for anyone who didn't "get Jesus up!"

Because Jesus Christ is the ultimate revelation of God, He must be the central focus of our worship. When Jesus Christ is the center, He is the focus that brings church unity. When our worship is God-centered and Christ-centered, when we're worshiping as individuals and as a group, unity is enhanced. Pastor and author A. W. Tozer explains this well:

> Has it ever occurred to you that one hundred pianos all tuned to the same fork are automatically tuned to each other? They are of one accord by being tuned, not to each other, but to one standard to which each one must individually bow. So one hundred worshipers met together, each one looking away to Christ, are in heart nearer to each other than they could possibly be were they to become "unity" conscious and turn their eyes away from God to strive for closer fellowship.[2]

Word-Centered

The early church's worship centered on God's Word. The apostle Paul instructed the young pastor Timothy, "Until I come, devote yourself to the public reading of Scripture, to preaching and to teaching" (1 Timothy 4:13). At the close of the first century, a church historian recorded for us that the Christians had continued this practice: "On the day called

Sunday, all who live in cities or in the country gather together to one place, and the memoirs of the apostles and the writings of the prophets are read, as long as time permits; then, when the reader has finished, the president speaks, instructing and exhorting the people to imitate these good things."[3]

The public reading of God's Word is important! At our church we stand for the reading of the Scripture for two reasons—first to get our attention and also to make the point that as a congregation we stand together under its authority. When Jesus was tempted in the wilderness, he showed us that the Scriptures are our very life when he quoted the words of Moses in answer to Satan's temptation: "It is written, 'Man does not live on bread alone, but on every word that comes from the mouth of God'" (Matthew 4:4; see also Luke 4:4; Deuteronomy 8:3). The Scriptures were life to Moses and food to Jesus! How about us? When the Scripture is read on Sunday morning, do we really believe that the words are essential for life itself? Think about it next time you gather for worship.

Service

It takes discipline to remember that what we are doing when we gather for Sunday morning worship is only an extension of what has been going on in our lives all week long. It is so easy to give way to thinking that says, "We worship on Sunday morning." To think that way suggests that we are not worshiping during the rest of the week. Sunday should be like every other day of the week except that we worship with the church gathered. But every day we can be singing hymns, reading the Scripture, and submitting our lives to the authority of God's Word. What we do on Sunday should help equip us to serve God throughout the week. Worship—whether by oneself at home, in the workplace, classroom, or with the church gathered—is consecration. Worship is serving God every day: "I urge you, brothers, in view of God's mercy, to *offer your bodies as living sacrifices*, holy and pleasing to God—this is your spiritual act of worship" (Romans 12:1, emphasis mine).

Every woman who calls herself a Christian must understand that worship is the ultimate priority of her life. Worship is what God wants from you and from me—every day. Jesus made this clear when He chided busy, frenetic Martha when she was so critical of her sister's sitting at Jesus' feet: "Martha, Martha . . . you are worried and upset about many things, but only one thing is needed. Mary has chosen what is better, and it will not be taken away from her" (Luke 10:41-42).

Mary chose the better part, and so can we. We must bring discipline to this matter of worship, for this is God's will for us in the Gospel.

RENEW YOUR MIND

Explain why it is possible to *feel* worshipful and not truly be worshiping? How is our obedience an act of worship? See 1 Samuel 15:22; Romans 12:1.

What does it mean to worship God "in spirit and in truth"? See John 4:21-24; 17:17.

How can you worship Christ in all of life? See Romans 12:1-2.

Understanding that worship must be Christ-centered (since He is at once our sacrifice, priest, and temple), how should we conduct our prayers, singing, and preaching?

What could you (and your family) do to be spiritually prepared for Sunday morning worship? Make a list, share it with your husband and children, and work together at implementing your plan.

CHARACTER

6

DISCIPLINE OF MIND

Submission's Education

Do not conform any longer to the pattern of this world,
but be transformed by the renewing of your mind.

ROMANS 12:2

The human brain has an astonishing capacity! It doesn't miss a thing. Capable of giving and receiving the subtlest input—from imagining a universe in which time bends to creating the polyphonic texture of a Bach fugue or transmitting and receiving a message from God Himself—it accomplishes feats no computer ever will.

But the human mind's potential reaches its height in the possibility of possessing the mind of Christ through the ministry of the Holy Spirit. Paul wrote, "But we have the mind of Christ"—and it's a mind that is constantly renewed (see 1 Corinthians 2:16 and Romans 12:2). No computer will ever be able to think God's thoughts or know the heart of God or do His works. But the human brain—that mystery residing between our ears—has this capacity. Actually, it's what the brain was created for—to have the mind of Christ.

Since the brain was created for this purpose, it's the great scandal of today's church that there are so many Christians without Christian minds—Christians who don't think, let alone think Christianly. There's a story about an old Quaker woman receiving a male visitor one afternoon. After tea the gentleman proceeded to talk about how he memorized poetry while shaving, and at breakfast he practiced Portuguese. He went on boasting about his use of time. The woman's simple but profound response was, "And when does thee think?"

In a book called *Recovering the Christian Mind*, Harry Blamires points out that while Christians may worship and pray as Christians, they are suffering from religious anorexia, a loss of appetite for growth in Christ.[1] God has given us this amazing instrument—the mind. We mustn't take it for granted. We need to program it wisely—never leaving it unguarded, unthinking, and undisciplined.

When we turn to God's Word, it's clear that the biblical writers understood this need. "Above all else, guard your heart," says Proverbs, "for it is the wellspring of life" (4:23). "For as he thinks within himself, so he is" (Proverbs 23:7 NASB). The Scriptures tell us that input determines output—that our mental programming determines production.

GOD'S COMPUTER PROGRAM

In one comprehensive sentence in his letter to the Philippians, Paul prescribes his personal mental program: "Whatever is true, whatever is noble, whatever is right, whatever is pure, whatever is lovely, whatever is admirable—if anything is excellent or praiseworthy—think about such things" (4:8).

God's programming guide is explicitly positive. He emphasizes what's true, noble, right, pure, lovely, and admirable. We all can choose a thought program that will produce a Christian mind. Our choices make all the difference to our minds.

Many women may feel defeated because their past has been such a series of bad choices. It's hard to believe that you can change when you've regularly chosen the impure, the illusory, the negative. But no one can rationalize her present choices by the past. As Christian women, we are free to have Christian minds! It's within our reach—and it's part of our discipline of godliness.

I learned a method from my husband that has been an invaluable help to me in disciplining my mind. During a Sunday morning sermon years ago, he made the point that if a person does something (i.e., reads a chapter of the Bible) for twenty-six days in a row, research shows that he has actually developed a habit. I'm the type that needs helpful suggestions like this. It gave me the encouragement to press on and not give up—"One down, twenty-five to go!"

Paul's positive programming guide demands rejection of negative input. He could also have written: "Whatever is untrue, whatever is ignoble, whatever is wrong, whatever is impure, whatever is unlovely, whatever is not admirable—if there is anything shoddy or unworthy of praise—do not think about these things." Paul was not naive; he knew about the dark side of human experience. But he chose not to make negative input a part of his mental programming.

So make this truth a foundation for your life as a godly woman: A Christian mind is impossible without the discipline of refusal. Part of having a Christian mind is saying no to ungodly influences.

The Power of Refusal

When our children were young, we did not own a television set. When they visited friends' homes where television was permitted, they were taught to politely refuse to join in watching programs that were off limits. When I think of what was on that list of rejected viewing, I'm alarmed at how much TV programming has degenerated. What offended us then would be considered tame these days. I wish I could say that we have remained as virtuous as we were twenty-five years ago. But we are not. Any who think that they have been able to keep their minds noble and pure in this culture, without rigorous discipline, are kidding themselves. In the years between 1970 and 2000, the standard of acceptability for TV content has dramatically dropped. What is disturbing is that Christian viewing habits have not only declined at the same rate as the secular, but the "difference between what we in the church now accept and what the world accepts is not as great as it once was."[2] Tragically, the Christian community is watching the same degrading programs as the rest of the world.

We do not need statistics to prove to us that TV is influencing our minds. All we have to do is notice how often a television is blaring in the background. However, as a grandparent, I am deeply concerned with a recent report of the Parents' Television Council. "The report revealed the following changes of content of prime time 'family hour' in the two years between 1997 and 1999:

Violence was up 86 percent.

Sexual content was up 77 percent.

Foul language rose 58 percent."[3]

This is alarming to say the least, but I'm not certain that even such statistics move Christian householders to make any concerted effort to change their viewing habits.

Some years ago media critic Malcolm Muggeridge said: "The one thing television can't do is express ideas. . . . There is a danger in translating life into an image . . . it is falsifying life." If you haven't noticed, television is all about image! Consider, by contrast, how God communicates with us: "In the past God spoke to our forefathers through the prophets at many times and in various ways, but in these last days he has spoken to us by his Son" (Hebrews 1:1-2).

One of the names of Jesus is the Word: "The Word became flesh and made his dwelling among us" (John 1:14). The words of the prophets and the Word (Jesus Christ) are God's chosen means of communicating with us. Words communicate ideas. This is important! As cultural observer and critic Kenneth Myers has said, "A culture that is rooted more in images than in words will find it increasingly difficult to sustain any broad commitment to any truth, since truth is an abstraction requiring language." As the images of television increasingly become the favored method of communication rather than words, people lose their capacity for reasoned thought. They therefore lose the ability to possess the mind of Christ.

If you doubt this is happening, think for a moment about the average church attender's ability to listen to a closely reasoned sermon. Now picture a family mindlessly staring at a television screen, hours on end, with barely a word spoken. What a frightening comparison!

Here's some radical advice: Turn off the TV. You'll be amazed at the time you've liberated for other tasks and for time with people. Even better, it will become virtually impossible not to become a deeper person and a more godly woman.

I'm not advocating that Christians stop watching all TV and movies. Christianity is by nature countercultural, but it is not anticultural. There are worthwhile things to view. But I am calling for gospel women to take control of their minds—what comes in and what goes out. If you can't control what you watch or read, then perhaps you need to remove the sources of temptation—that TV and those books or magazines. Jesus said, "If your right eye causes you to sin, gouge it out and throw it away" (Matthew 5:29).

Kent and I chose to raise our children without television intentionally, to create for them better opportunities for Christian mental programming. We have no regrets. It's not for everyone, but it may be for you.

Ours is a media age, but the psalmist offers some wise and timely advice for us: "I will walk in my house with blameless heart. I will set before my eyes no vile thing" (101:2-3). So let Christ be the Lord of your daytime and your prime time!

If you are married, schedule a confidential conference with your husband and prayerfully seek God's will regarding what's being watched and listened to in your home. If you are single, you likewise need to seek God's will over your mental input and output; find a friend to hold you accountable. Don't settle for being just like other Christian women. Be different because you have a Christian mind.

Intentional Programming

In Philippians 4:8, Paul recommends that we focus our minds on what is true, noble, right, pure, lovely, admirable, excellent, and praiseworthy. Then he gives his loaded command: "Think about such things."

I can spend hours in the pages of the latest garden catalog. The endless variety of plants, flowers, and trees takes my breath away—really and truly! I don't know what you daydream about, but I dream of acres of flowers and herbs, orchards and woodland plants. Almost every time I do, my mind goes to thoughts of God's creative powers. How does He design and manufacture something as fragile, detailed, and exquisitely hued as a stock of delphinium? How about the brilliance of the zinnia, the scent of basil, or the size of the redwood? I love to garden, but I adore the Master Gardener! We're to think about the wonderful elements God wants us to put into our minds. God calls us in His Word to a rigorous and positive discipline in this area.

Scripture Reading

The godly woman's discipline of the mind is achieved through a serious and continual exposure to God's Word. Helen Jensen, a pastor's wife and dear friend, is a godly woman who has developed this discipline. I can safely say that Helen has more of God's Word in her than any other woman I have ever known. She is a serious student of the Bible. When Helen studies a passage of Scripture, she often looks up every single listing in the concordance (the big one!) for the key words in the passage. She has so devoted her mind to this task that I believe it's given her a sharper ability to think clearly. She has so many biblical details stored in her "computer" that when her friends need a Bible fact, they're certain that Helen will know.

Helen's knowledge is not simply acquired knowledge; it is also applied knowledge. She knows God and desires nothing more than to do His bidding. She is beautiful! She has lived out the experience of the psalmist:

> *Oh, how I love your law!*
> *I meditate on it all day long.*
> *Your commands make me wiser than my enemies,*
> *for they are ever with me.*
> *I have more insight than all my teachers,*
> *for I meditate on your statutes.*
> *I have more understanding than the elders,*
> *for I obey your precepts. (119:97-100)*

This is all-important: You can never have a Christian mind without regular reading of the Scriptures and serious Bible study. Why is this? Because you cannot be profoundly influenced by what you don't know. If you are filled with God's Word, your life can then be informed and directed by God—your relationships at home, your parenting, your career, your ethical decisions, your internal moral life. The way to a Christian mind is through God's Word!

There's no need to be legalistic. The Bible nowhere commands that "good Christians must read the Bible through once a year." Some women can't read that well or that fast. Speed-reading is not the answer. As Lucy told Charlie Brown, "I just completed a course in speed reading, and last night I read *War and Peace* in one hour! . . . It was about Russia." The truth is, what Helen has practiced is available to all Christians. It isn't something for the elite or highly educated. You don't even need to be able to read.

My husband's brother is severely dyslexic. He learned to read only well enough to get along in his trade. When he became a Christian and gained a newfound motivation to know God's Word, he purchased Scripture tapes. His wife (who happens to be my sister) also reads to him. Many women listen to Scripture tapes while driving to work or in the car pool or while busy at home, fixing dinner, etc. The ability to read isn't essential to knowing God's Word. Just push the button and listen while the spaghetti sauce simmers.

Getting through the whole Bible once a year is a wonderful goal, if you can manage it. It requires only five pages a day and offers a reachable annual goal. Whatever your schedule or your reading ability, you must regularly read and study God's Word. If you don't, you are in effect "editing God" and will never have a fully Christian mind. Check out the resource section at the back of this book for a detailed plan you could use to help you read through the Bible in a year. I encourage you to give it a try!

If you are not in a group Bible study, join one. The guidance and accountability of such a group is invaluable to this discipline.

Christian Books and Good Literature

As well as reading God's Word, gospel women will want to read good books. Women are so busy today, they often think they haven't the time to read. But it is amazing how many books you can read in a year simply by reading a little each night before the light goes out. It would be easy to read a book a month with this method. That would be twelve books a year!

If you're the type who falls asleep after reading two paragraphs, keep a book in the car and read while you wait. That's one of the ways my daughter (the mother of seven children) finds time to read. In her case, she rarely falls asleep reading; on the contrary, she must discipline herself not to read too late, losing the sleep she needs to care for her busy family.

A trip to a bookstore is a big night out for members of our family. We often give gift certificates to a local bookshop, and finding just the right book is great fun. This past year the women in my family read books on home organization, gardening, parenting, and education. Just for fun every summer I read one of the latest political exposés. Someone always has at least one novel going, both Christian and secular—everything from classics like Jane Austen's *Pride and Prejudice* to the mysteries of

Dorothy Sayers. Christian devotional classics such as *My Utmost for His Highest* by Oswald Chambers and *Streams in the Desert* by Mrs. Charles Cowman have been favorites—as well as missionary biographies of women such as Amy Carmichael, Isobel Kuhn, Betty Stam, Gladys Aylward, and Ann Judson. Elisabeth Elliot, J. I. Packer, John Piper, and Chuck Colson ought to be on every Christian woman's reading list. They write to enrich our souls.

Why should we bother with Christian reading apart from Scripture? All the Christians who have come before us are offering a wealth of accumulated knowledge and wisdom. To feed on their ideas and experiences is to reject spiritual anorexia. Great Christian writing will magnify, dramatize, and illuminate life-giving truth for us. Others have walked the same paths we want to walk. They've chronicled the pitfalls and posted warning signs for us along the way. They've pointed the way in their descriptions of spiritual delights that will draw us onward and upward.

There is one Christian classic I return to again and again. I first read J. I. Packer's *Knowing God* as a young woman in my thirties. I never tire of it because its teaching about the attributes of God are just as significant to my life today as they were in 1973. The idea of God as Father came alive to me in the pages of this classic:

> If you want to judge how well a person understands Christianity, find out how much he makes of the thought of being God's child and having God as his Father. If this is not the thought that prompts and controls his worship and prayers and his whole outlook on life, it means that he does not understand Christianity very well at all. For everything that Christ taught, everything that makes the New Testament new and better than the Old, everything that is distinctively Christian as opposed to merely Jewish, is summed up in the knowledge of the Fatherhood of God. "Father" is the Christian name for God.[4]

To help point the way to some of the best reading out there, I've included a list of secular and sacred books of all types at the back of this book.

Women, once we've exercised that right of refusal, we can fill our minds with good stuff! Some of us read rapidly, some don't. But any one of us could commit to reading two or three really good books in the year ahead.

The human brain—three or four pounds of gray matter between our ears—yet what an amazing instrument it is and with what fabulous capacity! The mind is greater than any and all computers, because it can possess the mind of Christ and think God's thoughts after Him, hear His heart, and do His works. What an eternal tragedy it is to have such a mind and have it redeemed, and yet not have a Christian mind. Bring your mind under submission to the Gospel. Protect it! Say no to the spiritual wastelands that try to invade your home.

Make a conscious effort to submit to the Divine Programmer through reading His Word. Prayerfully commit yourself to reading and studying God's Word. Then read the great works of those who've gone before you.

What an opportunity—we can possess the mind of Christ! It is God's will for us in the Gospel.

RENEW YOUR MIND

Philippians 4:8 points your thought life toward positive ideals. How is it really possible to think about these positive things when the stresses and strains and disappointments of life are all around you?

What do Matthew 5:29 and Psalm 101:2-3 tell you about a disciplined mind? How can you live out these verses this week?

Check out Psalm 119:97-100. Are you doing what these verses prescribe? Why or why not?

If you have never read the Bible through in a year (or even two or three years), will you covenant with God to do it in order to become more familiar with the whole of Scripture and to hear God's voice better through His Word?

Name at least three Christian books that have made a major impact on your life. Identify two books you've been meaning to read (make one a classic) and set a deadline for reading them.

In what ways do you know you need greater discipline of mind? What are your greatest struggles in this area—unhelpful comparisons? self-pity? dwelling on past pain? pride? worry? something else? What can you do, practically and spiritually, to experience growth toward wholeness in these areas?

7

Discipline of Contentment

Submission's Rest

All my longings lie open before you, O LORD.

PSALM 38:9

O ur friend Libby is beautiful. A woman in her late twenties, she represents everything good about Gen-Xers. She is a graduate of an elite institution of higher education. She is "hip"—that is, in touch with her peers. She is intellectually curious. She keeps fit, both physically and spiritually. She is a faithful wife and a loving and conscientious mother. Best of all, Libby's life is all about the Gospel, and she is content. But there was a time in her life when the prospect of contentment was nearly lost.

Libby was raised in a Christian home with an enviable godly heritage. "I respect my parents' deep love for Christ," she says, "and the way they displayed that in our home while I was growing up." In this great environment, she accepted Jesus as her Savior as a young child. She knew in her head that she was a sinner and believed unwaveringly that Christ is the Son of God born to pay the price of her sin by dying on the cross. Throughout her early years and into college, she lived for Christ. As she matured, her faith also grew—in baby steps here and there. As she tells it, "I was comfortable in my life to have Christ by my side, and I was quite sure that I was acceptable to God. I was a 'happy' Christian."

But, as God would have it, her life took an unexpected turn. She and her husband moved from the suburbs to a large city and were bombarded with many alternatives to Christianity. For the first time in her life, as a wife and young mother, her faith began to waver. The alternatives suddenly seemed appealing, and the foundations of her life began to crumble.

"All my life," she recalls, "I had put myself in spiritually superior and morally invincible categories. Upon hearing about the failures of other believers, I would think to myself, *I would never do that!*" However, as soon as all of the props of cultural Christianity were knocked out from under her, she quickly lost her footing. She drifted into spiritual darkness, and she was actually standing at a crossroad.

Libby's whole demeanor changed during this period of time. Her appearance reflected the discontent in her soul. Black became her color of choice—even for lipstick. She was often sullen, rarely engaging in conversation. She avoided church and Christians as much as possible. Libby felt a longing deep within her, a restlessness, dissatisfaction.

WHAT IS CONTENTMENT?

One dictionary definition says that "contentment is desiring no more than one has; satisfied."[1] In the classic *The Rare Jewel of Christian Contentment*, first published in 1648, Jeremiah Burroughs defines contentment this way: "Christian contentment is that sweet, inward, quiet, gracious frame of spirit, which freely submits to and delights in God's wise and fatherly disposal in every condition."[2]

No one understood contentment better than the apostle Paul. He wrote to the Philippian church informing them that he had "learned to be content whatever the circumstances" (Philippians 4:11). Fortunately for us, he said that he had "learned" to be content. That means that there is hope for all of us who have at one time or another, like Libby, faced the monster of discontent.

Paul valued this Christian virtue so highly that he wrote Timothy, "Godliness with contentment is great gain" (1 Timothy 6:6). Dr. Martyn Lloyd-Jones, writing of Paul's instruction to Timothy says: "You remember also how he exhorts Timothy to take hold of this principle by saying: 'Godliness with contentment is great gain.' There is nothing like it, he says in effect; if you have that, you have everything. Paul had become an old man by then, and he writes to the young man Timothy and says: The first thing you have to learn is to be independent of circumstances and conditions—'Godliness with contentment.'"3

So godly contentment is independent of circumstances and conditions. Combine godliness with this kind of contentment, and you have a rare treasure indeed!

Contentment is in short supply today, however—outside or inside the church. According to 2 Peter 1:3, Christians have been given everything we need for life and godliness. If we have everything we need, why is it that so many of us are not content?

We come by it naturally. Eve had everything—the perfect husband, a beautiful environment, and—most astonishing—direct and daily fellowship with God. She walked and talked with Him. Until the time Satan appeared and spoke to her, she had always listened to and obeyed the voice of God. But then she listened to that contrary voice—the one that proposed the notion that God did not have her best interests at heart. The voice told her plainly that God was depriving her of something desirable: "Did God really say . . . ?" Something altogether unfamiliar began to stir in Eve's heart—discontent. She desired something she did not possess, something her loving Creator-God had chosen not to give her.

Interestingly enough, it wasn't the fruit itself that tempted Eve. Apparently, as long as Eve was listening and obeying God's voice, she took little notice of the forbidden fruit. She was utterly content. It was only after she listened to Satan's suggestion that she saw the fruit in a new light, as "good for food and pleasing to the eye, and also desirable for gaining wisdom" (Genesis 3:6).

We've all inherited Eve's problem. Libby was following in Eve's footsteps when the attractions in the city aroused discontent in her. Advertisers capitalize on the fact that the human heart is inclined to discontent; they're only too happy to inform us how to meet our inner longings. We're bombarded with visual images and alluring voices telling us that an exotic brand of hair color will make us irresistible to the opposite sex. We repeatedly hear and finally believe that a corporate job in an office on a floor above the glass ceiling will assure us of success in everyone's eyes, and variations along this theme ad nauseam. Everywhere we turn, we are told what we need to make us happy—something we don't already have.

It's difficult to tune out such voices all the time. We can't help but be influenced as the call to discontent is shouted from magazine pages, television, the workplace, and even the classroom.

Because I am the pastor's wife, I have spent much time over the years listening to women who are unhappy about some aspect of their life. Their dissatisfaction usually comes in one of four categories—their reputations, their marital status, their finances, or their children. Their concerns go something like this:

Reputation—desire other people to think that they are beautiful, intelligent, and successful.

Marital status—desire to be married, desire to be married to someone else, desire to change something about their husbands.

Money—desire for more, desire for husband to spend more or less, desire for children to have more. (I have never spoken to anyone who wanted less money.)

Children—wish they had some, wish they could change the ones they have, wish they could control children's decisions or circumstances surrounding children.

We naturally long for what we don't have!

Certainly it's fine to improve our quality of life. But the unchangeable factors in our lives ought to teach us that true contentment can only come from God—and that we must seek it in Him alone.

LONGINGS

As we study the discipline of contentment, it's important to recognize where those longings begin. Discontent can come from both godly longings and ungodly longings. When Libby was in the city, everyone and everything around her oozed pop sophistication. Alternative lifestyles offered excitement and forbidden pleasures. Life as a Christian seemed less than promised—stodgy and colorless. From deep within a longing to be free of restrictions overwhelmed her soul. She went through a long period of experimentation and increasing frustration.

Searching for rest from her inner struggle, she read 2 Peter 2:20-22. This passage describes believers who have received the Word of the Lord and are then re-entangled in the world. At the end of the passage they are compared to dogs that return to their own vomit. "I knew that was me," she says. "While I had the truth of God and the beautiful truths of the

Gospel, I was returning to the garbage this world had to offer and hoping to find meaning and fulfillment there." Pastor and author Phillip Jensen chronicles the irony of experiences such as Libby's in his book *Guidance and the Voice of God*:

> The non-Christian world likes to portray Christians as being trapped in a web of conformity, false morality and unhappiness, leading drab, pleasureless lives in the hope that somehow God will be impressed. The truth is that unhappiness is caused by sin, not by following God's ways. Sin destroys happiness; it destroys relationships; it deprives us of our freedom. The non-Christian world, enslaved as it is to sin, is full of broken lives and unhappiness.[4]

The truth is, the worst thing that can happen to a Christian who is longing for something outside of God's will would be for God to grant that desire! This was the experience of the nation of Israel before the exile: "But my people would not listen to me; Israel would not submit to me. So I gave them over to their stubborn hearts to follow their own devices" (Psalm 81:11-12).

When Christians seek satisfaction outside the will of God, many of them experience the same misery that Israel encountered. It must surely be "the greatest misery of all . . . for God to give you up to your heart's lusts and desires, to give you up to your own counsels."[5]

So when we experience discontent, we must ask ourselves some pointed questions: "What is the source of my longing?" and "Do I really want what I think I do?"

Godly Longings

The longing that has been placed in our hearts by God, for God, is a longing worth pursuing. Joyce Seelye, a member of our church, writes:

> I think *home* must be one of the sweetest words in the English language. It suggests belonging, care, comfort, peace, and safety. Several years ago I found myself drawing plans for a little home. I saw little houses for sale and wished I could see inside them and maybe buy one. Since we already had an adequate, comfortable

home with which I was quite content, I wondered what to do with this longing, so I went to God with the matter. Psalm 38:9 says: "All my longings lie open before you, O, LORD. . . ." And, as it usually happens, as I studied my Bible each day, I began to notice Scriptures about home, God's dwelling place:

"Look down from heaven, your holy dwelling place, and bless your people" (Deuteronomy 26:15).

"I long to dwell [make my home] in your tent forever" (Psalm 61:4).

"He who dwells [makes his home] in the shelter of the Most High will rest in the shadow of the Almighty" (Psalm 91:1).

"I will dwell [make my home] in the house of the LORD forever" (Psalm 23:6).

From time to time the longing returns, and I am reminded that heaven is my true and final home, the ultimate fulfillment of that sweetest of all words—*home*.

Joyce is right, for "the true Christian carries in his exiled heart a hunger that can only be satisfied by the fullness of God Himself and by his own country—his soul's true home."[6]

Longing for God is a proper longing. We were created for relationship with Him. But just as Joyce's longing for "home" periodically returns, our longing for God and His dwelling place will only be fully realized in heaven.

As a young woman I read Revelation 2:17 and longed for its promise: "He who has an ear, let him hear what the Spirit says to the churches. To him who overcomes, I will give some of the hidden manna. I will also give him a white stone with a new name written on it, known only to him who receives it." The mystery of receiving a stone with a new name written on it, a name known only to me and the Giver of the name, gripped my heart. Not Barbara, but a heavenly name chosen for me by my heavenly Father. That gift on that day will bring a satisfaction I'll never know on this earth. But I know it is coming! "For no matter how many promises God has made, they are 'Yes' in Christ" (2 Corinthians 1:20).

The psalmist David expressed such longings for God when he said, "As the deer pants for streams of water, so my soul pants for you, O God.

My soul thirsts for God, for the living God" (Psalm 42:1). Anyone who turns to God will be satisfied: "He will satisfy your needs in a sun-scorched land" (Isaiah 58:11).

When you find yourself discontented, stop and make a calculated evaluation of the longing. Is it a godly one—or ungodly? Will you yield to temptation in an attempt to satisfy your heart's desire, or will you turn to God and His Word for help?

CONTENT WITH PLENTY OR IN NEED

In his book *Spiritual Depression*, Martyn Lloyd-Jones poses an important question: Is it easier to be content with little or with much? Both are difficult. The apostle Paul's instruction is vital: "I have learned to be content whatever the circumstances. I know what it is to be in need, and I know what it is to have plenty. I have learned the secret of being content in any and every situation, whether well fed or hungry, whether living in plenty or in want. I can do everything through him who gives me strength" (Philippians 4:11-13).

Paul had learned the secret of contentment in plenty or in need. To be content with little is difficult for us because we fail to trust God to provide what we need. Instead we worry and plan. On the other hand, as Dr. Lloyd-Jones points out, "How difficult it is for the wealthy person not to feel complete independence of God. When we are rich and can arrange and manipulate everything, we tend to forget God."[7] So either way discontent always provides a temptation to sin by not depending on God.

Most women, however, feel certain they'd be quite content if they only had just a little bit more. But one woman has wisely said, "To be content with little is hard, to be content with much, impossible."[8] Apart from the only One who can satisfy us, we human beings are insatiable—we always want more. Solomon said it well: "All things are wearisome, more than one can say. The eye never has enough of seeing, nor the ear its fill of hearing" (Ecclesiastes 1:8). The more one has, the more one wants—nothing satisfies. So whether you are rich or poor, developing the discipline of contentment demands that we submit both our anxiety and our greed to the Lord.

THE SOURCE OF CONTENTMENT

It's a myth that people who are serious about the Bible are *serious* in general—long in the face and short on laughter. The fact is that women who love God and love His Word find sources of joy and satisfaction that surpass any the world has to offer. So it stands to reason that the rampant discontent among evangelical women stems from their shallow knowledge of the Bible.

We were made to know God! The knowledge of God is where satisfaction and pleasure are found. Here's a wise word: "Laughter and gladness are where joy, contentment, and gratitude overflow. But in an odd turn, these things proceed from an understanding of the truths of man's utter depravity and the salvation of the Lord."[9] Contentment is found in the knowledge of God!

James Packer says in his classic *Knowing God* that although many people do not see the practicality in a study of God and His attributes, every new discovery regarding God's character, in fact, graces our lives. He points, for example, to God's generosity toward us: "'The LORD is good to all: and his tender mercies are over all his works. . . . The eyes of all wait upon thee; and thou givest them their meat in due season. Thou openest thine hand, and satisfiest the desire of every living thing' (Psalm 145:9; 104:27 KJV). The psalmist's point is that since God controls all that happens in His world—every meal, every pleasure, every possession, every bit of sun, every night's sleep, every moment of health and safety— everything else that sustains and enriches life is a divine gift. And how abundant these gifts are!"[10]

How generous God is—and He is so much more! The Bible reveals all that we can know about God—His attributes and actions, His plans for time and eternity and where we fit into those plans. This is so obvious, but people fail to understand this simple truth. Christians have lost confidence in God's Word, as evidenced by the vast numbers who do not listen to it, read it, or study it—and most importantly apply its truths to their everyday lives.

Listen to God's Word

Does my critique of believers who don't pay attention to God's Word seem harsh? Often I've observed that people do not listen in church, and my sympathies are with those who, when they finally plop down in the pew, are completely exhausted from a week of work and a harried morning's rush to get to church. I am also sympathetic with those who have given up listening because the pastor is poorly prepared or has himself given up on preaching God's Word in favor of more popular themes. But when God's Word is preached, we must discipline ourselves to listen in spite of difficulties because listening is God's will for us. Hear Jesus' words: "*My sheep listen to my voice*; I know them, and they follow me. I give them eternal life, and they shall never perish; no one can snatch them out of my hand" (John 10:25-28, emphasis added).

A woman who works with children in our Sunday school program tells how God spoke to her through a phrase the children repeat each week. "It's time to put on our listening ears." At the same time, a passage of Scripture from her weekly Bible study came alive to her: "Guard your steps when you go to the house of God. Go near to listen" (Ecclesiastes 5:1).

Now when she sits in the pew at the beginning of the service, she consciously, silently prays, "Lord, I am here to listen." The Scripture goes on to say, "Therefore stand in awe of God" (Ecclesiastes 5:7).

Listening to God's Word is so important.

Study God's Word

Repeatedly throughout this book I encourage the study of God's Word. Bible study has never been easier than it is today. At any Christian bookstore there are endless guides and aids for help in personal Bible study. Almost every major city provides at least one of the Bible study organizations flourishing in this country today—Bible Study Fellowship, Community Bible Study, Precept Upon Precept Bible Studies, and Neighborhood Bible Studies. Many churches, such as my own, hold weekly Bible studies with childcare provided.

But these organizations are not necessary for the study of God's Word. All you need to do is set aside time to read the Bible with a pencil and paper in hand. London preacher and Bible teacher Dick Lucas provides these six basic questions that, if asked, will prove helpful:

1. What is the main point (or points) of the text?
2. How can you tell what the main point is?

3. How does your understanding of the text connect to what came immediately before and after?

4. Does this text tell us about or point us to Jesus? How?

5. What are the surprises in this text?

6. What is the application of this text? How do you know?

Get the big picture. After applying these questions to the text you are studying, ask this question: "How is the text tied to the context of the whole Bible?" This will help you avoid getting bogged down in the small details and enable you to gain an understanding of how a smaller section of the Bible fits into the big picture.[11]

As you study God's Word, you will come to know and love it! You will "eat" God's words (Jeremiah 15:16) and find them satisfying: "Jesus answered, 'It is written: "Man does not live on bread alone, but on every word that comes from the mouth of God"'" (Matthew 4:4). God's words are everlasting ("Heaven and earth will pass away, but my words will never pass away" [Matthew 24:35]), and God is the source of the wisdom you need: "Lord, to whom shall we go? You have the words of eternal life" (John 6:68).

Apply God's Word

Knowledge without application is lethal. Although there are far more women than men who attend Bible study on a regular basis, it is not necessarily true that it is doing them much good.

"We must learn to measure ourselves, not by our knowledge of God, not by our gifts and responsibilities in the church, but by how we pray and what goes on in our hearts. Many of us, I suspect, have no idea how impoverished we are at this level."[12]

This is where Libby got off track. She had been taught well, but she failed to trust what she knew to be true. Knowledge without application is one of the greatest dangers in the Christian community—following close behind a loss of confidence in God's Word. Knowledge for the sake of accumulated information leads only to pride and arrogance, both of which are the enemies of God. Applying our knowledge of God to our circumstances is the key to contentment.

When Paul wrote from prison that he had "learned to be content whatever the circumstances," he then added, "I can do everything through him who gives me strength" (Philippians 4:13). Paul applied his dynamic knowledge of God to his circumstances—and he was content.

From an anonymous eighteenth-century woman (A Poor Methodist Woman was her pen name) comes a luminous, haunting declaration of contentment in God alone. For me, her words have become the ideal.

> *I do not know*
> *when I have had happier times*
> *in my soul*
> *than when I have been sitting at work,*
> *with nothing before me*
> *but a candle and a white cloth,*
> *and hearing no sound*
> *but that of my own breath;*
> *with God in my soul*
> *and heaven in my eye.*
> *I rejoice in being exactly what I am*
> *—a creature capable of loving God,*
> *and who, as long as God lives,*
> *must be happy.*
> *I get up*
> *and look a while out the window.*
> *I gaze at the moon and stars,*
> *the work of an Almighty Hand.*
> *I think of the grandeur of the universe*
> *and then sit down*
> *and think myself*
> *one of the happiest*
> *beings in it.*

The rare jewel of Christian contentment will be yours when all that God is and all that He has done in Christ Jesus fills your heart. We may lack many things in this world, but as godly women we must work to develop the discipline of contentment. For this is God's will in the Gospel.

RENEW YOUR MIND

What are some aspects of the "great gain" that comes from "godliness with contentment" (1 Timothy 6:6)?

Why must godly contentment be independent of circumstances and conditions?

What characterizes godly discontent? What longings are godly ones? See Psalm 42:1; 61:4; 119:18-20.

How can you connect God's Word (your knowledge of Him) with your own areas of discontent?

If contentment is found in a growing knowledge of God combined with trust in God regardless of your circumstances, what is missing from your Christian life when you are discontented—knowledge or trust?

8

DISCIPLINE OF PROPRIETY

Submission's Behavior

❧

*Whatever happens, conduct yourselves in a manner
worthy of the gospel of Christ.*

PHILIPPIANS 1:27

We all have had the experience of pouring ourselves a cup of coffee and sitting down in front of the TV for a little diversion, clicking to a talk show, and hearing the host question a woman about her sex life. The exchange is degrading and frankly embarrassing. So we flip to another channel, and there to our amazement we hear couples revealing painful family secrets. We change the channel to view a discussion with young girls and their mothers. The mothers are defending their daughters' rights to dress indecently!

In disgust we turn off the television. Such a smorgasbord of swill was virtually unknown thirty years ago. Why? Because though our culture was not Christian, it still benefited from the rich Judeo-Christian heritage that graced our society with a sense of propriety.

Propriety—it's an old-fashioned word. It means "characterized by appropriateness or suitability." It seems a perfect word for describing what Paul means when he tells believers to act "in a manner worthy of the gospel" (Philippians 1:27).

The discipline of propriety is simply behaving in ways appropriate for Christians—actions that don't bring shame to the Gospel and to Christ. Propriety elevates our words, our appearance, and our attitudes. But propriety doesn't begin with these outwardly measurable signs. Propriety is a matter of the heart.

THE HEART OF THE MATTER

Author Bob DeMoss writes, "Your heart is the core of your being. It's the essence of who you are. It's where your mind and will, your emotions and convictions come together to shape what you believe and the choices you make."[1] He's saying that our behavior is determined by what is in our heart. Scripture backs up this idea: "As water reflects a face, so a man's heart reflects the man" (Proverbs 27:19).

Behavior dictated by the heart sounds fine—except that our hearts have a fatal flaw: "The heart is deceitful above all things and beyond cure. Who can understand it?" (Jeremiah 17:9).

What if we weren't gospel women? Apart from the Gospel, the best we could do to master what is in our hearts would be to refine our civilities and manners. But patting ourselves on the back because we're "not that bad" is false comfort because the most cultivated sensibilities can never get to the core of the problem in our deceitful, incurable hearts. Only the Gospel can get to the heart of the matter.

The heart! It's the place where we are born again. "That if you confess with your mouth, 'Jesus is Lord,' and believe in your heart that God raised him from the dead, you will be saved" (Romans 10:9).

Once we've confessed and believed in our hearts, the Word of God helps us address our deep need for an ongoing conversion of heart: "For the word of God is living and active. Sharper than any double-edged sword, it penetrates even to dividing soul and spirit, joints and marrow; it judges the thoughts and attitudes of the heart" (Hebrews 4:12).

When the Word of God begins its gracious surgery on our hearts, it is painful. It demands submitting to God's will in areas that we either deny exist or that we'd prefer to think are none of His business.

THE PROPRIETY OF OUR APPEARANCE

From the day a girl first opens a fashion magazine until the day she dies, clothes are a major topic of discussion. Surprisingly, for all we talk about clothes, the Bible says little on the subject. Yet what it does say is important.

Jesus taught that we shouldn't worry about our clothes the way pagans do, who run after such things, saying, "What shall we wear?" (Matthew 6:25-34). He was addressing a lack of faith in God for basic needs. When most of us fret over clothing, it usually has nothing to do with a basic need and everything to do with impressions we wish to create or the way we hope to feel about ourselves.

Celebrate the Difference

The Bible's primary instruction about our dressing speaks to the differences between men and women: "A woman must not wear men's clothing, nor a man wear women's clothing, for the LORD your God detests anyone who does this" (Deuteronomy 22:5).

This verse isn't about whether or not a woman can wear jeans (I have a few well-worn pairs myself!). It doesn't impose an impossible list of do's and don'ts. This passage is about a principle. Later when we discuss the discipline of marriage, we'll explore the value that God places on the differences between the sexes. Blurring that difference offends God. Christians should celebrate the difference. But how?

Will Hollywood help us? Historically they've cashed in on gender differences. Marilyn Monroe is virtually a monument to feminine curves. Hugh Hefner parlayed gender differences into an industry by unveiling them. No blurring of the differences here.

But, ironically, for some time now, it has also been "in" to *deny* the differences. Feminists certainly haven't helped us celebrate the difference. Rather they have brought about an enormous change in women's fashion, resulting in many women looking like soldiers in Mao's army! Critics wryly note that feminists "gag on the very word *feminine*."[2]

Together Hollywood image-makers and feminists influence women's clothing choices from early on. From adolescence we open our closets and make decisions about the image we want to project. "Effect" controls our choices: "Should I dress for men or women? Should I dress for power? for sophistication? for seduction?"

The gospel answer is "none of the above!" Christian women dress to please God. As Christ changes our hearts, we hear His voice above the clamoring of fashion magazines and promises of power. As our hearts are changed, we increasingly cherish being a woman.

Have you thanked God for making you female? If not, stop now and do so. Begin to make a habit of it. Rather than worshiping womanhood, worship its Creator! A heart of gratitude will surely begin to be reflected in your appearance. Your heart will be drawing from a source above the world around you—the life-giving source of the Word of God.

Dress with Modesty

Edward Sanford Martin puts it beautifully: "There is nothing the matter with girls. . . . They are a good invention of the kind and the kind is indispensable and has never been beaten. If you don't think so, there is something the matter with you. When a race or a nation doesn't think so, it is an infallible symptom that there is something amiss with that nation. There isn't any surer test of the progress of any people in civilization than its appreciation of girls."[3]

The Word of God addresses what women wear precisely *because it values girls.* Celebrating gender differences highlights a woman's value. Modesty is intrinsically elevating: "I also want women to dress modestly, with decency and propriety, not with braided hair or gold or pearls or expensive clothes, but with good deeds, appropriate for women who profess to worship God" (1 Timothy 2:9-10). We've already noted that propriety means characterized by appropriateness. If you attend a formal occasion, such as a wedding, you dress up. Your attire shows proper respect for the bride and groom. So "dressing down" on that occasion would not be worthy of the Gospel.

As to "modestly, with decency," both *modest* and *decent* are synonyms for the word *chaste.* "Chaste primarily implies a refraining from acts or even thoughts or desires that are not virginal or not sanctioned by marriage vows."[4] Dressing modestly then means to wear clothes that do not arouse thoughts or actions that promote sensuality.

If you are blind or from another planet, you may conceivably have missed the fact that modesty has disappeared. It is dead and buried! If you don't think so, go shopping with a teenager. The fashion gurus have made sure that every item of clothing today's teen girl might need was designed to provoke thoughts that are other than virginal. It calls to mind the prophet Jeremiah's exclamation: "Are they ashamed of their loath-some conduct? No, they have no shame at all; they do not even know how to blush" (Jeremiah 6:15).

I've noticed that some young Christian women have reacted to the pressure by donning oversized, baggy, mannish clothing. In their desire to please the Lord, they find it easier to wear unbecoming clothes than to think through what is feminine and unprovocative.

Of course, there are many young women—Christian and non-Christian—who do not dress seductively. Common sense is enough to tell the thinking young woman that modesty protects the value of women. In her book *A Return to Modesty*, Wendy Shalit writes: "Certainly sexual modesty may damp down superficial allure, the kind of allure that inspires a one-night stand. But the kind of allure that lasts—that is what modesty protects and inspires. Modesty damps down crudeness; it doesn't damp down Eros. In fact, it is more likely to enkindle it."[5]

So there's the challenge—to dress in a way that is *feminine, appropriate,* and *modest.* We gospel women must begin with our hearts, allowing God's Word to search out the thoughts and intentions that influence our wardrobe. We must also turn our attention to the beauties that God values most in us—beauties that have little to do with clothing.

Dress with Strength and Dignity

Proverbs 31:15 celebrates a woman who is virtuous in God's eyes. She is "clothed with strength and dignity"—not to be confused with power dressing! Power dressing is dressing with the intent of intimidation—a show of power over a person from whom you hope to gain something. Instead, when gospel women dress with strength and dignity, they are reflecting their created position and rank as women of God.

We women are God's image-bearers; that's where our dignity comes from. First God made us in His image; then He bought us. Christ's purchase made us children of God, joint-heirs with Him—a position of highest rank. The woman clothed with "strength and dignity" will behave in a manner worthy of her honored position. She knows who she is, and she carries herself with that assurance—not to impress or intimidate anyone but to honor her Creator and Redeemer.

Beauty That Counts

Peter points the way to a better kind of beauty than that which the fashion magazines promise: "Your beauty should not come from outward adornment, such as braided hair and the wearing of gold jewelry and fine clothes. Instead, it should be that of your inner self, the unfading beauty of a gentle and quiet spirit, which is of great worth in God's sight" (1 Peter 3:3-4).

Such beauty does not rely on external helps; it's deeply rooted in faith and trust in God. No matter how many charge cards you may have, you cannot purchase this beauty; it's priceless! It's a beauty that grows as our hearts respond in ongoing surrender to God's will for us. Each time you act in obedience to God's Word and will for you, you experience an amazing renewal: "Though outwardly we are wasting away, yet inwardly we are being renewed day by day" (2 Corinthians 4:16).

The Bible likens the application of God's Word to our lives to the act of dressing. So as we follow God's directive, it is good to visualize ourselves "putting on" the good things of God.

> *Put on the new self, created to be like God in true righteousness and holiness (Ephesians 4:24).*

> *Put on the full armor of God so that you can take your stand against the devil's schemes (Ephesians 6:11).*

> *Put on the new self, which is being renewed in knowledge in the image of its Creator (Colossians 3:10).*

> *The night is nearly over; the day is almost here. So let us put aside the deeds of darkness and put on the armor of light. (Romans 13:12)*

> *Therefore, as God's chosen people, holy and dearly loved, clothe yourselves with compassion, kindness, humility, gentleness and patience. Bear with each other and forgive whatever grievances you may have against one another. Forgive as the Lord forgave you. And over all these virtues put on love, which binds them all together in perfect unity (Colossians 3:12-14).*

> *Clothe yourselves with strength. Put on your garments of splendor (Isaiah 52:1).*

Clothe yourselves with humility (1 Peter 5:5).

Clothe yourselves with the Lord Jesus Christ, and do not think about how to gratify the desires of the sinful nature (Romans 13:14).

I also want women to dress . . . with good deeds, appropriate for women who profess to worship God" (1 Timothy 2:9-10).

Discipline your hearts so that you "dress" in a manner worthy of the Gospel!

THE PROPRIETY OF OUR WORDS

Propriety also extends to the things that we say. The Scriptures are explicit as to how godly women (in particular, leaders' wives) should use their words: "In the same way, their wives are to be women worthy of respect, not malicious talkers but temperate and trustworthy in everything" (1 Timothy 3:11).

Respectability is the operative quality here, and my husband, the scholar, tells me that in the original language *respectability* is defined by what it is *not*. This respectable woman is not a malicious talker. She is respectable because her words are not malicious but temperate (restrained) and trustworthy (true).

True and restrained words are always wise words: "Reckless words pierce like a sword, but the tongue of the wise brings healing" (Proverbs 12:18). True and restrained speaking is worthy of the Gospel. As with our appearance, our words must not bring disgrace to Christ. The godly woman's words are true words, spoken wisely. They are sweet to the hearer: "Pleasant words are a honeycomb, sweet to the soul and healing to the bones" (Proverbs 16:24).

James writes of the tongue that is used for destructive purposes: "Consider what a great forest is set on fire by a small spark. The tongue also is a fire, a world of evil among the parts of the body. It corrupts the whole person, sets the whole course of his life on fire, and is itself set on fire by hell" (James 3:5-6). Wow! The tongue holds such awesome potential for harm. What a warning to every woman who desires to please God.

Gossip

The age-old way the tongue destroys is through gossip that often cannot be undone. A physician in a Midwestern city was slandered by a disgruntled patient who tried to ruin him professionally through rumor—and nearly did. Several years later the gossiper had a change of heart and wrote the doctor asking his forgiveness, and the physician forgave her. But there was no way she could stop or erase the story she'd started, and neither could he. As Solomon sadly observed, "The words of a gossip are like choice morsels; they go down to a man's inmost parts" (Proverbs 18:8). Gossip was greedily picked up and stored away by the hearers like tasty tidbits. Vigorous denial would only have brought more suspicion. The damage was done. Hereafter the innocent doctor would look into some of his acquaintances' eyes and wonder if they had heard and believed the lies.

Gossip often veils itself in certain phrases:

"Have you heard . . . ?"

"Did you know . . . ?"

"They tell me . . ."

"Keep this to yourself, but . . ."

"I don't believe it's true, but I heard that . . ."

"I wouldn't tell you, except that I know it will go no further."

Of course, the most infamous such rationalization in Christian circles is, "I am telling you this so you can pray." It sounds pious, but the heart that feeds on evil reports leaves flaming fires in its wake. Oh, the heartache that comes from the tongue.

Flattery

Gossip is saying behind a person's back what you would never say to her face. Flattery is saying to a person's face what you would never say behind her back. The Scriptures warn us repeatedly against flatterers, for they are destructive people who carry a legion of unwholesome motives: "Whoever flatters his neighbor is spreading a net for his feet" (Proverbs 29:5). "A lying tongue hates those it hurts, and a flattering mouth works ruin" (Proverbs 26:28). "May the LORD cut off all flattering lips and every boastful tongue that says, 'We will triumph with our tongues . . .'" (Psalm 12:3-4).

Criticism

Fault-finding seems endemic to believers. Perhaps this is because a little righteousness can be easily perverted into an overweening sense of self-righteousness and judgmentalism. Once while John Wesley was preaching, he noticed a woman in the audience who was known for her critical attitude. All through the service she sat and stared at his new tie. When the meeting ended, she came up to him and said very sharply, "Mr. Wesley, the strings on your tie are much too long. It's an offense to me!" He asked if any of the women present happened to have a pair of scissors in their purses. When the scissors were handed to him, he gave them to his critic and asked her to trim the streamers to her liking.

After she clipped them off near the collar, he said, "Are you sure they're all right now?"

"Yes, that's much better."

"Then let me have those shears a moment," said Wesley. "I'm sure you wouldn't mind if I also gave you a bit of correction. I must tell you, madam, that your tongue is an offense to me—it's too long! Please stick it out. . . . I'd like to take some off."

On another occasion someone said to Wesley, "My talent is to speak my mind."

Wesley replied, "That's one talent God wouldn't care a bit if you buried!"

Diminishment

James also forbids any speech (true or false) that runs down another person: "Do not speak against one another" (4:11 NASB)—meaning, literally, "Do not speak down on one another."

Certainly no Christian should ever be a party to slandering another's reputation. But many Christians feel it's fine to convey negative information as long as it's true. Somehow passing along damaging truths feels almost like a moral responsibility! By such reasoning, denigrating gossip (of course it is never called gossip!) is deemed okay if the information is based in fact.

Then there are folks who won't denigrate other people behind their backs but are quite ready to do it face to face—as if driven by a "moral" compulsion to make others aware of their shortcomings.

It can be equally destructive to minimize others' virtues and accomplishments with a superior glance or tone of voice or putdowns such as "What a nice *little* piano" about your Steinway. Diminishing others with words may stem from a need to make ourselves feel bigger or better, like the Pharisee who thanked God he was not like other sinners "or even like this tax collector" (Luke 18:11).

Cutting remarks also come from too much empty talk. When you run out of worthwhile ideas and issues to discuss, stop talking: "The heart of the righteous weighs its answers, but the mouth of the wicked gushes evil" (Proverbs 15:28).

A Warning from Jesus

Jesus cuts through our feeble excuses and gets to the heart of our problem with a scathing blow to our hypocrisy: "Make a tree good and its fruit will be good, or make a tree bad and its fruit will be bad, for a tree is recognized by its fruit. You brood of vipers, how can you who are evil say anything good? For out of the overflow of the heart the mouth speaks. The good man brings good things out of the good stored up in him, and the evil man brings evil things out of the evil stored up in him. But I tell you that men will have to give account on the day of judgment for every careless word they have spoken. For by your words you will be acquitted, and by your words you will be condemned" (Matthew 12:33-37).

Again our hearts! The problem lies in the core of our being, and our words are constantly revealing what's there. Russian writer Turgenev once said, "I do not know the heart of a bad man, but I know the heart of a good man—and it is terrible!" Over and over again, my words painfully reveal my heart's need of the Gospel and of Christ, whose words revealed the truth and beauty of His heart. If it weren't for Him, I couldn't bear the burden of my sin—in particular, the sins of my mouth. "May the words of my mouth and the meditation of my heart be pleasing in your sight, O LORD, my Rock and my Redeemer" (Psalm 19:14).

THE PROPRIETY OF ATTITUDE

The Gospel brings us to our knees. In the moment that faith is born, we submit to truth about God but also to truth about ourselves. The Gospel humbles us. We admit our own lack of goodness as we submit to the One who is perfectly good and worthy of praise.

If only that moment of true humility would remain with us through-out our lives. But as long as we are on this earth, pride continues to rear its ugly head in our hearts. Pride is the attitude of the ungodly. Humility is the hallmark of godliness.

Of course, pride isn't always easy to recognize, and humility can be so costly. My Bible study coleader, JoAnn, found her life transformed when she recognized her pride and pursued a proper attitude. She tells her own story:

One particular year was filled with disappointments. Little things—and then bigger things. The final straw occurred when a ministry was taken from me. I reached the end of my reserves. I responded in self-pity, anger, defensiveness, bitterness, and resentment. Not on the outside, of course. Outside I was gentility personified.

Those I considered to be responsible were enemies. I couldn't entirely hide what was in my heart from them. I let them know by my silence and facial expressions that I didn't like them, and I rejoiced inwardly when they suffered or experienced any diffi-culties. My revengeful attitude extended to my family members and friends of those I dubbed enemies.

A struggle ensued within me that went on for years. I knew that the Scripture clearly teaches that we are to love and forgive. And so I struggled between getting even and forgiving.

My struggle extended to my attitude about God. It seemed to me that ministry was being dangled in front of me like a carrot and then snatched away. What kind of a God would do this? I stopped reading the Bible and praying.

These struggles continued for a very long time. One day I asked myself what I had accomplished for God. The answer stunned me: It was wood, hay, and stubble.

Sometime later I decided to set aside a day to pray. In the course of the day I made a list of undesirable characteristics I saw in myself—an excessive need for approval and affirmation, a critical spirit, bitterness and resentment, striving for center stage, and a competitive spirit. I decided these were "weaknesses." There was no immediate change in my behavior after that day, but I now see that there was a softening of my spirit and a growing hunger for God.

Six weeks later, during a Sunday morning Communion service, God spoke to me through Psalm 22 with its description of Jesus' suffering and the horror He felt when God forsook Him. I thought of the many times I had sought intimacy with God and of all the frustration and isolation I'd felt and realized that my experience was nothing compared to what Jesus voluntarily experienced on the cross. The words of Hebrews 5:7 crossed my mind: "During the days of Jesus' life on earth, he offered up prayers and petitions with loud cries and tears to the one who could save him from death, and he was heard because of his reverent submission."

It occurred to me that although Jesus was heard, His request was not granted. I began to see what Jesus' death really cost Him. That list of "weaknesses" I had made for myself were not weaknesses. They were symptoms of a serious sin—pride.

I was overwhelmed with the realization of my sin. "Oh, Lord, I don't know what to do," I prayed. "Such sin is too much for me to handle. You'll have to take it away." This prayer marked a major change in attitude. I was asking God to change me, not trying to change myself so that He would be satisfied with me.

All of the people I had harbored so much bitterness toward came to mind. I knew I had to ask their forgiveness—each one. I got in touch with all of the people within two days. After talking to the last person, I was overwhelmed with a sense of God's presence. There was a release and an inner joy. I was conscious of a great love for God and for other Christians.

In the succeeding weeks I became aware of changes occurring in the inner workings of my heart. There was a tenderness, a new willingness to give to others, and a great compassion for those who were suffering in any way. I was also conscious of an overwhelming love for God. I had fallen in love with God. And I'm still in love with Him!

Years later, while talking with a former acquaintance, she said to me, "I don't know what's happened, but you're a changed person."

I was one of the people JoAnn visited that long-ago day, which involved confession, tears, forgiveness, and reconciliation. Since that time she has served as a model to me of a woman who continues to submit her heart to the scrutiny of God's Word and allow God to do His exquisite surgery. I cannot tell you the extent of the influence she has had in helping me become a godly woman. Her Bible study lessons and evangelistic lunches, her teaching on prayer, and her insights into using hospitality for the sake of the Gospel have marked my life.

Heart Healing

Allowing the Word of God to assess the thoughts and attitudes of our hearts is difficult indeed. It is painful. Some of you may be realizing that your heart is sick and that you have never found the magic potion to heal it. No matter how hard you try, you cannot do the things you ought to do or even what you want to do. This heart condition is called sin. Many good church women try to "be good" without ever truly being converted; they never get a new heart that is inclined to do good. You can develop a refined external civility, but it is impossible to change the source of the problem—your heart. Only God in Christ can do that, and, praise God, He is willing.

Living out the discipline of propriety means acting in a way worthy of the Gospel in dress, speech, and attitude. If your behavior is worthy of the Gospel, the source of that behavior will be a heart changed by the Gospel. Is your heart truly converted? Have you ever authentically bowed your knee in humble submission to Jesus Christ as Lord? If you have any question, reread "Two Ways to Live" at the end of chapter 2. Make certain that this question is settled today.

If you are confident that you are a Christian, this matter of the heart is an ongoing housekeeping matter. Consider the words of the psalmist:

> *How can a young man keep his way pure?*
> *By living according to your word.*
> *I seek you with all my heart;*
> *do not let me stray from your commands.*

I have hidden your word in my heart
that I might not sin against you.
Praise be to you, O LORD; teach me your decrees.
With my lips I recount
all the laws that come from your mouth.
I rejoice in following your statutes
as one rejoices in great riches.
I meditate on your precepts and consider your ways.
I delight in your decrees;
I will not neglect your word. (Psalm 119:9-16)

May the words of my mouth and the meditations of my heart
be pleasing in your sight, O LORD,
 my Rock and my Redeemer. (Psalm 19:14)

RENEW YOUR MIND

As you examine your heart—where propriety begins—what surgeries has the Holy Spirit already performed there? What areas do you think still require change? See Proverbs 27:19, Jeremiah 17:9, Romans 10:9-10, and Hebrews 4:12.

Does your apparel reflect your desire for modesty and appropriate femininity? Does your outward appearance reflect your "new life" as a believer (Ephesians 4:24; Colossians 3:10)?

What aspects of "spiritual dress" do you most need to add to your wardrobe—compassion, kindness, humility, gentleness, or patience (Colossians 3:12)?

Gaining mastery over what we say remains a lifelong challenge. Generally, is your conversation temperate (restrained) and trustworthy (true)? Why does 1 Timothy 3:11 point out "malice" as a specific danger in our words? Think back to some recent conversations and check them for the insidious problems of gossip, flattery, fault-finding, or diminishing others. Pray Psalm 19:14 to the Lord.

Because pride is so close to our hearts, it's especially difficult to discern this attitude. How does spending time with God help you see yourself with appropriate humility? Would you consider your attitude before God one of "reverent submission"?

9

DISCIPLINE OF PERSEVERANCE

Submission's Challenge

Let us run with perseverance the race marked out for us.

HEBREWS 12:1

Pastor Scott Willis and his wife, Janet, together with six of their nine children, piled into their minivan, buckled up, and left their home on Chicago's south side for Wisconsin. It would turn out to be a day of excruciating pain and horror. While driving north on Interstate 94 in Milwaukee, the van ran over a large piece of metal that punctured the gas tank, immediately turning the vehicle into an inferno. By the time the van stopped and the parents fell out, their children were hopelessly trapped. Six of their children went home to be with the Lord that day.

You'd think the Willises would conclude that their God was far away at that moment. Yet the burned, bandaged couple, still in physical pain, gave witness to God's grace at a news conference. Janet relates that when she looked back toward the van and began screaming, Scott touched her shoulder. "He said, 'Janet, this is what we've been prepared for.' And he was right. He said, 'Janet, it was quick, and they're with the Lord.' He was right."

In their shared hospital room Scott and Janet comforted themselves by watching videos of their children, reading passages from God's Word, and talking openly about what had happened.

The Willises' testimony amidst the tears and heartache is amazing. "I know God has purposes and God has reasons," says Scott. "God has demonstrated His love to us and our family. There's no question in our mind that God is good, and we praise Him in all things."

"It's His right," agrees Janet. "We belong to Him. My children belong to Him. He's the giver and taker of life, and He sustains us."[1]

With these words, Janet and Scott Willis demonstrated to the world and particularly to believers what it means to "run with perseverance the race marked out for us."

When that drama unfolded on national television, an icy fear gripped my heart. I suspect that most Christian women quietly prayed something like, "Dear God, please don't ask that of me!" The Willises' amazing faith poignantly revealed the shallowness of our own—the tentative commitment that lets us fall apart if we experience even the inconvenience of losing the car keys.

Faith in the goodness of God in the face of extreme adversity doesn't just happen. It grows out of a discipline of perseverance in the day-in, day-out grind of everyday life.

WHY PERSEVERE?

To persevere means "to persist in a state, enterprise or undertaking in spite of counterinfluences, opposition or discouragement."[2] The *Dictionary of Biblical Imagery* says that "perseverance is rooted in confidence in the Lord. It is produced by suffering (Romans 5:3; James 1:3) and produces character, 'so that [we] may be mature and complete, not lacking anything' (James 1:4; Romans 5:4)."[3]

Let's face it right up front: Suffering is associated with the development of perseverance. As we understand better what Scripture teaches about the spiritual benefits of perseverance, we can look to the future with hope instead of fear. There are three specific reasons for our suffering:

Suffering is God's means of perfecting us.
Suffering is a means of spreading the Gospel.
In persevering through suffering we see God.

God's Means of Perfecting Us

As Christians we are already perfectly acceptable to God through faith in the death and resurrection of Jesus. Christ's righteousness has become our own. What is achieved through perseverance is not righteousness but maturity. This maturing process regularly involves testing.

Two words are used in Scripture for testing. The first likens what happens to us in trials to what happens to metal when it is refined. Heat is applied, and the dross comes to the top and is skimmed off, making the substance purer. The other word for testing means to tempt, and the goal of the tempter is destructive. Christians must persevere through many trials and temptations if we would grow mature and be refined.

The life of the apostle Peter is a grand example of a life transformed through testing. Scripture carefully portrays Peter as very human—someone we can all relate to. He comes to Christ in loving submission, but with the passing of time Peter succumbs to independence and self-reliance.

Peter had walked away from the family business in order to follow Jesus and was with Jesus for three years of intense discipleship. On the eve of Christ's crucifixion, Peter boldly announced to Jesus: "Lord, I am ready to go with you to prison and to death" (see Luke 22:33, 57). Yet just as Jesus had predicted, the next day Peter cowardly denied that he even knew who Jesus was with these bitter words: "Woman, I don't know him."

However after the Crucifixion and Resurrection, we see another Peter. Absolutely fearless, he preached before a crowd and made this bold accusation: "Therefore let all Israel be assured of this: God has made this Jesus, *whom you crucified*, both Lord and Christ" (Acts 2:36, emphasis mine).

At the end of his life, the now wise old apostle exhorted the church with a gentle and fatherly tone: "All of you, clothe yourselves with humility toward one another, because, 'God opposes the proud but gives grace to the humble'" (1 Peter 5:5).

Peter had been perfected through the trials and temptations he suffered. He persevered. He endured hardship. He didn't give up through failure, fears, and the repeated attacks of Satan. The words of Jesus to Peter in the Upper Room give us insight into what God was doing: "Simon, Simon, Satan has asked to sift you as wheat. But I have prayed for you, Simon, that your faith may not fail. And when you have turned back, strengthen your brothers" (Luke 22:31).

God's will for Peter's perfection included his being sifted by Satan. Before the sifting came, it first passed through Christ's prayers and the merciful hand of God. That is how it is for all of us.

When you feel that you are in the sifter, don't lose sight of the reality that God is in control and that Christ and the Holy Spirit are praying for you—just as they did for Peter. Remember that Christ "is able to save completely those who come to God through him, because he always lives to intercede for them" (Hebrews 7:25).

Romans reveals to us the Spirit's incredibly intimate work of intercession on our behalf: "In the same way, the Spirit helps us in our weakness. We do not know what we ought to pray for, but the Spirit himself intercedes for us with groans that words cannot express. And he who searches our hearts knows the mind of the Spirit, because the Spirit intercedes for the saints in accordance with God's will" (Romans 8:26-27).

As we take to heart the reality that both Jesus and the Holy Spirit pray for us, we are empowered to persevere. My dear friend Nancy tells of a period beginning in January of 1995 when a sequence of events and circumstances began that shook nearly every aspect of her previously comfortable life. Her husband changed jobs within his company and then changed places of employment twice. Both of her children changed schools. Then she changed places of employment. They left one church for another. Most critical of all were serious health issues that arose in their immediate family, demanding every bit of Nancy's time and energy. Each day brought new challenges and fears to her life.

Before this all began, Nancy had chosen Luke 22:31-32 as her verse for the year: "Simon, Simon, Satan has asked to sift you as wheat . . . but I have prayed for you . . ." Nancy remained in the sifter for five years! She was acquainted with fear, discouragement, deep sadness, and uncertainty. But throughout this time she took comfort from the reminder that just as Christ prayed for Peter, He was praying for her as well.

Nancy now triumphantly says, "Knowing that He is at God's right hand, offering intercessory prayer for me was my strong anchor throughout the storms. The knowledge of Jesus' prayer shifted my focus from the storms, raging around and within, *to God's will for me*. When the path ahead was unclear and it seemed as if God were silent for a long time, or when circumstances overwhelmed me and I felt like crying enough! this verse turned my heart from fear to faith. God's purpose for the sifting was to prove and perfect my faith. That perfection is not to be completed in this earthly life. But here and now, He gives everything we need to face whatever sifting He allows—He gives Himself."

A Means of Spreading the Gospel

A faith that perseveres through suffering makes a powerful statement about the object of such faith. When Scott and Janet Willis proclaimed to the world that "God is good," the world listened. Their perseverance served as a brilliant spotlight illuminating the Gospel.

The book of Revelation describes how human beings naturally respond to suffering in its depiction of that day when God's wrath will be poured out. The ungodly refuse to repent and glorify God. Instead they curse the God of heaven because of their pain (cf. Revelation 16:8-11, 21).

Indeed, the human response to pain and suffering is to curse God. Persevering faith, like that of Janet and Scott Willis, shouts for our attention and hallows (sanctifies) God's name because it is immovably fixed in absolute confidence in the Lord. As seventeenth-century writer Jeremiah Burroughs put it: "He whose contentment is of grace is not disquieted and keeps his heart quiet with regard to vexation and trouble, and at the same time is not dull or heavy but very active to sanctify God's name in the affliction he is experiencing."[4] The Willises sanctified God's name in their affliction.

I learned about this kind of faith in a hotel room in Israel. My husband and I had arrived late the night before and were awakened with an early morning call. Kent expected to hear the voice of a missionary friend who was to give us our first tour of the Old City in Jerusalem, but instead we heard our youngest son's anxious voice conveying the worst news we have ever received. His brother was in the hospital, and the doctors had just informed him they didn't know if he would survive. Unable to get a return flight home until midnight, we spent the longest day of our lives in deep agony of soul—praying for the life of our dear son.

I opened my Bible for help to a passage of Scripture I'd been studying in preparation to teach a women's Bible study—the fourteenth chapter of John, one of the most comforting passages in Scripture. The radio Bible teacher, Dr. A. C. Gaebelein, was fond of recounting that among his family treasures was a German Bible that went back many generations. He said one could open that Bible to some pages that looked as if the book had just come off the press. But when they opened to John 14, the pages were spotted, soiled, and worn from the tears of generations.

I found more than comfort in John 14 that day as I read: "Do not let your hearts be troubled" (John 14:1). I knew from study that the idea communicated is, "Don't let your heart shudder." Jesus was saying to the disciples (in light of His imminent death), "It may look like your world is falling in, and all is lost, and the darkness is going to engulf you, but don't let your heart shudder." But my heart *was* shuddering in deepest fear.

Christ goes on to explain how to keep your heart from being troubled: "Trust in God; trust also in me." So simple. I had just learned that the tense of the verb "believe" meant to keep on believing in God—to keep on believing in Jesus—and the emphasis is specifically for times of trial.

Jesus was telling me that dark day in Israel to persevere through my fears by believing true things about God—to keep on believing all that I had learned about His sovereignty, His omniscience, His omnipotence, His mercy, and His loving grace. But Jesus did more for me that day than tell me not to give up. He showed me how.

As I read on in that passage, I was comforted—not as one might expect by the familiar promise of a place prepared in heaven for me or of the coming Comforter. I was comforted by Jesus' behavior.

Jesus knew when He left that upper room with His disciples that He would face His greatest test of persevering faith—remaining resolute to do God's will in facing the cross. The last twenty-five words of John 14 shot off the page and into my heart like a bullet hitting its mark: "The world must learn that I love the Father and that I do exactly what my Father has commanded me. Come now, let us leave" (John 14:31).

The world learns through our determined, loving obedience to God's will in the face of adversity that God is worth it! I knew in that hotel room that my actions and my words would tell those around me what I really think of the Lord Jesus Christ. My husband and I had fervently prayed long before this day that our children would be spared the tragedy our son was facing. But the answer from heaven to us was no! What would I do? Would I toss in the towel, crying that God had let us down or that our prayers were useless? Would I inform my husband that I had reached the limit of what could be expected in my walk of faith? If

I chose that path, the message to the world and the church would be clear: God isn't worth it!

As we keep on believing when the answer is no, we demonstrate to the world the value of Christ. Our actions in such times validate the reality of the Gospel to a watching world.

With God's Word as my comfort and guide, Christ's example to follow, and His Spirit's help, I found comfort. By His grace, I kept on believing that God is good and that He is worthy of my loving obedience. There was no escaping the pain—either for us or our son. But one day at a time—sometimes one hour at a time—our faith persevered. After long months of hospitalization and medical help, the dark day passed, and our son has been fully recovered for years now. God showed Himself faithful to our family again and again.

In Persevering We See God

Peter also tells us that our "enemy the devil prowls around like a roaring lion looking for someone to devour" (1 Peter 5:8). Satan hopes to bring people so low that they curse God and spread the devouring delusion abroad.

The book of Job begins with a scene in heaven as Satan appears before God and asks Him, "Does Job fear God for nothing?" (1:9). The cynical question reveals Satan's view that man is absolutely self-centered and self-serving, even if he appears to be a faithful worshiper of God, as did Job. Satan asserts that if God stretches out His hand and strikes everything Job has, Job will curse God to His face (1:11). Job didn't curse his God. Instead he saw God for who He is and blessed His name.

It is through times of difficulty that we best learn of God's character and love because God then has our full attention. The most dramatic test for me began in February 1996. With Kent by my side, I checked into the hospital for what was supposed to be routine surgery. It never occurred to me that I would be fighting for my life in just a few hours.

My life was preserved that day by sovereign providence because God had orchestrated many people and events over years of time so that all would come together in time to save my life.

My life's preservation began years before when my niece on a whim moved nearby and took a job as a lab technician at our local hospital. One slow night she and another bored technician ran blood tests on each other, and she learned that she had a rare clotting disorder. Shortly afterward my niece moved to the East Coast.

On the morning of my presumed simple surgery, that other lab technician, Suzanne, went to make a bank deposit at a hospital ATM and walked through a part of the hospital where she normally didn't go. She saw my husband there and offered to stop by for a quick visit with me the next morning.

After my surgery the doctor reported that all was well, so Kent went home for a quick shower. Returning, he was met by our worried daughter, who informed him that I was back in surgery, which should take about "fifteen minutes." Those fifteen minutes became five interminable hours. Kent's associate pastor, Larry Fullerton, and his wife, Susan (a physician), joined Kent in the long wait. In spite of repeated blood transfusions, I continued to decline.

In the morning Susan left to go to work, but as she approached her car, she realized she had locked her keys inside. She had to retrace her steps to my hospital room to get Larry's keys. As they walked together to the car, Larry asked his wife what she thought was going on. She told him the problem had to do with my blood not clotting.

Returning to my room, Larry greeted my brother, who had just arrived. As Larry briefed him, Suzanne, my niece's friend from the lab, stopped by to see me—without her manager's approval! At that point in spite of continuous transfusions, I was near death. Shocked to walk in on the family crisis, Suzanne quietly slipped out.

As she left, she overheard Larry repeat to my brother the information his wife had given him: "There seems to be a problem with her blood clotting."

In an instant Suzanne remembered those long-ago blood tests. She recalled that my niece had been warned by a blood specialist that if she ever suffered a serious physical trauma, she could bleed to death without the proper treatment.

Suzanne ran to the lab, switched on her computer, and got both my own and my niece's lab reports on the screen. The pathology was identical! Suzanne raced to the critical care unit and excitedly tried to explain all this to the nurse, who thought she was delirious. She dashed back to her supervisor, who did take her seriously and got the attention of the team of doctors working on my case.

Without time to test me, the doctors took Suzanne's word for it. On the advice of a lab technician who recognized one of a list of blood disorders they verbally tossed at her, the doctors administered the one and only remedy for the rare blood disorder, hypofibrinogenemia.

Without a doubt, the doctors said, Suzanne saved my life. And she may have saved the lives of several of my family members also, since subsequent testing has revealed that my mother, aunts, two sisters, a brother, one daughter, and three grandchildren have the same life-threatening genetic disorder.

What happened to me was an empirically verifiable miracle of divine providence! Count up the people involved, the timing, the events. God designed it all—down to keeping the lab so busy that Suzanne was prevented from visiting me until that precise moment when Larry Fullerton would answer my brother's question within earshot of Suzanne.

Suzanne didn't save my life. God did! God raised the shade of eternity for a brief time and let our family and church family have a peek at how His loving care for me throughout the nitty-gritty of everyday life for years before came together on that critical day.

The word *providence* comes from two Latin words: *pro* (before) and *video* (to see). So when we speak of God's providence, we are referring to His seeing all things beforehand and His sovereign arrangement of all things. The mathematical probability of these events coming together in this way are astronomical! Only God could have arranged it, start to finish.

Job, who suffered the loss of everything—family, wealth, possessions, and the respect of his wife and friends—spoke these beautiful words: "My ears had heard of you but now my eyes have seen you" (Job 42:5). He praised God for the chance to see God at His incredible work!

I can say, as the psalmist David did, that "it was good for me to be afflicted" (Psalm 119:71). In the weeks, months, and years of my recovery, I confronted physical challenges that peeled away nearly every layer of confidence in the flesh. Most difficult are the lingering effects of oxygen deprivation. Concentration problems made reading (a lifelong pleasure) impossible for years. Characteristically agile-minded, I now have problems with short-term memory, leaving me frustrated and embarrassed. But in the midst these insecurities, I have turned and continue to turn to the Scriptures for peace. The Lord has given me a greater vision of Himself. I know the Lord in ways that I had not formerly known Him. The Scriptures wonderfully convey my experience:

> *He did this so that all the people of the earth might know that the hand of the LORD is powerful and so that you might always fear the LORD your God. (Joshua 4:24)*

> *When my life was ebbing away, I remembered you, LORD, and my prayer rose to you, to your holy temple. Those who cling to worthless idols forfeit the grace that could be theirs. But I, with a song of thanksgiving, will sacrifice to you. What I have vowed I will make good. Salvation comes from the LORD. (Jonah 2:7-9)*

> *I am the LORD, and there is no other; apart from me there is no God. . . . I form the light and create darkness, I bring prosperity and create disaster; I, the LORD, do all these things. . . . Turn to me and be saved, all you ends of the earth; for I am God, and there is no other. (Isaiah 45:5, 7, 22)*

> *Among the gods there is none like you, O LORD; no deeds can compare with yours. All the nations you have made will come and worship before you, O LORD; they will bring glory to your name. For you are great and do marvelous deeds; you alone are God. Teach me your way, O LORD, and I will walk in your truth; give me an undivided heart, that I may fear your name. I will praise you . . . with all my heart; I will glorify your name forever. For great is your love toward me; you have delivered me from the depths of the grave. (Psalm 86:8-13)*

> *The God who made the world and everything in it is the Lord of heaven and earth and does not live in temples built by hands. And he is not served by human hands, as if he needed anything, because he himself gives all men life and breath and everything else. From one man he made every nation of men, that they should inhabit the whole earth; and he determined the times set for them and the exact places where they should live. God did this so that men would seek him and perhaps reach out for him and find him, though he is not far from each one of us. For in him we live and move and have our being. (Acts 17:24-28)*

For when David had served God's purpose in his own generation, he fell asleep. . . . (Acts 13:36)

As the heavens are higher than the earth, so are my ways higher than your ways and my thoughts than your thoughts. (Isaiah 55:9)

The secret things belong to the LORD our God, but the things revealed belong to us and to our children forever. (Deuteronomy 29:29)

Here is a God who is *in control*. He knows what He is doing, using everything at His disposal to accomplish His purposes for this world—and for me. Because He deemed it necessary to afflict me in order to teach me, then I must wholeheartedly agree with the psalmist: "It was good for me that I was afflicted." Submitting to God in my trials—trusting God to be God (good, wise, merciful, just, kind, lovingly all-knowing, and all-powerful)—is what the discipline of perseverance is about. This discipline is necessary if we would see more of God.

HOW DO WE PERSEVERE?

My illness, my heartaches, my trials—they will, of course, be different from yours. It's important to remember that each of us is called to run a different race. I'm not running the same race as the Willis family. But whatever difficulties come our way—broken relationships, infertility, loneliness, failure, illness, financial struggles, religious persecution—all of us will need to persevere. And likely your suffering won't be anything particularly dramatic, perhaps only a daily commitment to *seemingly* insignificant and distasteful duties.

So we must put aside comparisons with others and instead keep our own race and reward before us, as the apostle Paul did: "I have fought the good fight, I have finished the race, I have kept the faith. Now there is in store for me the crown of righteousness, which the Lord, the righteous Judge, will award to me on that day—and not only to me, but also to all who have longed for his appearing" (2 Timothy 4:7-8).

The eternal reward—the glories of heaven—has inspired many remarkable women such as Helen Roseveare, the missionary who was kidnapped and suffered the agony of rape while praying for her captors, or Elisabeth Elliot, who returned to bring the Gospel to the very same Auca Indian tribe who had savagely murdered her husband and five other missionaries.

All agree that the toughest part of the race is the middle. At the beginning you have energy and enthusiasm. You feel you can do anything. But as the race wears on, you begin to grow weary. It seems so long since the race began, and the finish line seems so far away. Each step you take becomes more painful. But then comes the point when you can see that the end is drawing near. The reward is just around the bend, and you receive that merciful "second wind" that spurs you on to the goal—the Lord Jesus Himself.

What can keep you going in the middle of the race? Jesus. Think of Him, "who for the joy set before him, endured the cross." We too must "consider that our present sufferings are not worth comparing with the glory that will be revealed in us" (Romans 8:18). Don't give up!

Keep on looking to Jesus: "Consider him who endured such opposition from sinful men, so that you will not grow weary and lose heart" (Hebrews 12:3).

Women, it takes discipline to accept the challenges of suffering in a way that glorifies God. But perseverance is a discipline we all can develop by daily submitting to God's will—whatever irritating, insignificant duties or grand-scale tragedies we may suffer—for this is God's will for us in the Gospel. Listen to Paul: "I consider my life worth nothing to me, if only I may finish the race and complete the task the Lord Jesus has given me—the task of testifying to the gospel of God's grace" (Acts 20:24). And now I join Paul and say, "May the Lord direct your hearts into God's love and Christ's perseverance" (2 Thessalonians 3:5).

RENEW YOUR MIND

How do Romans 5:3-4 and James 1:3-4 connect suffering with character or maturity? What is the "root" of perseverance that makes it possible for the believer to endure difficulties?

How has the Spirit of God "perfected" you through certain trials or tests? Can you see any parallels to what happened in the life of the apostle Peter? See Luke 22:31-32.

When have you seen a believer's testimony of faith during a time of suffering have an impact on those around him or her? What difficulties are you currently enduring? Ask the Lord to give you an unshakable confidence in Him that will have a role in spreading the Gospel.

When has a time of trouble given you a clearer view of who God is? What did you see—His power? His compassion? His nearness? His sovereignty over details? Can you think of any Scriptures that support your answer?

What keeps you going when you're "in the middle of the race," so to speak (see 2 Timothy 4:7-8; Romans 8:18)?

Read "What I Do with the Hard Things in My Life," p. 243.

RELATIONSHIPS

10

DISCIPLINE OF THE CHURCH

Submission's Framework—God's Family

*I am writing you these instructions so that, if I am delayed,
you will know how people ought to conduct themselves
in God's household, which is the church of the living God,
the pillar and foundation of the truth.*

1 TIMOTHY 3:14-15

A friend of mine tells me that when he was a college student, a popular bumper sticker boldly stated: "Jesus Christ, Yes—The Church, No!" Though the bumper sticker is long gone, that sentiment has trickled down to a pervasive attitude of "Jesus Christ, Yes—The Church, When I Need It and on My Terms."

These days church attenders are infected with a virus of conditional loyalty that has produced an army of church hitchhikers. The hitchhiker's thumb says, "You buy the car, pay for repairs, upkeep, and insurance, fill the car with gas—and I'll ride with you. But if you have an accident, you are on your own, and I'll probably sue." Many churchgoers have a similar agenda: "You go to the meetings and serve on the boards and committees. You grapple with the issues, teach and entertain the children, and I'll come along for the ride. But if things do not suit me, I'll criticize and complain and probably bail out. My thumb is always out for a better ride."

This "McChristian" mentality constantly checks to see what's new on the menu, just in case there's a better deal down the street. "McChristians" have a telling vocabulary, using phrases such as "I go to" or "I attend" but not typically using the words "I belong to" or "I am a member of."

If you're a tried-and-true long-term member of a church, the following may or may not surprise you. "A 1999 George Barna Research poll showed that one in seven Americans changes their church affiliation every year, while one in six rotates between churches."[1]

So here in the first decade of the new millennium, there's a phenomenon that would have been unimaginable in any other century—churchless Christians. There is a vast herd of professing Christians who exist as nomadic hitchhikers without accountability, without discipline, without discipleship, without fellowship, living apart from the regular benefits of the ordinances.

As to why the church has fallen on such hard times, historians tell us that an overemphasis on the "invisible" body of Christ by evangelical leaders produced an ingrained disregard for the visible church. Dr. Robert Saucy writes: "As for membership in an invisible church without fellowship with any local assembly, this concept is never contemplated in the New Testament. The universal church as the universal fellowship of believers met visibly in local assemblies."[2]

My husband points out that another reason for the dechurching of many Christians is the historic individualism of evangelical Christianity and the grassroots American impulse against authority. The natural inclination is to think that you need only an individual relationship with Christ and no other authority.

But women who are committed to putting every area of our lives under the discipline of the Gospel must determine to submit to God's idea of the church—and to come to value church as God does.

The church was God's idea in the first place; He instituted it. Acts 20:28 addresses the shepherds of "the church of God, which he bought with his own blood." The church must be important to every believer "because it is of supreme importance to Jesus Christ himself."[3] After all, He "loved the church and gave himself up for her" (Ephesians 5:25). Do we dare devalue what Christ cherishes?

Christ treasures the visible church. He values the structure of the "assembly" or "gathering," as the word *church* literally means

(Deuteronomy 4:10; 9:10; 31:30; Matthew 18:17; Acts 5:11; Romans 16:5; 1 Corinthians 1:2; Ephesians 1:22; 3:10; Hebrews 12:23). The visible church is, therefore, the gathering of the people of God. Whether there are two or three believers meeting or five thousand, Christ is there: "For where two or three come together in my name, there am I with them" (Matthew 18:20). There's something special, valuable, about the gathering of believers, as opposed to simply the individual operating alone.

Some of the other ways this gathering of believers, the church, is described in Scripture are the body, the family, the household, the bride, the building, the flock, the temple. The fact that Scripture reaches for so many descriptive terms to describe the church shows us its importance. God wants us to treasure the visible church. We will examine the first three—the body, the family, and the household.

THE BODY

Because the church is "the gathering of God's people," the church is about relationships. This is especially clear in the comparison of the church to a body. Just as a physical body is intricately interconnected, the church too depends upon the proper function of each individual part. When one part fails, the entire body is affected.

My husband recently broke a few of his ribs by taking a spill—over the dog!—on ice-covered ground. Although the injury site was his upper left back, the pain radiated to his chest. In compensating to protect the injured rib, one set of muscles after another began to ache in sympathy. He had trouble sleeping. He avoided coughing, sneezing, or laughing at all costs!

In the same way, individual church members are so amazingly interrelated that the health of the whole depends on the healthy function of each of us. This is the great challenge, of course, because we believers come from such varied backgrounds and bring our individual baggage with us through the church doors. So even though we are different, we must work together in harmonious relationships, each carrying out functions that are our given responsibility and gift. This is why it's so critical to mend the misunderstandings and tend the wounded and broken parts; we can't afford to impair the proper function of Christ's body! "The key issue is the quality of relationships and mutual responsiveness that believers have with each other (Romans 12:3-8 and 1 Corinthians 12:12-31)."[4]

What's the most important part of a body? The head, of course, because the body can't function at all without a head. Jesus Christ is the head of the body. "And God placed all things under his [Christ's] feet and appointed him to be head over everything for the church, which is his body, the fullness of him who fills everything in every way" (Ephesians 1:22-23). And also from Ephesians: "Instead, speaking the truth in love, we will in all things grow up into him who is the Head, that is, Christ" (4:15). Colossians points to Christ as well: "And he is the head of the body, the church" (1:18).

Your body functions best when each member takes its cues correctly from your brain. In the same way, we function in proper relationship with one another in the body of Christ when each of is taking our "cues" from the head—Jesus Christ.

THE FAMILY

I'm thankful that the church is also portrayed as a family—the family of God—because it takes our interdependence a step beyond the use of our interrelated gifts and mere function. A family, after all, is about loving relationships.

An Eternal Family

Of course I remember with absolute clarity the births of my four children. From the moment each entered this world, they began a host of relationships—with mother, father, sisters, brothers, grandparents, aunts, uncles, and cousins.

Becoming a member of God's family also takes place at birth—when a person is born again, "born of the Spirit" (John 3:5-8). It doesn't happen by the signing of papers or by majority vote; it happens when an individual accepts Christ as Savior and Lord. Immediately that person is born into a family with enormous potential for relationships!

Jesus made a rather startling statement about the family of God: "Then Jesus' mother and brothers arrived. Standing outside, they sent someone in to call him. A crowd was sitting around him, and they told him, 'Your mother and brothers are outside looking for you.' 'Who are my mother and my brothers?' he asked. Then he looked at those seated in a circle around him and said, 'Here are my mother and my brothers! Whoever does God's will is my brother and sister and mother'" (Mark 3:31-35). Those of us who love and value our human families might find that this sentiment offends our sensibilities. Jesus gives the eternal family of God priority over earthly family ties.

After the encounter with the rich young ruler, Jesus gave His disciples more insight into this family: "'I tell you the truth,' Jesus replied, 'no one who has left home or brothers or sisters or mother or father or children or fields for me and the gospel will fail to receive a hundred times as much in this present age (homes, brothers, sisters, mothers, children and fields—and with them, persecutions) and in the age to come, eternal life'" (Mark 10:29-30).

By sharing the same spiritual Father, our relational dynamic is far greater than that in our earthly family. It's difficult for us to accept this truth because our own families mean so much to us. But it is true! Even the chosen words for our church family are significant. Jon Dennis, our former colleague and fellow pastor, tells me that the term "elder" is a family-based term, like grandpa! So an elder is to be a godly and wise leader who eagerly protects his church family.

The relationships in the family of God are eternal, unlike those of our earthly families. Mary Lou Bayly, a widow in our church, reminds us that earthly marriage is temporal (Matthew 22:30). After years of serving the Lord as a wife, Mary Lou was comforted by a more enduring reality when her loving husband, Joe, died. She called her "assignment" as a wife and mother of seven children "richly rewarding." "But I am no longer a wife," she said. "There's a wonderful security in remembering that my relationship to Jesus Christ is my real identity, and no one can take that away from me."

Mary Lou has voiced an important spiritual truth: Our church familial relationships will never end! Our relationship as sisters and brothers sharing the same Father will exist for eternity.

Nurture and Instruction

The church, as God's family, is beautiful. I have had many spiritual mothers, fathers, aunts, uncles, sisters, and brothers over the years, and these family members have nurtured and instructed my soul.

Mrs. Thorne, the superintendent of the primary Sunday school department, had hair like an angel—finely combed rows of white waves. She taught me an old-fashioned hymn that even today I often find myself singing:

> Let the beauty of Jesus be seen in me,
> All His wonderful passion and purity.
> Oh, thou Spirit divine, all my nature refine,
> Till the beauty of Jesus be seen in me.

Mrs. Coleman, my fourth grade Sunday school teacher, was the "mother" who coached me in Bible memory work. She saw to it that I memorized several psalms (the 23rd, 100th, and 121st), the Lord's Prayer, and the Beatitudes. She rewarded me then, but many years later I am still reaping the benefit of God's words logged into my memory bank. I thank God for her nurturing of my young soul.

Mrs. Boxley faithfully managed Vacation Bible School each summer. What a thrill it was for me when I graduated from student to teacher's helper, giving me the privilege of joining the ladies (and Mrs. Boxley) in the kitchen for prayer and coffee. I was impressionable, and the hard-working example of this "jolly aunt" left its mark on me.

Larry Sharp was my "big brother" and youth leader. After the evening service, he'd take us in his old Chevy for fries and a coke. Then each Wednesday evening he patiently and tenaciously taught us junior highers about the tabernacle of the Old Testament. How the sacrifice of Christ came alive to me, even at that age! I thank God for the ministry of Larry Sharp, a loving member of the family.

Other times I've been the giver—nurturing, teaching, praying for, and encouraging members of God's family. This give and take among "family" is the atmosphere that allows us to grow and for fellowship to thrive.

Fellowship

The church, as the family of God, provides us with one of the sweetest of God's gifts to His children—fellowship. Theologian J. I. Packer points out the presence of fellowship in "the first description that the New Testament gives us of the life of the young church. 'They devoted themselves to the apostles' doctrine and fellowship' (Acts 2:42)."[5]

Packer goes on to explain that the fellowship is aimed in two directions—one vertical and one horizontal. Believers fellowship with each other (horizontal) because we share the same Father God (vertical). Fellowship with God our Father nurtures fellowship with each other. Fellowship is a family thing! And it is far more than a warm greeting on the way out the church door or a chat over coffee. "It is the habitual sharing, the constant giving to and receiving from each other, which is the true and authentic pattern of life for the people of God."[6]

Anyone who has spent an evening with Christian friends considering the mysteries of God, how to live in light of them, and the glories that await us, knows this is true. The disciples on the Emmaus road expressed it for all of us when they said of Jesus' teaching: "Didn't our hearts burn within us . . . ?"

I recall a night in a home just outside London, seated around a table in a tiny dining room. Several pastors and their wives had traveled to attend a conference on the Bible. Our host and hostess had prepared an authentic English Christmas feast, plum pudding and all. But as wonderful as the meal was, it was not the highlight of that evening. It was the spiritual feast we remember with delight. Crowded shoulder to shoulder, citizens of the world and more importantly of the next world, we dreamed together about sharing the good news of God's Gospel. "Devoted to doctrine," we experienced fellowship! And it was wondrous.

THE HOUSEHOLD OF FAITH

Who wouldn't want to be blessed with a family that provides a place to use one's gifts for the glory of God, opportunity for receiving and giving loving care and nurture, and enlightening relationships that are eternal? But "as in any family, relationships are maintained by members behaving appropriately to one another."[7] So we must consider "the correct behavior of members in the household of God."[8]

This is an issue that particularly interests women in our contemporary culture. Godly women who are committed to submitting to God's order and rule must come with open hearts to the New Testament teaching about a woman's behavior in the family of God.

Paul wrote to Timothy, a young pastor, "I am writing you these instructions so that, if I am delayed, you will know how people ought to conduct themselves in God's household, which is the church of the living God, the pillar and foundation of the truth" (1 Timothy 3:14-15). Paul draws attention to the fact that just as there is a God-given order for our earthly families, there is a similar order for the church family. Since we discuss much of Paul's instruction for women elsewhere in this book, we will consider the more controversial words here: "A woman should learn in quietness and full submission. I do not permit a woman to teach or to have authority over a man; she must be silent. For Adam was formed first, then Eve" (1 Timothy 2:11-13).

Since this is only a small section of a chapter in a much larger book, my comments can hardly be comprehensive. I realize of course that these words set off red flags in many minds. These are difficult words—especially today when women value and exercise their freedoms in so many ways. But our commitment to bring our lives under the discipline of the Gospel requires us to receive all of what God has given us in His Word.

Actually bringing the Gospel to bear in this area of life for today's Christian woman is no different from any other area in which she struggles to submit to God's will. The discipline of the church demands that we hear and obey the "hard parts" of the Word of God in the church, as well as those that are easier to appropriate. John Piper writes in *The Pleasures of God* about welcoming the difficult teachings of Scripture:

> Can controversial teachings nurture Christlikeness? Before you answer this question, ask another one: Are there any significant biblical teachings that have not been controversial? I cannot think of even one, let alone the number we all need for the daily nurture of faith. . . . As much as we would like it, we do not have the luxury of living in a world where the most nourishing truths are unopposed. If we think we can suspend judgment on all that is controversial and feed our souls only on what is left, we are living in a dream world. There is nothing left.[9]

The instruction to women in 1 Timothy to "learn in quietness and full submission" directs our attention to our heart attitude about male leadership in the church. This passage reminds me of the admonition we considered in the chapter on propriety to "walk in a manner worthy of the gospel." Our outward actions and words always reveal what is in our hearts. Do you believe God has your best interest at heart? Can you trust His wisdom in establishing order in the church? If so, quietness and submission will not be a problem.

In order to understand the prohibition, "I do not permit a woman to teach or have authority over a man; she must be silent" (v. 12), we must note what it does *not* say. My husband explains in his commentary *1 & 2 Timothy and Titus*[10]:

> These instructions do not prohibit a woman teaching or having authority in the marketplace, or the academy, or the public square. They are about order in the church. Neither do these directives allow any man within the church, by virtue of his gender, to exercise authority over women in the church. Such more generally explicit authority only exists within the sacred covenant of marriage and family, and then is only to be exercised with the self-giving spirit of Christ (cf. Ephesians 5:22-23).
>
> Note also that Paul's instructions have nothing to say about male and female equality. Such equality has been established from the beginning in Genesis 1:27 by virtue of man and woman being created in the image of God. And the mutual spiritual equality and status of men and women "in Christ" were given spectacular expression by Paul himself *earlier* in Galatians 3:28.
>
> So now, how is Paul's prohibition of women teaching and exercising authority over a man to be understood, especially since the words "to teach" and "to have authority" contain no negative connotation like "dominate" or "domineer"? The answer is that the word "to teach" and its noun forms "teaching" and "teacher" are used in the New Testament to describe careful and authoritative public doctrinal instruction[11] (cf. 1 Timothy 4:11-16; 2 Timothy 3:16; 2 Timothy 4:2).
>
> What then is prohibited is *preaching*, such as is enjoined in Paul's charge to Timothy, "Preach the Word; be prepared in season and out of season; correct, rebuke and encourage—with great patience and careful instruction" (2 Timothy 4:2). Also prohibited is the *teaching-elder* role of authoritatively defining and expositing the apostolic deposit. This is the realm of male elders who are "able to teach" (1 Timothy 3:2). Again, the text is also very clear that attitude is of paramount importance—submis-

siveness to leadership—"A woman should learn in quietness and full submission" (v. 11). Thus a critical, argumentative attitude is excluded. Bottom line: women must not preach or exercise elder-like rule.

The God-given reasoning behind Paul's prohibition is, "For Adam was formed first, then Eve. And Adam was not the one deceived; it was the woman who was deceived and became a sinner" (vv. 13-14). Paul grounded the ordering of authority in the church upon the order of creation *before* the Fall—Adam came before Eve. John Stott says of this appeal to creation order:

> All attempts to get rid of Paul's teaching on headship (on grounds that it is mistaken, confusing, culture-bound or culture-specific) must be pronounced unsuccessful. It remains stubbornly there. It is rooted in divine revelation, not human opinion, and in divine creation, not human culture. In essence, therefore, it must be preserved as having permanent and universal authority.[12]

In a later wide-ranging interview with *Christianity Today*, he strongly restated his position:

> But then I can't dismiss masculine headship in the cavalier way in which some evangelical feminists do. There is something in the Pauline teaching about headship that cannot be ignored as a purely cultural phenomenon, because he roots it in Creation. We may find his exegesis of Genesis 2 difficult—that women were made after men, out of men, and for men—but he does root his argument in Creation. I have a very high view of apostolic authority. I don't feel able to reject Paul's exegesis.[13]

Neither can we. We must joyfully live out God's good order. It is best for us, for the church, and for the needy world! We miss the point of verse 13 entirely if we think that Eve was more gullible than Adam, and that is why she "was deceived and became a sinner." Eve's sin was not naivete, but a willful attempt to overthrow the creation order. She hoped, in eating from the tree, that her eyes would be opened and that she would be like

God (cf. Genesis 3:5). As Phillip Jensen explains: "Eve's sin involved overturning the order of creation and teaching her husband. Similarly, Adam's sin came from 'listening' to his wife, in the sense of heeding and following her instruction. He was taught by her, thereby putting himself under her authority and reversing God's good ordering of creation."[14]

Hard Truths, Good Truths

Many volumes have been written to address the objections to the apparent meaning of Paul's teaching in 1 Timothy—and to support it. As a woman who longs to bring every area of life into submission to the lordship of Jesus Christ, you must give this issue your attention. As Dr. Piper pointed out, we don't have the luxury of picking and choosing what we like in Scripture and disregarding whatever appears unpleasant to us. The godly woman will come to love God's truth: "His commands are not burdensome"(1 John 5:3). Theologian Peter Bolt puts it well: "Isn't all of God's Word good for us, whether its first taste is bitter or sweet—a sensation which so often depends upon what else we have been chewing previously? It shouldn't be tampered with, or rejected, or grudgingly accepted. It should be willingly embraced as a gift of life from our loving Creator and Redeemer! Whatever the Word of God says, surely it should be received as gospel—God's good news! It drips with sweet honey from God's honeycomb."[15]

Don't hesitate to take your rightful place in the body of Christ, the family of God, the household of faith. So much of your life as a nurturer and gifted servant of God will be lived out within the relationships you'll find there. Don't forsake the assembly of believers, for this is God's will in the Gospel.

RENEW YOUR MIND

Why aren't more people making a commitment to one good church?

According to Hebrews 12:22-24, what spiritual treasures are found in the church? Put these in your own words, and then thank God for each one of them.

What does the image of the church as Christ's body suggest to you

(Ephesians 1:22-23)? His temple (Ephesians 2:19-22)? His bride (Ephesians 5:25-33)?

What do your attitudes toward church and toward Christ have to do with each other?

What tempts you to disobey Hebrews 10:25? What spiritual benefits might you miss out on by staying away from Christian gatherings?

"On the most elementary level, you do not have to go to church to be a Christian. You do not have to go home to be married either. But in both cases if you do not, you will have a very poor relationship." How do regular attendance and participation strengthen your relationships with God, with family members, and with other believers? Be specific.

List the strengths and weaknesses you see in your church. Now write down the ways you are personally contributing to each of these and also specific ways you can be part of changing the weaknesses.

Do you struggle with Paul's teaching in 1 Timothy 2 regarding a woman's behavior and role in the church family? For further study, check out 1 Timothy 3:15, 1 Peter 3:1-7, Ephesians 5:22-33, Colossians 3:18-19, and 1 Corinthians 11-14. You might also read *Women, Creation, and the Fall* by Mary Kassian, *Recovering Biblical Manhood & Womanhood* edited by John Piper and Wayne Grudem, and *Man & Woman in Christian Perspective* by Werner Neuer.

11

DISCIPLINE OF SINGLENESS

Submission's Framework — Singleness

*Nevertheless, each one should retain the place in life
that the Lord assigned to him and to which God has called him.*

1 CORINTHIANS 7:17

Of my sixteen grandchildren (so far), nine of them are girls, and each girl is an utterly original individual.

Catherine Rose, at thirteen, is as romantic as her name. A nice combination of artistic creativity and intellectual curiosity, she is often found stitching a fine piece of handwork or curled up with a good book. Our budding Shakespeare, she writes all of the family plays.

Tagged "Queen Caroline" by my husband, Caroline is a fascinating blend of regal strength and humor. A keen observer, her conversation and wit are always interesting. She is noted for her eagerness to help others and truly has a serving heart.

Jessica, with eyes of translucent turquoise, is also noted for her writing, musing for long hours over paper and pen. After years of competing athletically with her two older brothers, she's become a "can-do" girl who steps up to challenges with a fierce determination.

Amanda's heightened sense of audio perception allows her to mimic almost any accent. With nearly perfect pitch, she sings like an angel. She remembers with precision the kinds of detailed information that escape most people.

Isabel is a wonder. Her whisper-thin frame and enormous blue eyes make her appear fragile and waiflike. But she's a strong girl with well-thought-out opinions that she isn't timid about sharing! Her intensity is matched by a dry wit and a twinkle in her eye. Add to all of this her barefoot tree-climbing skills, and we have a champion.

Undauntable Paige has no intention of remaining status quo. She has no concern about appearing unconventional. With the gift of comedy, she possesses the ability to turn a situation on its head for a good laugh. Paige is very comfortable in her own skin.

Lilly is a love. Dramatic is an understatement regarding her exuberance for life, her affectionate nature, her affable ways, and her teasing eyes. Lilly celebrates every member of her family—including the pets.

Adorable Samantha, at three, is the youngest of five siblings. She has *joie de vivre* and always wakes up on the right side of the bed. Spend a minute with Samantha, and you'll be smiling.

Hannah, the baby, delights in new words and in attempting to keep up with her older brothers and sister. The unfolding of her personality is a pleasure to behold.

I love watching these girls change and grow on their way to becoming the women God has planned for them to be. You may think that perhaps I cherish hopes that each of these young women will grow up to meet their individual Prince Charmings, marry, and provide me with plenty of great-grandchildren. Not necessarily. I hope that my granddaughters will mature with the understanding that singleness is not something to avoid at all costs, but that singleness is in fact a desirable option for their lives, particularly in view of the Gospel.

Here's what I do hope for my lovely, original granddaughters—that each will come to know Christ early and go on to full lives of service for Him.

A BETTER LIFE

Everything in our culture—books, movies, recreational pastimes—tend to push the idea that sex and romance are the ultimate pursuit. Even our evangelical churches—though in reaction to the demise of family life and the alarming escalation of divorce in our country—have overemphasized family life to the point that singles feel out of place. Many single Christian women have received from the church what feels like a loud-

and-clear message that their singleness is "something to be fixed." My friend Lois Hagger, a single woman who has given this a lot of thought, claims that even believers are "indoctrinated by our relationship- and sex-worshiping culture." Lois has been my number-one source for understanding singleness in light of the Scriptures.

What does our life guide, the Bible, say? First Corinthians 7:40 declares that it is *better* to be single than married. Better! Shake yourself loose from the ideas of the world around you and look to God's Word to see the single life described as an assignment, a calling, and a gift.

An Assignment

God assigns each person to be either married or single. Paul writes, "Each one should retain the place in life that the Lord assigned to him and to which God has called him" (1 Corinthians 7:17). What does it mean to be assigned a position? Generally speaking, the word *assign* is used with regard to a post or duty. A duty is "an obligatory task, conduct, service or function that arises from one's position in life."[1] In other words, God has a task for us to accomplish by means of our marital status.

A Calling

That same verse, 1 Corinthians 7:17, refers to that assigned position as a calling. When someone is called, she has been invited or summoned to a particular ministry. First we see God in a military sense assigning us to report for duty, and then we see Him gently beckoning us to minister alongside Him—all in regard to our marital status.

Your marital status is not an accident; God planned it. Acts 17:24-28 reveals God's sovereignty—that He is a God who is in charge:

> *The God who made the world and everything in it is the Lord of heaven and earth and does not live in temples built by hands. And he is not served by human hands, as if he needed anything, because he himself gives all men life and breath and everything else. From one man he made every nation of men, that they should inhabit the whole earth; and he determined the times set for them and the exact places where they should live. God did this so that men would seek him and perhaps reach out for him and find him, though he is not far from each one of us. For in him we live and move and have our being.*

God doesn't need our service; He chooses to involve us in His plans. He even determines our time and place in history in order that the circumstances He assigns us might drive us to Him. My hope for my granddaughters is that they will understand that life is not about getting God to give them what they want; life is about discovering where they fit into God's plan, whether single or married.

A Gift

The New Testament's attitude toward being single is very positive. Besides being assigned by God and a calling of God, singleness is a gift from God. Paul, speaking about this matter says, "But each man has his own gift from God; one has this gift, another has that," meaning, among other things, either marriage or singleness (1 Corinthians 7:7).

Jesus, when questioned by the Pharisees about divorce, said that the only justification for divorce is marital unfaithfulness. Shocked, the disciples responded: "If this is the situation between a husband and wife, it is better not to marry" (Matthew 19:10). Jesus doesn't disagree. Instead he says: *"Not everyone can accept this word, but only those to whom it has been given.* For some are eunuchs because they were born that way; others were made that way by men; and others have renounced marriage because of the kingdom of heaven. The one who can accept this should accept it" (Matthew 19:11-12, emphasis mine).

Paul and Jesus are saying the same thing: Singleness is a gift—a gift for the kingdom of God. Unlike an assignment to duty or a calling to ministry, a gift is a grace. A gift often implies special favor by God. The favor of singleness means God has bestowed dignity and honor to a position that had formerly been regarded as less than desirable. I want my granddaughters to receive the gift of singleness joyously if God graciously gives it to them.

The Unwanted Gift?

I've occasionally heard single women question whether or not God has given them the gift of singleness. Usually they conclude that because they are not happy being single, they must not have the gift.

But guess what—I've also heard women ask, "How do I know if I have married the right man?" And I've answered them, "If you're married, he is the right man." Whether or not things are going well in the marriage, and whether the two partners like it or not, they are assigned and called to their married position.

The gift of singleness is not always a permanent state, but it's a fact. If you're single right now, God in His providence has settled that fact. That's why in the capstone verse for this chapter Jesus says, "Each one should retain the place in life that the Lord assigned to him and to which God has called him."

Maybe this sounds unpleasant to you. Obedience often feels that way initially. But remember what the apostle John testifies: "This is love for God: to obey his commands. And *his commands are not burdensome*" (1 John 5:3, emphasis mine). In fact, they are delightful: "Blessed is the man who fears the LORD, who finds great *delight* in his commands" (Psalm 112:1, emphasis mine); " . . . your commands are my *delight*" (Psalm 119:143, emphasis mine); "All your commands are trustworthy" (Psalm 119:86).

The good gift of singleness doesn't seem to jive with what God clearly states at creation—that it was "not good for the man to be alone" (Genesis 2:18). Renowned pastor and theologian John Piper speaks to this point:

> Well, is it good or not good to be alone? If it is not good—not God's will—how can it be called a 'gift from God'? How could Jesus, who never sinned, have chosen it for Himself? How could Paul say it was a great asset for ministry?
>
> . . . Genesis 2:18 was a statement about man before the Fall. Perhaps, if there had been no Fall, there would have been no singleness. Everyone would have had a perfectly compatible personality type for someone else; people and situations would have matched up perfectly; no sin would have made us blind or gullible or hasty; and no great commission—no lostness, no famine, no sickness, no misery—would call for extraordinary measures of sacrifice in marriage and singleness. But that is not our world. So sometimes—many times—it is good for a person to be alone.[2]

Dr. Piper is not saying that the single person doesn't need relationships of many kinds. He is pointing to the goodness of the single person's state because of the ministry possibilities inherent in it.

In an article in *Discipleship Journal*, Albert Hsu makes this interesting point: "Without demeaning marriage, the New Testament gives a new dignity to singleness. Both states are now equally valid ways to serve God. If the Old Testament seems to value marriage more than singleness, the New Testament brings them onto an even level."[3]

Where does the merit in singleness come from? It derives its dignity and honor from association with the kingdom of God. So when a single person recognizes that his or her marital status is a gift from God for the sake of the Gospel, it is truly a grace in that person's life.

THE SINGLE ADVANTAGES

My friend Lois has shown me the grace of the single life. A beautiful red-head, Lois has spent the last fifteen years of her life discipling women university students through Bible study, training them to be godly women.

Lois became a Christian through the ministry of the Navigators. When she was thirty-five years old and a nurse by profession, she returned to university studies in order to become a missionary. While a student herself, she was challenged by the pastor of the church she was attending to get involved in the ministry to students. She accepted the challenge and has been an effective worker for the Gospel ever since.

Lois is loved and respected by the people who work alongside her. They report that she not only models godly living but also a "sanity" in ministry that has prevented the burnout that can overcome gospel work-ers. She keeps this sanity in her ministry in several ways. She has a sense of her limits; when she needs a day off, she takes one—or even two. She maintains friendships apart from her work. She has cultural interests, specifically art and ballet. She regularly plays on a league basketball team.

And Lois is not obsessed with marriage. Like most single people, she must deal with loneliness and other problems, but I see no evidence of self-pity in her. She understands that married women have their own set of struggles—whether it's the exhaustion and time constraints of caring for small children, the pain of an unhappy marriage or divorce, or diffi-culties and disappointments with older children.

Lois makes a point of focusing on the advantages of being single. When I asked her to share those advantages, here's the list she gave me:

1. I can change plans at a moment's notice. It would be common courtesy to let a roommate know my whereabouts, but I don't need her approval.

2. My personal time is my own. I have more time to do things I want to do than my married friends do.

3. I, and I alone, decide how I will use my money. I only have to consult the Lord about my budget. I also generally have greater amounts of discretionary money at my disposal than most of my married friends, so I can be quite generous with it.

4. " . . . An unmarried woman or virgin is concerned about the Lord's affairs: Her aim is to be devoted to the Lord in both body and spirit. But a married woman is concerned about the affairs of this world—how she can please her husband" (1 Corinthians 7:34-35). Because I am single, I can give my undivided devotion to the Lord. Because I am in ministry, I am able to use the majority of my time serving the Lord while my married friends must spend a majority of their time caring for the needs of family and children. But even if I were not in ministry, my free time is still more available to use for the Lord than my married friends' time, for the same reason.

SINGLE, BUT NOT ALONE

In Genesis 2 God provided marriage as a solution to the human need for relationship and intimacy. But throughout the New Testament, the family of God is presented as a place of fellowship. Human families are wonderful, but every believer is part of a more important family, one that belongs to our heavenly Father.

Remember the rich young ruler? Mark 10:17-31 records his reluctance to give up what was dear to him in order to follow Jesus. The disciples respond to Jesus by saying, "We have left everything to follow you." But Jesus corrects them: "I tell you the truth, no one who has left home or brothers or sisters or mother or father or children or fields for me and the gospel will fail to receive a hundred times as much in this present age (homes, brothers, sisters, mothers, children and fields—and with them, persecutions) and in the age to come, eternal life." He holds out the promise of greater blessing.

Paul envisages that family needs will be met by the family of God.

Do you take the family of God seriously? Both married and unmarried people can find there the satisfaction and joy of family relationships. A whole chapter of this book emphasizes a woman's God-given role as nurturer—and not solely in terms of mothering. The church offers the ideal scenario for women to fulfill this inborn passion for caring for others.

Single women needn't be alone at church or at home. Well-chosen roommates can be a provision of the Lord. Lois tells me that a roommate can be a source of accountability for how her private life is lived.

Sexual loneliness, of course, is not something that the church can assuage for the single person. And the joys of sexual union enjoyed by husbands and wives seem, to the single person, the most important advantage that they are denied. Sometimes that longing takes the single person right into temptation. "In fact, it is to relieve loneliness—deep, personal loneliness—that many single people seek refuge in sex. In sex, there is intimacy, relationship and emotional nudity. Sex creates a bond with someone. It forges some kind of relationship. Used outside God's framework, however, it is also damaging. It bonds us to someone who may pull away (sometimes only too quickly), leaving us scarred and even more alone than before."[4]

Ada Lum talks about single women respecting and valuing their sexuality:

> The single woman needs to respect herself as a sexual being whom God created. She is not less sexual for not being married. Sex has to do with biological drive for union with one of the opposite sex. Sexuality has to do with our whole personhood as a woman or a man. It has to do with the ways we express ourselves in relation to others. It has to do with being warm, understanding, receptive sexual beings when we relate to another female or to a child or to a man who is the least prospect for a husband! . . . I try to treat him as I do my two brothers. I enjoy Leon and Dick. I respect them. I like to hear them talk about masculine things in masculine ways. I am pleased when they treat me thoughtfully. . . . With care and discretion a single woman can and should be a real woman to the men around her.[5]

A BRIGHT FUTURE

I don't know whether God will give my nine granddaughters the gift of marriage or the gift of singleness. I do know that I long for them to embrace whatever gifts He has chosen for their lives. I have great confidence that He loves them far more than I do and that His plans for them are loving and gracious. I do not know the future, but I have already seen God's love and grace at work in their young lives.

Remember Isabel, who appears so fragile but is strong and determined? She began life with a medical condition that demanded an enormous struggle on her part to survive. God developed her strengths through this trial.

Amanda's acute sense of audio perception has developed because her vision is impaired. She has very limited sight in only one eye. God's plans for Amanda have not been thwarted but intentionally developed through adversity.

Both Caroline and Lilly are adopted. They have literally been plucked out of one situation and placed into the home of believing Christians for an eternal purpose. Their unique circumstances are developing them for an assignment for the Gospel that only God could have planned.

You see? The sovereign God is in charge, and His plans for our lives are wonder-filled. Nothing about us has taken God by surprise, nor has He planned to deny anyone less than the best. If God has graciously given you the gift of singleness, embrace it for the sake of the Gospel because it is there, in the Gospel, that life comes together.

RENEW YOUR MIND

(A Checklist from Lois Hagger)

Have you fallen into the habit of considering singleness a disability? Shake yourself loose from the ideas of the world around you and look at 1 Corinthians 7:40. How is the single life described as an assignment, a calling, and a gift?

Have you taken a passive role rather than expanding your interests and contacts? Read books, go to plays, join a club, take up gardening—try something new. Invite others to do something with you. Make a list of everything you'd like to do and then put a few dates on the calendar and begin planning.

Have you been so busily on the lookout for a life partner that you've missed enriching friendships? How could you pursue some new friendships, especially in the family of God? Read Romans 16:3-16, noting the family of God at work. The Gospel is the family business, and we are all part of the business. Ask yourself, "What can I do to help the family?" Get active in a Bible study group. Become a member of a Bible-teaching church—this is not optional.

Check your life for patterns of self-pity or envy of those who are married. Search out some young mom at church who could use a break from the kids and offer to care for her children for a few hours. This will give you an up-close reminder of the struggles of women who are married with children.

Are you tempted to date unbelievers? Don't get involved! Most Christian women married to non-Christians will tell you they never planned to marry an unbeliever. The fact is, people marry people they allow themselves to date.

Do you indulge yourself in any secret or hidden life you wouldn't want others to see? Repent and then confide in someone you can trust in order to establish accountability. Check out the parable in Luke 18:9-14.

All believers, both married and single, are waiting. All are enduring and persevering through their own unique trials for the blessed hope. Waiting is a very active occupation for believers. As we wait, we're to grow in godliness and live self-controlled, upright lives in this present age—for the sake of the Gospel (see Titus 2:11-14). Are you prepared to wait?

12

DISCIPLINE OF MARRIAGE

Submission's Framework—Marriage

*The LORD God said, "It is not good for the man to be alone.
I will make a helper suitable for him."*

GENESIS 2:18

If you are married, have been married, or hope to be married, how would you characterize a successful marriage? Many would envision, say, premarital counseling, a beautiful wedding with family and friends, decent jobs, enough money for a home of their own, and two or three children.

But Christian women who accept the challenge of bringing every area of life under the discipline of the Gospel must be prepared to look to God's Word for their standards for marital success. The discipline of marriage requires *holiness,* and God's plans for a woman's role in marriage must be unchanging.

In Ephesians the apostle Paul compares a married couple to Christ and His bride, the church—and he calls it a mystery! It is a mystery— one we can explore given the Old and New Testament passages describing the union of a man and woman.

Every generation has brought its expectations to marriage. My own mother, when she married in 1934, planned a beautiful wedding and looked forward to a life of helping and respecting her husband, who would love her and provide for their family. What actually happened during the forty-six years of my parents' marriage did not live up to either one's expectations, and yet each of them would have counted their marriage a success—and a blessing.

A Successful Marriage?

On a sunny April morning in 1934, a California family gathered flowers and greenery in their well-tended garden in preparation for the wedding of their much-loved daughter, Lula Anne. The bride, her mother and father, five younger sisters and a brother, aunts, uncles, and cousins helped to hang garlands and fashion an arbor of roses under which the shy couple would stand before the minister and make their holy vows the next day.

That night, exhausted after long hours of hard work and laughter, they fell into bed in eager anticipation. To their disappointment, they awoke to the dark, thunderous downpour of a spring storm. The garlands had been ripped from the branches and the arbor toppled by the high winds. Plans hastily changed. They prepared the house for the festivities in what little time remained before the ceremony would begin. The few photos of that event were snapped when the rain stopped momentarily and everyone dashed outside. They show a young man and woman in black and white against a background of gray, an image of a marriage beginning.

The best man and his wife planned to drive the couple to their honeymoon destination—no simple task in 1934. The California coast highway to Santa Barbara was roughly paved, and the car's inferior tires resulted in more than one unplanned stop. After several hours the wedding party was too weary to complete the drive. They parked at the side of the road and fell asleep. In the dark of that first night the bride's suitcase was quietly lifted out of the car as they slept. The thief took the few precious things she'd saved up for her wedding night. For the second time in less than twenty-four hours, the young bride, my mother, cried.

Father's name was Wilfred. He had a twin brother named Willard, and everyone on the farm called them "Will-Work" and "Won't-Work." From childhood my father worked hard and valued a job well done. As a child, I remembered that nickname as I observed the amazing energy he brought to any task. An unskilled laborer, he worked at whatever job was available—as a gardener at a bird sanctuary, digging ditches for highway drainage systems, and most often in the lumber yards. The nature of the work often put him in danger, and he suffered more than one serious accident.

After the birth of my younger sister, a load of lumber fell on Dad and crushed his ankle. Even with a huge cast on his leg, he was determined to work, hobbling around to help Mom hang out the laundry. During that time, my mother drove an ice cream truck from nine in the morning until nine at night to provide our family of seven with $6.00 a day—enough to feed us, barely. My mother and father simply did what was necessary. I'm sure there were tears, but I rarely saw them.

When I was twelve, my father became a Christian. Among my most treasured memories is the day of his conversion when he came through the door with a tear-stained face and hugged my mother. Those were the happiest days of my childhood. Dad would report regularly at dinner how he was working to clean up his language and how his coworkers teased him. He'd recall his attempts to witness to his buddies. Most of all, he radiated joy.

That summer the church I'd been attending on my own had its annual all-church picnic, and for the first time Mom and Dad came. There was fried chicken and potato salad, apple pie, and watermelon. Dad played volleyball with his Sunday school class. His laughter still echos in my soul.

The day after the picnic there was another accident at the lumber yard. This time my dad nearly lost his hand to a power saw. The following year he endured many surgeries. While undergoing physical therapy, he memorized Scripture. He received a leather New Testament with his name inscribed in gold as first prize in his Sunday school class memory contest.

As difficult as the physical pain had been to endure, the pain that faced my father in the days ahead was far greater. Now this hardworking laborer could no longer use his hands to provide for his wife and children. The attorneys protected the interests of the lumber company, and my father was left crippled and penniless. From the day the court handed down the decision, my father worked at the only job he could get—washing dishes.

My older sister recalls a day in a restaurant when she was out with friends, and a pitcher of Coke was knocked over. Laughing and having a grand time, they barely noticed the arrival of the man sent to clean up the mess. As he mopped, my sister looked up into the anguished eyes of our father. She was humiliated, and he was tortured by her embarrassment.

With his role as provider stripped away, my father grew increasingly depressed. He began drinking heavily. Eventually he ended up on skid row in Los Angeles. During the years that he was separated from our family, people told my mother to give up on Dad. She didn't; she clung to her chosen role of helping and respecting her husband by ensuring that we children spoke of our father with love and respect. When he was diagnosed with emphysema, he came home. Mother lovingly nursed him the last eleven years of his life.

My children's memories of their grandfather are from those eleven years. They adored him—this cheery invalid who made great chili and loved Grandma. My father died blessing my mother, as well as the Lord she had so faithfully followed in obedience to the vows she had taken those many years before.

When Dad died, my mother wept. The lover with whom she had shared so much—love, pain, sacrifice, failure, disappointment, forgiveness, laughter, and hope—the partner with whom she'd shared the sweetness and challenges of parenthood was gone.

But there were also tears of joy because my mother had the satisfying knowledge that they had ended well. In spite of the many difficulties of their journey together, Mom and Dad parted without bitterness, leaving their children a heritage of blessing.

By today's standards, and indeed compared to the humble hopes they'd begun with, my parents lacked all the things deemed necessary for success in marriage. Father had received no earthly reward for his hard work, much less for his good intentions and desire to be a Christian husband after he was converted. Disaster was followed by despair—for long, lost years. Mother, who had never anticipated being a single parent or the family's sole breadwinner, found herself in that lonely situation.

But my mother's faithfulness to her marriage vows, made before God, preserved her marriage. Her faith in Christ helped her to serve, respect, bless, and forgive her husband.

A BIBLICAL STANDARD FOR A WIFE'S ROLE

Essential to bringing our marriages under the discipline of the Gospel is a biblical understanding of our roles in marriage. With such knowledge, we then can live out God's plan for marriage, sometimes with difficulty, as my mother had to, in the real world and with flawed people.

Surprisingly, in a time when Christians have more money and more education and certainly more resources such as books, videos, counselors, and support groups to advise them, many young couples lack the most important ingredient for the success of their Christian union—a biblical understanding of their roles. Certainly the time-honored passages of Scripture that teach married people how to relate to one another haven't changed. But the church's shifting view of that teaching has left couples indecisive and confused.

Consider how marriage vows have changed over the years. Sentimental and generic, they typically lack a solidarity with the past that reflects the lifelong commitments made by our parents and grandparents. In a *Time* magazine editorial, "The Hazards of Homemade Vows," Lance Morrow warns: "Some couples remain tempted today by the opportunity a wedding offers for self-expression. It is a temptation that should be resisted. . . . A wedding is public business. That is the point of it. The couple are not merely marrying one another. They are, at least in part, submitting themselves to the larger logics of life, to the survival of the community, to life itself."[1]

Yes! As Christians, our marriage vows ought to reflect what the Bible teaches about the responsibility of both husband and wife. Historically, the Christian marriage vows were rooted in Scripture, especially in the last half of Ephesians 5. Every Christian couple ought to understand and, I think, even commit to memory the directives given there. Those sacred words compass the foundational discipline of marriage—teaching us that the marital relationship must reflect that of Christ and His bride, the church. Christ and His holy church model the sacrificial love and submission that we seek to build into our marriages.[2]

Hear God's Word: "Wives, submit to your husbands as to the Lord. For the husband is the head of the wife as Christ is the head of the church, his body, of which he is the Savior. Now as the church submits to Christ, so also wives should submit to their husbands in everything . . . and the wife must respect her husband" (Ephesians 5:22-24, 33b).

The apostle Paul calls this a profound mystery. The mystery is more than profound. It is spectacular! The mystery of marriage did not begin when Christ came and established His church. It began centuries before. It was God's plan from the beginning. So if you want to understand the New Testament teaching on marriage, you must begin with the Genesis account of creation.

THE OLD TESTAMENT FOUNDATION

In her best-selling book, *A Return to Modesty*, young Jewish author Wendy Shalit argues that "people today have missed the fact that our differences are key to our relationship." She explains: "The sexual revolution seems to have failed mostly because it ignored the differences between the sexes. . . . Not only do we think there are differences between the sexes, but we think these differences can have a beautiful meaning—a meaning that isn't some irrelevant fact about us but one that can inform and guide our lives. That's why we are swooning over nineteenth-century dramas and clothing."[3]

She's right. And we who believe God's Word don't have to guess or wonder about the meaning of those differences. The first chapters of the book of Genesis give us a "better understanding of the profound and complex order which makes sense of the differences between men and women,"[4] and therefore of the roles of husband and wife.

Unity

The intriguing words of Genesis 1:26 provide essential information about God—and because we are made in His image, about ourselves. Listen to the mystery in God's declaration: "Let *us* make man in *our* image." When God speaks of Himself in the plural (*us* and *our*), we learn that though God is One, He is not alone. Whatever else it may mean to be made in God's image, this verse makes it clear that we are *made for relationship*.

The astonishing truth then is: "Like God, mankind is both unified and diverse. We know from the rest of Scripture that the three persons of the Godhead (Father, Son, and Holy Spirit) are nevertheless a single God, and that from all eternity they have enjoyed relationship with each other. Mankind is created in this image, with separate persons (male and female) created to enjoy a deep unity."[5] This unity goes deeper than the bond with one's own flesh and blood. The moment I held each of my newborn children in my arms, a powerful bonding took place. They were from my flesh. I am close to them, interwoven with them. Yet I am not "one flesh" with them; I am one flesh only with my husband. The sexual union between husband and wife makes two literally become one—body and soul. As the years go by, we become more and more one flesh as there is an exchange of soul, a mutual appropriation of each other's lives.

Genesis 1:27 goes on to say: "So God created man in his own image, in the image of God he created him; male and female he created them." The use of the biological terms "male" and "female," rather than "man" and "woman," shine a spotlight on gender differences—physiology and function. Understanding the differences will help us appreciate Paul's command in Ephesians to "submit to" and "respect" our husbands. Such an understanding will give young women what Wendy Shalit is looking for—a sense of the relevance of gender differences to their lives.

Diversity

In the words of Claire Smith in her article "Two Commands to Women," "God is a God of order, and we were created for relationships that reflect his order and purpose."[6] Even within the Trinity there is an order to the relationship. Scripture reveals differences in the roles of the Father, the Son, and the Holy Spirit. These differences are not demeaning. Theologian Wayne Grudem explains it like this: "It is the Father that planned redemption and sent his Son into the world; the Son obeyed the Father, accomplishing redemption for us; and the Spirit brings to completion the work that has been planned by the Father and begun by the Son. The Father directs and has authority over the Son, and the Son obeys and is responsive to the directions of the Father. The Holy Spirit is obedient to the directives of both the Father and the Son."[7]

Made in God's image, men and women are also equal but different. Equal before God as persons, we have been given distinctly different roles. In the marriage relationship, man is to lead, and woman is to follow his lead. In the beginning Eve rebelled against God, rejecting His will regarding the forbidden tree and then encouraged her husband to *follow her lead*. When Adam joined her, *failing to lead his wife in godliness*, they overturned the good order of creation. Ever since that day there has been war between the sexes.

COUNTERCULTURAL WOMEN

To live out biblical standards for roles in marriage, however, is to swim upstream against culture. And it's not only secular society that angrily reacts against the idea of differing roles. There is also widespread confusion among believers on Scripture's teaching on the subject. A recent article in the *Chicago Tribune* quoted a woman from a Christian organization: "[We do] not believe that marriage is about subordination, but mutuality. Intimacy is impossible when you subordinate to anybody else. That is not what the Bible says, and we don't think that's how God intended us to live."[8]

Excuse me! We know from the very first book of the Bible that "intimacy through subordination" is not only possible, but it is God's plan for us—modeled after the intimacy that exists in the Godhead. So for me, as a Christian woman, submitting to my husband is not an option; it is obediently following God's plan for order in marriage, a plan that has existed from the beginning.

The wonder of my wedding night—my face warm with the flush of timidity and embarrassment that came with the vulnerability I was experiencing for the first time—is a sweet, lingering memory. My husband and I had begun to explore the mystery that God wondrously provided for us. From the beginning God made us in His image, male and female—equal but different. And when we women live out this profound mystery, we are pleasing God by living out His beautiful order.

There's only one problem, and it's a big one: We don't live in an ideal world or with ideal men who perfectly follow the Ephesian instruction to love their wives as Christ loved the church and laid down His life for her. Like Adam, many husbands fail to lead (or sacrificially love). And like Eve, many wives rationalize about submission, inwardly mouthing Satan's condescending question, "Surely God didn't really say that!"

But God did say it, and the New Testament's passages on marriage consistently root their teaching in Genesis.

NEW TESTAMENT GUIDANCE

Three of the New Testament passages that call women to submit to their husbands include an important and instructive phrase. Ephesians 5:22 says, "Wives, submit to your husbands *as to the Lord*." Colossians 3:18 similarly reads, "Wives, submit to your husbands, *as is fitting in the Lord*." These parallel phrases serve as reminders to all wives that submission in marriage must be with the same loving wholeheartedness with which we submit to the Lord. When we submit to our spouses, we are once again agreeing with God that His beautiful ordered plan is worth obeying and the mystery worth preserving. By so doing we once again acknowledge that Jesus is Lord.

The third passage, 1 Peter 3:1, says, "Wives, *in the same way*, be submissive to your husbands. . . ." This essential phrase from Peter, "*in the same way*," holds the key to empowering us to do what we ought when it seems impossible.

In the chapter that precedes 1 Peter 3 (1 Peter 2:13-25), Peter teaches all believers that submission to every authority instituted by God is essential. "For it is *God's will* that by doing good you should silence the ignorant talk of foolish men," states 1 Peter 2:15. The apostle goes on, "But if you suffer for doing good and you endure it, this *is commendable before God*" (v. 20). God's will and pleasure are always the defining factors for behavior choices.

Wonderfully, Peter points to Christ as an example of the beauty and effectiveness of submission:

> To this you were called, because Christ suffered for you, leaving you an example, that you should follow in his steps. "He committed no sin, and no deceit was found in his mouth." When they hurled their insults at him, he did not retaliate; when he suffered, he made no threats. Instead, he entrusted himself to him who judges justly. He himself bore our sins in his body on the tree, so that we might die to sins and live for righteousness; by his wounds you have been healed. For you were like sheep going astray, but now you have returned to the Shepherd and Overseer

of your souls. Wives, in the same way be submissive to your hus-
bands. . . . (1 Peter 2:21—3:1)

It could be that you and I have often read this command to wives as a stand-alone idea, apart from the preceding verse. But "in the same way" connects us to the example and person of Jesus! We are to submit to our husbands in the same way that Christ submitted to God's will and went to the cross; He kept on "entrusting Himself to Him who judges righteously" (NASB). Jesus' persistent faith in God's goodness and wisdom in everything was unflinching. Obedience to God's will was His primary concern.

Obedience to God's will was Eve's point of failure. She doubted God's goodness and wisdom in denying her the tree of the knowledge of good and evil. Through the Gospel, we who are Eve's daughters are now also children of God, and we've been given the power to live like Christ. But obedience is still up to us.

Submission to our husbands begins and ends with trusting God—Eve's point of failure. My mother began and ended by trusting God—no matter how dark her trials. I cannot recall her ever questioning God's love or care for her or for her family.

So that word that today's Christian women struggle over, *submit*, is still God's Word for us: "Wives, in the same way be submissive to your husbands."

HELPER

From the very beginning, a woman's purpose was clearly defined. God took a look at Adam and said, "It is not good for the man to be alone. I will make a helper suitable for him" (Genesis 2:18). So why does our blood pressure rise at the mention of the word *helper*? It's a cultural norm for us to associate weakness and even inferiority with the one who assists. No one wants to play second fiddle. But the fact is, without a second violin there is no harmony.

What is helping supposed to look like—then and now? With what task, for instance, was Eve supposed to help Adam? She was to assist him in carrying out God's order to rule and subdue the earth. But she failed God when she led Adam to join her in submitting to Satan. We modern daughters of Eve must not fail as did our mother. Our task is to encourage our husbands to obey God's Word and will for their lives.

I first began to understand this concept in a personal way when my husband was a young pastor in California. I'd noticed that when things were going well at church, he was pretty upbeat; but when things went wrong, he was easily discouraged. If church attendance was up, he was up; if it was down, so was he. Then the numbers went down—for a long time. He didn't confide in me, but he was seriously wondering whether he should continue in the pastoral ministry.

One night after the children were soundly sleeping, he began to reveal his misery to me. My attempts to console him were met with depressing responses. When I said, "Honey, your sermon really spoke to me last week," he responded, "Yes, but I'll just be on trial again next week." I tried again: "Just think of Noah. He preached 120 years without a single convert!" Kent's dark-humored response was, "Yes, but there wasn't another Noah across town with the people flowing into his ark."

Finally I stopped offering advice and simply listened. The words he spoke that night were those of a man who had lost sight of what biblical ministry is all about. A combination of secular ideas presented to us by church growth experts coupled with his own fear of failure had propelled Kent into a desperate search for success. As he recited his negative observations of ministers and ministry in general, he found himself coming to a conclusion he didn't want to admit. It had been growing in him for a long time, and it was terrible: "God has called me to do something He hasn't given me the gifts to accomplish. Therefore, God is not good." In aching desperation he asked me, "Barbara, what am I going to do?"

When we think back to that long-ago night, Kent tells me that if I had answered him in any other way than the way I did, it would have been all he needed to "hang it up." If I had joined him in bitter recriminations and complaints about our situation, he might have quit the ministry and spent the rest of his life attempting to prove his worth and God's injustice.

But, thanks to God, my answer was full of hope in God. "I don't know what you're going to do, but for right now, for tonight, hang on to my faith, because I believe. I believe that God is good. I believe that He loves us and is going to work through this experience. So hang on to my faith. I have enough for both of us."

Together we turned to the Bible, searching for God's view of success.

Together we found it—and it didn't look much like the up-and-down numbers game we'd been playing. The truths we found have served as a polestar in our life that we return to together again and again. Whether it be marriage or ministry, success is defined by knowing and obeying God's will as revealed in His Word.

This was the first time that I became aware of the powerful role I have as my husband's helper. It was also at this time that I discovered something beautiful about gender roles. In John 14:16 Jesus comforts his disciples with the promise of the Holy Spirit, referring to Him as "another Helper" (NASB). By addressing the Holy Spirit as a helper, Jesus forever elevated the position of the one who assists. Trace the Holy Spirit's actions through the New Testament, and you'll find the Spirit repeatedly encouraging, comforting, coming alongside, and helping. The work of the Holy Spirit, the Helper, is beautiful! And women are never more regal and lovely than when they follow His example, cherishing their responsibility as helper.

So Christian wives must never resent or despise the term "helper" or consider it demeaning. To help is divine! There is no better word to describe the role of a wife than "helper."

A GENTLE AND QUIET SPIRIT

Most women today care something about the way they look; beauty is so important to our society! But again God's idea of what's beautiful is countercultural. The beauty God desires for wives is the result of trust and obedience—a gentle and quiet spirit.

> Your beauty should not come from outward adornment, such as braided hair and the wearing of gold jewelry and fine clothes. Instead, it should be that of your inner self, the unfading beauty of a gentle and quiet spirit, which is of great worth in God's sight. For this is the way the holy women of the past who put their hope in God used to make themselves beautiful. They were submissive to their own husbands, like Sarah, who obeyed Abraham and called him her master. You are her daughters if you do what is right and do not give way to fear. (1 Peter 3:3-6, emphasis mine)

Gentleness, or meekness as many translations have it, isn't weakness or spinelessness or timidity or even niceness. This word in classical Greek was used to describe tame animals, soothing medicine, a mild word, and a mild breeze.[9] It is a word with a caress in it.[10]

Gentleness also implies self-control. Aristotle said that gentleness is the mean between excessive anger and excessive angerlessness. So the person who is gentle is able to balance his anger. He controls it.

Meekness/gentleness is strength under control.[11] The gentle woman is strong! She is in control of her fears. She is as strong as steel. Jesus tells us in the third Beatitude, "Blessed are the gentle, for they shall inherit the earth" (Matthew 5:5 NASB). Jesus calls himself gentle: "Take my yoke upon you and learn from Me, for I am gentle and humble in heart" (Matthew 11:29 NASB). And in 1 Peter the holy women of old, and in particular Sarah, are examples of this gentle beauty. We learn from this passage then that a gentle and quiet spirit is a direct result of Sarah's trust in God while submitting to her husband.

This is a beauty that most of us living in the early part of the new millennium hear little about. We have plenty of magazines and exercise gear infomercials to keep us up to date on how to cultivate beauty and keep our bodies fit and trim. We take skin care very seriously—using exotic ointments and lotions to protect us from exposure that causes the premature wrinkles. We make sure we are color-coordinated. And if our bank account permits, we seek procedures that offer a few more years of youthful appearance. We do all of this in the pursuit of the beauty the world esteems and yet ignore the convicting passages of Scripture that tell us where the beauty that God values resides.

RESPECT

Earlier we touched on that important passage on marriage in Ephesians 5. The end of that passage focuses attention on another wifely attribute that God considers important: ". . . and the wife must respect her husband" (Ephesians 5:33b).

Most women seem to think their husbands must earn respect before wives can give it. They couldn't be more wrong. Even when a husband is utterly *not* respectable, his wife can honor him by respecting his position. Sarah understood this: "She lived with a flawed man who asked her to do something unthinkable, yet she didn't hold this horrendous failure over him the rest of his life but restored her respect for him in her heart and lived with him, calling him, 'Master.'"[12]

Remember the story of my mother? Just as she never questioned God's goodness and care for us, she seemed always to hold fast to her love and respect for Dad. She wouldn't tolerate bad talk about him from us children or from anyone else. I have no memory of her ever speaking a critical word about my father. Even when he was at his worst—which could be pretty bad—he could always be sure that Mom's love and respect for him was steady.

My mother's spirit paid off in a surprising dividend over time to the marriage and the family. Because of her faithfulness and forgiveness he was restored to our family for that eleven years before he died. Because of Mother's choice to respect Dad, her children and grandchildren have memories of a positive relationship with him. We remember the little things—like huge anniversary cards with the almost illegible script of his crippled hand, and dinners prepared with great effort for her to come home to after her work as a janitor at a preschool.

Too often these days we hear of love that is only conditional: "I'll love you as long as you love me." But my mom understood that real love stands apart from circumstances and sees the object of love with all its flaws—and loves anyway. Real love is intentional, an act of the will. It's respect that's given because it's the Lord who requires that respect be given.

When I hear women whining about their husbands' faults to friends, and I catch myself speaking to my husband in tones that don't sound honoring, I want to shout, "Stop! Stop yourself, Barbara! Think of the consequences!" Our attitudes and words are teaching the next generation.

Where have you learned to speak to and about your husband? From television talk shows or sitcoms—or from God's Word? Giving loving respect to your husband is God's will—even when he doesn't deserve it. Watch your actions and listen to your words. God sees and hears.

A GOAL FOR LIFE AS A WIFE

When Eve was tempted, she wanted what God in His goodness had not given her. Things haven't changed. Sometimes I desire an easier, quieter life. At times I long to be free from other people's problems. And I despair at the constant bombardment of voices telling me I should pursue personal power and prestige. I know such thinking is foolish. A wise woman once told me that today's woman in search of equality often overlooks the one thing she needs most—an equality of commitment to know God and to obey His voice. The fact is, if she shares this commitment with her husband, or even, as my mother did for many years, holds it alone, she has the crucial ingredient for a fulfilling and joyous life.

Our evangelical church can appear to be a community of sound marriages. It looks so good on the surface—extensive educations, financial security, elegant homes, gracious churches, beautiful people, and marriage therapists for when there's a bump in the road. But how does God measure our marriages? Not by those standards!

My parents' marriage was a far cry from the neat evangelical package I've described. Yet there was a genuineness and beauty in the promises made and kept by this laboring couple who faced what seemed like insurmountable odds. The result has been a harvest of grace, and I am part of it.

Kent and I have been married for thirty-eight years. We have four grown children and sixteen grandchildren. Together we have tried to live out the directives of God's Word about marriage. Our struggles have been far different from those of my parents, and yet through them our commitment has grown, like my parents', into a deep and abiding love for each other. Our mutual commitment to live in accordance with God's plan for husband and wife has enabled us to experience a joyous unity—something rare and beautiful in this broken world.

My deepest regrets are for the times when I've failed the Lord by not being a respectful and submissive helper. My greatest joys have been the direct result of living in accordance with God's plan for me as a woman, made in His image—equal but different.

During the time that my husband and I worked to establish a biblical view of success, I sought to answer for myself, "What is my goal as a wife?" What I decided that day, twenty-five years ago, remains the same today: One day I want to hear God say to Kent, "Well done, good and faithful servant. Enter into the joy of your Master." As Kent's helper in this life, those words will be my joy.

Sisters in Christ, we must discipline ourselves to submit to God's will for our marriage relationships—to live as our husbands' helpers, submitting to and respecting their position, gracefully developing a gentle and quiet spirit. This is God's will in the Gospel.

RENEW YOUR MIND

What expectations did you bring to marriage? How does the goal of holiness figure into your current expectations (see Ephesians 5:22-31, especially 27-28)?

As a Christian, you must accept the authority of God and make it a life goal to submit every area of your life to His rule and order. What understanding do you glean from Genesis 1:26-28; 2:7, 18-25; 3:1-7, 14-17 and Ephesians 5:22-24 about God's order for authority in marriage? What does submission mean in specific terms for your marriage?

If you and your husband are "equal but different," why do you think God created an order for the marriage relationship? How does this order reflect the order in the Godhead?

How do you react, gut-level, at being termed your husband's "suitable helper"? How does understanding the role of Holy Spirit as "helper" dignify this role for you (see John 14:16)?

Why is gentleness countercultural for women in today's society? Why is a woman's gentleness her true beauty (1 Peter 3:3-6)? Who is the prime example for gentleness (Matthew 11:29)?

Why must you respect your husband whether or not he has earned your respect (see Ephesians 5:33; 1 Peter 3:6)? Take an inventory of your own recent actions and words. Do they show respect for your husband?

In view of the Gospel, what are your personal goals as a wife?

13

DISCIPLINE OF NURTURING

Submission's Caress

*Adam named his wife Eve, because she would become
the mother of all the living.*

GENESIS 3:20

The screaming headline was tabloid-size: I WAS DESPERATE FOR A BABY, AND I HAVE THE MEDICAL BILLS TO PROVE IT." Thus began Charles Krauthammer's feature article in the *Washington Post*.[1] The article went on: "Some love-struck movie star? a lesbian celebrity? No. It was Germaine Greer, icon of twentieth-century feminism. 'I still have pregnancy dreams,' she confessed, 'waiting with vast joy and confidence for something that will never happen.'"

What irony! Ms. Greer, in Krauthammer's words, "is the great exemplar of the fiercely independent, aggressively sexual new woman. Iconoclastic to the point of ferocity, she reveled in her lovers and in telling about them." In 1970 Ms. Greer wrote in *The Female Eunuch* that women should view motherhood as a handicap and pregnancy as an illness. Greer urged women to be "deliberately promiscuous" and to be certain not to conceive children.[2]

Krauthammer's article continues: "The one adjective rarely attached to Ms. Greer was domestic. And now she reveals the hollowness that haunts her, the terrible sorrow she feels at what she lost: her chance for motherhood. Many years ago, she now writes, she cared for the infant daughter of a friend. 'Ruby lit up my life in a way that nobody, certainly no lover, has ever done. I was not prepared for the incandescent sensuousness of this small child, the generosity of her innocent love.'"

Why the change of heart? Why would a woman so rabidly against mothering be experiencing the agonizing loss of the very thing she despised? Because motherhood is the essence of womanhood.[3] I believe that whether or not a woman has children, she is called to embrace the discipline of nurturing. This aspect of womanhood goes far beyond the physical bearing of children.

NURTURE IN OUR NATURE

The word *nurture* originated from the Latin word meaning "act of nursing, to suckle or nourish."[4] In our English language its broader meaning includes "to further the development of, to train."[5] Nurturing is essential for everyone's well-being. It follows then that if a woman's gentle nurturing touch is missing, society will surely degenerate. You don't have to look far for evidence that this is happening all around us. The world's children are crying out for a womanly, nurturing touch. But to submit to God's plan for the maternal essence of our being takes discipline, especially in light of our culture.

God's Word teaches that nurturing life is uniquely female. We are all daughters of Eve, whose name, we are told in Genesis 3:20, means "mother of all living." Each of us, like Eve, has been given a body designed to nurture life. We are reminded of this every month with the storing and passing of blood necessary for the nourishment of the unborn. Our breasts are likewise given to nourish the newborn. Those who become pregnant and give birth experience the full realization of these gifts and make the wondrously personal discovery that an infant is wholly dependent on the mother's body for life itself.

But there are many women who never give birth, whose nurture will necessarily extend to those who are not her children. It isn't the actual process of pregnancy and childbirth that makes a daughter of Eve a nurturer. Germaine Greer glimpsed this when something beautiful was aroused in her as she cared for little Ruby. What is the quality that makes a woman a life-giver?

The Bible teaches that all women are created to "mother," to nurture life. Mothering is more than the mere mechanics of uterus and breast; it is far more profound. And women become more womanly when they mother.

We have all heard about couples who were able to conceive their own child shortly after having adopted another. This is more than coincidence. A recent study suggests that the mother's act of nurturing and caring for the adopted child causes female hormones to be released in her body, which creates more favorable conditions for conception. Nurturing, acting like a mother enhances her womanhood.

Is it possible that what Germaine Greer experienced while caring for little Ruby actually resulted in releasing her suppressed womanliness? I believe so.

SAVED THROUGH CHILDBEARING?

A complex passage of Scripture emphasizes the importance of nurturing. In 1 Timothy 2:15 Paul advises, "But women will be saved through childbearing—if they continue in faith, love and holiness with propriety."

Many today avoid this passage because it is out of sync with our culture, which is so careful to define a woman's place and position apart from any nurturing role. On the surface "saved through childbearing" also appears to contradict the crucial teaching of the New Testament— that we are saved by God's grace alone and not by our actions.

Of course, Paul does not mean that Christian women will be "saved" from death in childbirth. Countless godly women have died while giving life to a child. The context clearly indicates that Paul is speaking of being "saved" in a spiritual sense. We also know that women who have never given birth are heirs of salvation. So then what does the apostle mean?

In the immediate context of this passage, Paul is instructing us about the behavior of godly women as distinct from that of godly men, especially in reference to how we should behave at home and in the church. Paul directs our attention back to Creation and the ordained differences between Adam and Eve from the very beginning. He uses childbearing as a universal example of the God-given difference between the roles of men and women. Men don't give birth.[6] Therefore, when Paul says, "women will be saved through childbearing," he means that *by living out their God-given roles and not seeking a man's role, they will more likely remain in the heart attitude that invites salvation and its attendant blessings.* The essential attitude here is one of submission. Of course, godliness for both men and women always begins with submission to God's will. But in this text, we women are encouraged to submit to the God-given nurturing realm for which we were designed, willingly abiding in the four virtues of "faith, love, and holiness with propriety."

An Unchanging Principle in Changing Times

Being gospel women means that we are committed to evaluate our thoughts and actions only by the standard of God's Word, being determined not to be "conformed to this world" but "transformed by the renewing of our minds" (Romans 12:2). This necessarily involves being aware of and informed about the world around us. We must continually evaluate popular ideas, holding them up against the measure of God's Word.

I well remember as a young mother trying to understand and live out what the Bible says about the value of mothering as compared to the radical new thinking sweeping our country. It was the mid-sixties. Kent was in seminary and working swing shift in a factory in east Los Angeles to provide for our young family. There he met a law student who was working to finish his degree and to enhance his wife's already successful career. Their ambitions precluded thoughts of parenthood or spiritual issues. Concerned, we reached out to them, but we met excuses and demurrals. Such a contrast in values.

Graduation came, and we went our separate ways. While we grew our family, they grew their fortune. The newspapers reported that the woman, now world-famous, had an abortion so that she could pursue her goals *unhindered.* Later there was national news of their divorce and her new companion—her lesbian lover. Of course, the story was reported without critical comment, for she was living out the values of the culture of the day. Tragically, she had rejected not only her realm of motherhood, but also the realm of salvation.

Women, we must cultivate *nurturing* spirits whether single or married. This has nothing to do with whether or not I am a mother. Nurturing is my responsibility before God as a human being and in particular because I am female. The context for where and how I will care for others will be dictated by where God places me—in a home, in a school, in a hospital, in the inner city, wherever. Someday I will answer to God for how I nurtured life on this planet.

Certainly mothering and nurturing will not save us physically or spiritually. But the cultivation of a mother's heart and a nurturing role under God will place our submissive souls in the way of salvation and of the greatest use to the kingdom.

NURTURING THE NURTURING INSTINCT

As I have mentioned, it takes great effort to develop the nurturing instinct in ourselves and others, primarily because all around us women are intentionally being encouraged to reject roles of service and caring. Barbara Dafoe Whitehead writes in her brilliant article "The Girls of Gen-X" that Gen-Xers are the heirs of what she calls the "girlhood project" to reeducate them. "The girlhood project," Whitehead writes, "was rooted in rebellion against traditional conceptions of girlhood. . . . Feminists called instead for a new single sexual standard based on traditional boyhood. In their play and pursuits, little girls were to be made more like boys. . . . Today, all that is naturally womanly—especially anything related to childbearing—is treated by elites as something to be managed, minimized, and somehow overcome."[7]

We must be informed and intentional as we train our daughters (and the young girls in our lives) to be godly mothers for the kingdom of God. If we don't train our daughters, they will be trained by default—by the world's agenda.

Consciously look for evidences of the nurturing instinct in your daughters or other young women you know and cherish the differences. My own two daughters were both little nurturers as children, but they showed it in such different ways. Heather loved baby dolls, playing "mommy" for hours, tending to the needs of her "babies." But Holly was not interested in dolls. Instead, her attention was lavished on baby rats, birds, cats, bunnies, and turtles. She once trapped a wild parrot that flew into our California garden by patiently putting food and water out for him until she could entice him into a cage. "Big Bird" remained her pet for eight years.

We didn't attempt to make Holly take up dolls or encourage

Heather to love animals. We helped them to flourish—and nurture—as God made them, different from one another. Both expressions of nurture were part of their training in understanding their femaleness. We wanted them to be aware that the world offers women various avenues for mothering.

Nurturers at Home

My adult daughters are now busy mothers who work to nurture life both at home and in the broader world, and they are facing pressures I never knew. I reared my four children during a time when most mothers were full-time, stay-at-home moms. I took for granted the support I received from other neighborhood moms as we worked together to protect and instruct the children in our neighborhood. Though ideas were quickly changing, mothers enjoyed a high regard for the work they performed for society. And, of course, the church was of greatest support.

Today's mothers are pulled in many other directions—and typically away from at-home tasks considered too humble or too selfless for twenty-first-century women of status, sophistication, and power. Today's mothers are isolated and unsupported by popular culture in the work of mothering.

We must become convinced in our souls that nurturing is a supremely elevated role. And we need to proclaim that truth to the women around us, emphasizing that the role of mother is an incredible privilege. We older women carry a God-given responsibility to help younger women with families so that they do not become overwhelmed with the mothering task, for it is great (Titus 2:3-5).

Nurturers Outside the Home

Twenty-five years ago a friend of our family—Deborah Bayly—created a school in Chicago's inner city for children who had dropped out of the school system. No longer able to attend public school for various reasons, teenagers have been given another chance at the Lakeview Academy. Deborah is an excellent teacher, but she has gone far beyond the teaching role in caring for her students. Deborah nurtures her teens in ways many of them would never have experienced.

She patiently teaches her students how to read a city map. Then, money in hand, they venture out on the public transportation system, going from place to place as directed until they return triumphantly to Deborah at the end of the lesson.

Deborah invites these city kids out to her mother's home in the country where they have lunch and play games. In teaching them to read, she shows them how to read a recipe and prepare a meal. And, yes, when they fail to do their assigned work, she chides and disciplines them like a mother. And like a loving mother, she encourages them when they're down. Deborah Bayly, a single woman, has never borne a child, but she is mother of many!

Sharon Luthey loved all animals as a child, but she adored horses. When she was a student at Wheaton College, she used to visit me and tell how she longed to be a mother, but she also felt the call of God to go to Mongolia as a missionary.

Sharon understood that if she went to Mongolia, her opportunities for marriage and family would diminish. Nevertheless, she obeyed God and set off for the Himalayas. Today Sharon uses her unique, gentle, nurturing personality in ministering to young Mongolians. Her family looks different from mine, but God has given her children of all ages. She is a mother indeed. (Incidentally, God remembered her love of horses. She rides with the wind over the Mongolian countryside.)

Nurturing Appropriate Priorities

Mothers are in the divinely given position to model for their girls the value and richness of the nurturer's role. One of my most treasured memories is of a day shortly after the birth of my youngest brother. I was fourteen years old. My mother had worked outside the home—by necessity. So for me, coming home from school usually meant entering an empty house with breakfast dishes waiting to be washed and no aroma of the dinner to come. But on this day, I heard my mother's voice as I approached the front door. She was singing a lullaby. The house was bright and tidy and redolent with wonderful aromas from the kitchen. Mother was rocking my baby brother. She looked happier than I had ever seen her. From that moment, I knew that there was no place on earth my mother would rather be than at home caring for us. Of course, she had no choice; she worked outside the home until she was sixty-five years old. But the dreadful thought that my mother's job was more important to her than I was never crossed my mind. Her attitude was so utterly powerful. It has marked me for life.

A beautiful newly married woman told me privately that she didn't know if she wanted to have children. She'd been raised on the mission field. Over the years her missionary mother had repeatedly told her and her sister that she wished she had never had them because they took so much time away from her "ministry." She made them feel guilty for thwarting her career.

Whether you work in or outside your home, discipline yourself to convey biblical truth about the value of nurturing to those around you— even when you are exhausted from your duties. Admittedly, this is harder for single working women, but it can be done.

NURTURING THE FORGOTTEN CHILDREN

Let the needs of children penetrate our hearts! Never in history has there been a greater need for a woman's nurturing touch. There are more orphans, foster children, and single-parent homes than ever before. The suburbs are as bleak as the inner cities when it comes to neglected and unwanted children. The nightly news bears appalling reports of child abuse all around the globe. The need for nurture is desperate.

God's Word repeatedly instructs His people to care for the needy and suffering, especially widows and orphans. James 1:27 says, "Religion that God our Father accepts as pure and faultless is this: to look after orphans and widows in their distress." Jesus Himself said, "And whoever welcomes a little child like this in my name welcomes me" (Matthew 18:5).

The Scriptures clearly direct us to care for the "fatherless" children of the world. In our culture many children are being raised by single mothers—women whose desperate straits are not unlike those of the widows of biblical times. As nurturers, we must find concrete ways to support and help divorcees, widows, and single moms in their job of caring for their children.

As Christian women, we surely ought to know the value of adoption, considering that we are "adopted" into God's family ourselves! Ephesians 1:5-6 joyfully declares, "In love he predestined us to be adopted as his sons through Jesus Christ, in accordance with his pleasure and will—to the praise of his glorious grace, which he has freely given us in the One he loves" (see also Romans 8:23). Clearly, God elevates adoption as a divine way of creating a family.

A well-known Hollywood comedian recently asked on a late-night talk show, "If all the anti-choice people care so much for children, how come they aren't emptying the orphanages?" Ouch! Certainly there are many who have stepped out of their comfort zone and given a needy child a home. But what a powerful witness it would be to the world if even one out of four Christian families would give a needy child a home. Such Christlike love would change the face of the church—not to mention the world—forever.

It is a contrived secular myth that there are not enough children to go around for families wishing to adopt. The truth is that the number of older adoptable children, plus children exposed to alcohol or drugs during pregnancy, children of minorities, children with special medical needs, and children with physical or mental handicaps is far greater than the number of families willing to adopt. If we believe every human life is valuable and precious, we must do more than just nod assent.

My own family has experienced the privileged joy of welcoming adopted children. Three of my sixteen grandchildren came to our family in this manner.

Fellow pastor Steve Krogh and his wife, Lois, wrote to us, relating their stirring testimony of how God prepared their hearts to receive a seventeen-year-old orphan into their family. They'd read about the difficulties believers faced in southern Sudan and began to pray for the Christians caught in the civil war. Here in their own words is how God led them:

> When headlines in our local newspaper informed us that eighty "lost boys" from Sudan were going to be resettled here, we wondered if this might be the hand of God directing our lives. We made a few phone calls, asked a lot of questions, gathered pages of information, prayed with our family and church elders, and then began the process of becoming foster parents for one of these boys.
>
> There was never one defining moment when we decided this was God's will for us. We just kept walking forward in the path

that more and more seemed like the "good works" that God had foreordained for us to walk in.

And so in less than a week, we will welcome Emanuel into our family. All we know of him we have learned from a Red Cross questionnaire. At seventeen years old, he has been an orphan and without siblings for about eight years. He has seen the cruelties of war firsthand. He has known nothing but poverty. He said he desires to study in America to become a pastor. The rest of his story and the adventures that await us once he joins our family we will only know as we walk together the path ahead.

. . . God has quieted my fears of the unknown with the continual reminder of His sovereignty and sufficiency. Instead of my natural disposition to worry and attempt to control my circumstances, God has thrilled my heart with the experience of knowing Him and seeing His control over all things. With joy and peace we await His prepared gift, handed to us in His wisdom and love.[8]

For single women, for women struggling with infertility, and even for women who are already mothers, the joys of nurturing precious lives far outweigh the difficulties. Although many have been put off by adoption agency procedures, lack of space, and finances, it has been my children's experience (and the experience of other adoptive parents) that when you are willing, God provides.

There is a wide-spread misconception that the responsibility for children without families falls to those who have exceptional parenting gifts or only to those who already have children. But, married or not, mothers or not, we must trust God to enable us to nurture as He has called us to do! God the Father will give us the strength, the wisdom, the resources, and the support we need to raise forgotten children for the glory of God. In fact, through nurturing each child that God brings to us in the love and admonition of the Lord, we are expanding the kingdom dramatically. Just think—every child who grows up learning of the love of Jesus Christ through a family has the potential to reach many others for Christ in his or her lifetime—far more than any one person could ever reach on her own.

UNASHAMED OBEDIENCE

To live out of sync with culture takes courage. When we become Christians, we are called to take up a gospel-life that is radically countercultural. We begin to treasure things that those who have their hearts set on earthly things do not understand. St. Paul's declaration, "I am not ashamed of the gospel of Christ" (Romans 1:16), reminds us that the preaching of the Gospel is foolishness to the world.

Unbelievers may view us as fools, and if this world is all there is, then we are indeed fools to do anything other than think of ourselves first and get the best life we can experience. But in Christ, our life is not about what we get, but what we give. Life is about living in submission to His will regardless of what it may cost us. God's will for women since the beginning is to nurture.

Mothering is at the essence of womanhood. To live out life as a nurturer in this self-centered, godless culture will cost you. But the rewards, as Germaine Greer so belatedly discovered, are rich indeed.

RENEW YOUR MIND

Why is nurturing not confined to mothering your own children? Can you think of times when you have nurtured others (not your own children)?

What does the apostle Paul mean when he claims that "women will be saved through childbearing" (1 Timothy 2:15)? How does that point women toward nurturing?

Whom does James 1:27 instruct Christians to care for?

What contemporary issues attract your God-given instinct to protect and preserve the young? How are you involved in doing this?

How can you influence other young women to value the role of nurturer in a society that devalues it persistently? How is nurturing commonly devalued?

What did God speak to you about most specifically or most powerfully in this chapter? Talk to Him about it right now!

MINISTRY

14

DISCIPLINE OF GOOD DEEDS

Submission's Industry

*For we are God's workmanship, created in Christ Jesus
to do good works, which God prepared
in advance for us to do.*

EPHESIANS 2:10

Good deeds aren't as popular as they once were. But there was a time when our society highly valued good works. Historian Joan Jacobs Brummberg's *The Body Project: An Intimate History of Girlhood* "meticulously documents the downward slide of girls' aspirations and ambitions over the past century, from improving one's character through good works to improving one's body through grueling workouts."[1] The development of character through selfless acts of charity has been replaced by the vain pursuit of a sculpted body. We once valued what women did; we now value what women look like. Unfortunately, this is not just a problem belonging to our secular culture. It's often true of the church as well.

These days selfless acts are rare enough to be newsworthy. Sometimes Oprah Winfrey's show features women who have acted in selfless ways. Invariably tissues come out of handbags all over the audience. However, the response seems to be purely emotional—and fleeting. When the show is over, the sacrifice is quickly forgotten; it rarely inspires change in the hearts of those who wipe away sentimental tears.

But we gospel women have also had a sacrifice modeled for us. Our lives have been changed by Christ's sacrifice on our behalf. Our response has nothing to do with sentimental emotions; it requires a practical, rubber-meets-the-road reaction of good deeds. Read Ephesians 2:10 in its context: "For it is by grace you have been saved, through faith—and this not from yourselves, it is the gift of God—not by works, so that no one can boast. For we are God's workmanship, created in Christ Jesus to do good works, which God prepared in advance for us to do" (Ephesians 2:8-10).

While we are not saved by works, we *were* created for good works. Like the God in whose image we were created, we were designed to work, to create. Good deeds are the redeemed heart's response of gratitude for the gift of God's grace. Good deeds are not an option for Christians. We cannot fail to follow Christ's example. Good deeds are our way of life.

The remarkable flow of thought in the second chapter of Ephesians goes from amazing grace to amazing work. First, the good news of salvation defines us as human beings: We are His workmanship! The best translation of that word *workmanship* is given by F. F. Bruce: "His work of art, his masterpiece."[2] We are God's works of art. We were created in His image. Then, even better, we were recreated in Christ Jesus! Paul describes it this way: "Therefore, if anyone is in Christ, he is a new creation; the old has gone, the new has come!" (2 Corinthians 5:17).

Perhaps you don't feel like a masterpiece because of difficult and painful experiences that have made you question your own worth. Don't overlook this beautiful truth of Scripture: You are His "workmanship"— His masterwork of art.

Ephesians 2:10 points to the purpose of our creation and recreation—good deeds. The Gospel defines us and then explains what we are supposed to do. Paul's great statement here capsulizes God's role in our salvation and our responsibility to God. So what does the privileged position of masterpiece require of us? Once we have been saved by His grace, we must work. Works are a sign that we are His workmanship! "No one more wholeheartedly than Paul rejected good works as a ground of salvation; no one more strongly insisted on good works as a fruit of salvation."[3] Authentic believers, in response to God's grace, work for Him.

Think of it! In God's great plan, there are good works prepared before the foundation of the world, waiting for you and for me to carry out. They have been prepared for us by design. And we unique individuals have been designed with these specific tasks in view.

THE SCOPE OF GOOD DEEDS

Good deeds are important to God, and Scripture makes it clear that good works should also be important to us. God's Word lays out clearly and comprehensively the value of good works in our lives, showing that good deeds have implications for our *reputation*, our *appearance*, and our *means*.

Our Reputation

In describing the qualifications a widow must have in order to be put on the church's benevolence list, 1 Timothy 5:9-10 gives us further clues about good deeds: "No widow may be put on the list of widows unless she is . . . *well known for her good deeds*, such as bringing up children, showing hospitality, washing the feet of the saints, helping those in trouble and devoting herself to all kinds of good deeds" (emphasis mine). This verse makes it unquestionably clear that in the early church a godly woman had to have a reputation for her good deeds.

Tabitha met this standard well. "In Joppa there was a disciple named Tabitha (which, when translated, is Dorcas), who was always doing good and helping the poor" (Acts 9:36). If someone had to describe you in only one sentence, wouldn't you wish for a lovely line like this one? This verse shows us what it means to have a reputation for doing good deeds. Even two millenniums later, Dorcas is known for her good works.

In my own church, Carol Carlburg is such a woman. Carol seems tireless in her labor for anyone in need at our church. Her home-cooked, graciously served meals have been enjoyed by thousands. Her work with the handicapped in our area is widely known. Before recycling was widespread, Carol drove around town on Tuesday mornings gathering the newspapers put on curbsides for disposal. The small amounts of money she collected at recycling centers for the newspapers were donated to missions. Over the years those few weekly dollars added up to a surprising total. And there is hardly a two-year-old in our church family who doesn't know Mrs. Carlburg from Wednesday morning Kids Korner, the children's program provided for mothers in Bible study.

Henrietta Mears's reputation for good deeds for the sake of the Gospel is legendary. The influence of one woman, single her entire life and handicapped by serious eye problems, is truly amazing. In her own words, Miss Mears put forth her vision: "The first thing I did in Hollywood was to write out what I wanted for my Sunday school. I set down my objectives for the first five years. They included improvements in organization, teaching staff, curriculums, and spirit. I wanted a closely graded program, teaching material that would present Christ and his claims in every lesson, a trained teaching staff, a new education building, choirs, clubs, a camp program, a missionary vision, youth trained for the hour."[4]

And that is exactly what Henrietta Mears accomplished. According to distinguished author and theologian Dr. Wilbur Smith: "She was the inspiration and genius of the great Sunday school of the First Presbyterian Church of Hollywood with its some 6,000 members! . . . She was the founder of Gospel Light Publications, whose literature has done so much to save many Sunday schools from compromising or destructively liberal Sunday school study books. She saw come into reality her vision of a Bible conference center at Forest Home, where, I think it can be said, a greater work has been done each year in the College Briefing Conference than in any similar gathering since those conferences held at Northfield by Dwight L. Moody.[5]

Miss Mears wasted no time sitting around feeling sorry for herself because she wasn't married or because she was visually impaired. She believed the Gospel! She knew that in the Gospel, she was "created in Christ Jesus to do good works, which God prepared in advance for [her] to do" (Ephesians 2:10). Long after her death, her reputation for good deeds lives on.

What are you known for? If people made a list of your pastimes, would any of them include labors for the kingdom of God? We gospel women must determine to develop the discipline of good deeds. Paul, in his advice in Titus 3:8, says, "And I want you to stress these things, so that those who have trusted in God may be careful to devote themselves to doing what is good. These things are excellent and profitable for everyone."

Our Appearance

We've already given ample attention to our appearance as we considered the discipline of propriety. But one very important phrase in Timothy's instruction regarding women's clothing was not addressed. We are to adorn ourselves with good deeds. "I also want women to dress modestly, with decency and propriety, not with braided hair or gold or pearls or expensive clothes, but *with good deeds*, appropriate for women who profess to worship God" (1 Timothy 2:9-10, emphasis mine).

So how can we clothe ourselves in good deeds? First, we should consider what we must not do. From Paul's description, we do not spend excessive time or money on our appearance. Our primary attention and emphasis shouldn't be on the external things—that is, what we wear—but on what we do. Our good deeds determine our apparel.

So how does Carol Carlburg dress for success? Blue jeans and a sweatshirt for collecting newspapers, no doubt! A washable dress maybe for serving up a meal after a funeral or wedding. When she dresses for good deeds, she'll dress for the occasion! On any Wednesday evening at our church, you'll find women dressed appropriately for all kinds of good deeds. Lorraine, who's busy with girls in our club program, might wear overalls and a T-shirt. Jan, who works with the evening businesswomen's Bible study, might wear dress slacks and a sweater. Nancy dresses like the banker she is; she's putting her banking expertise to work helping families organize their finances. Apparel options are as varied as the good deeds their wearers do. Our clothing should enhance our good deeds, not overshadow them. And our appearance should reflect our labor for the Lord.

Revelation 19:6-8 describes what we will wear on that great and glorious day at the wedding of the Lamb to His bride, the church. "'Hallelujah! For our Lord God Almighty reigns. Let us rejoice and be glad and give him glory! For the wedding of the Lamb has come, and his bride has made herself ready. Fine linen, bright and clean, was given her to wear.' (Fine linen stands for the *righteous acts* of the saints)" (emphasis mine). Someday my garments will be woven from the good deeds I offered to the Lord as a child of God on this earth. If ever there was a time to be dressed appropriately, this will be it! Good deeds are important to God, and they should be at least as important to us as what we wear each day.

Our Means

We are to use our resources—our wealth—for good deeds. Listen to Paul's instruction in 1 Timothy 6:17-19: "Command those who are rich in this present world not to be arrogant nor to put their hope in wealth, which is so uncertain, but to put their hope in God, who richly provides us with everything for our enjoyment. Command them to do good, to be rich in good deeds, and to be generous and willing to share. In this way they will lay up treasure for themselves as a firm foundation for the coming age, so that they may take hold of the life that is truly life."

Selina Hastings was a rich woman—the Countess of Huntingdon, born in 1707 in Leicestershire, England. When she was converted, she "cast herself fully upon Christ for life and for salvation. . . . Full of this joy and peace, she resolved there and then to dedicate her life to Christ and to His service."[6] The remainder of her life was the fulfillment of her resolve.

Selina Hastings used both her position and her means to do good deeds for the sake of the Gospel. She bought properties and built chapels across England and then provided them with godly gospel-preaching pastors. When she could not find enough pastors, she opened a theological college for their training. She went so far as to provide a suit of clothing for each student at the theological college for each of their three years of study. That's practical empowering!

Lady Elizabeth Catherwood says this of Lady Huntingdon: "Now she did not open all her churches easily; money did not just come simply to her. She was, for example, only able to build the Brighton church by selling all her jewels. . . . She gave her money generously—100,000 English pounds then must be millions now—and she gave it all from her own funds."[7] The scope of the countess's influence is staggering. George Whitefield and Charles and John Wesley were a few of the men she enabled to minister. Her interest in missions made its way across the Atlantic to America in her support of George Whitefield and his mission to our forefathers. She also helped with missions to the Jews.

Lady Catherwood continues: "All her life, too, she worked assiduously to help people. She said once, 'I am connected with many'—that meant her position in society—and she used that. She got involved in parliamentary acts, and when the Archbishop of Canterbury was behaving in a totally unseemly way in Lambeth Palace, she sent to the King himself to tell him to stop! She used her influence, because everything she had was given to God; so she used it, and God blessed it greatly."[8]

If you are a woman of means or position, God has given you those blessings for a purpose. I challenge you to step out from the crowd of those who give only a small percentage of their wealth for good deeds and follow the example of Selina Hastings, whose chief concern was to make the Gospel known! Use what you have in doing good deeds until it truly costs you something.

But women who have little in the way of monetary blessing have equal opportunity to be generous. Most women today are familiar with Christy, the heroine of a book and subsequent television movie and series. Christy was a real woman in real circumstances, married to a minister who spent forty years serving congregations in small communities and living frugally. Her story is told by her daughter, Catherine Marshall, who portrays her mother's amazing ability to use her meager means generously in good deeds.

"Though we did without many things, Mother always provided us with a feeling of well-being. One way she did this was the unique manner in which she contrived to give to others. Out of our meager pantry she would send a sick neighbor a supper tray of something delicious she hand-prepared—velvety-smooth, boiled custard; feather-light homemade rolls—served up on our best china and always with a dainty bouquet from our garden."[9]

One day, when my children were young, I walked to a neighbor's house to call them home for dinner. As soon as I entered the house, I could smell something delicious cooking. Entering my neighbor's kitchen, I asked, "What's for dinner?" To my amazement, it was a simple pot of shredded carrots seasoned with a bit of onion and butter. That was dinner for their family that night—only those carrots. It was the end of the week, and a bag of carrots was all that remained in the refrigerator. I was shocked that Jan's family would be eating only shredded carrots for dinner, but her attitude was even more surprising—and instructive. I had always looked up to Jan, who was five years older than I, and she taught me something important that day. Jan chose to be thankful, with no hint of self-pity or even a suggestion that shredded carrots for dinner wasn't as worthy as a full-course meal.

That picture of Jan's beautiful strength in refusing to feel sorry for herself inspired me! I saw how self-pity can paralyze a woman and put on blinders that prevent her from seeing beyond herself to the needs of those around her.

The remedy for self-pity, according to Catherine Marshall's mother, was giving. "Only unconsciously were we aware of it, but Mother was providing us constantly with an object lesson in giving. The message: no matter how little you have, you can always give some of it away. And when you can do that, you can't feel sorry for yourself, and you can scarcely consider yourself poor."[10]

We women of the twenty-first century have so much! It's so easy for us to fall into the trap that says: "I will give when I get ahead." Or to constantly compare our own means with those who have more than we do. Rather let's agree to put on an opposite mind-set, always comparing ourselves to those who have far less than we do. The truth is, as Catherine Marshall's mother taught her, no matter how meager your means, there is always something you can give to someone in need.

Take a look in your pantry. Could someone be blessed by your preparing a little something for them out of your abundance? How about your closets? Is there something there that someone needier than your family could use? Christians are never poor. Our problem is that we fail to understand that what we have or do not have has been given us by God for a purpose. We may be temporarily given the opportunity to persevere through difficult times, but no matter how long those times may last, we are children of a King. We are on a comparatively short journey to our Father's home, where we will be greeted with all the splendors that heaven can afford.

When we do look around, it's easy to find folks in our sphere of influence who are truly poor and needy. Again hear Catherine Marshall: "Mother offered her services to the county welfare board and to our surprise (but definitely not hers!) was given a job to help improve conditions in any way she could. Day after day, she would send us off to school in our hand-me-downs and our artfully patched clothing, and then she would go off to help what she called 'the poor people.'"[11]

THE PURPOSE OF GOOD DEEDS

Just as good deeds are important to God with regard to their scope, they are also important to Him in respect to their purpose for the church, the world, our sanctification, and God's glory.

For the Sake of the Church

There is a shocking passage of Scripture in Galatians: "Let us not become weary in doing good, for at the proper time we will reap a harvest if we do not give up. Therefore, as we have opportunity, let us do good to all people, *especially to those who belong to the family of believers*" (6:9-10, emphasis mine).

This passage knocked me off my feet because it points so directly to the priority of exercising good deeds first within our church family. For years I've considered evangelism the highest endeavor a Christian can undertake, so this really got my attention. We can't neglect to care for those outside the faith, but our family—that is, the family of God—comes first.

In the Resources section of this book, there is a list of most of the verses that speak to Christians about good deeds. In many cases, the deeds that are described are those done in the service of a family. Good deeds are important to God because they nurture and care for the needs of His family here on earth. God's purpose for good deeds, however, goes beyond His own family.

For the Sake of the World

The Old Testament speaks again and again of the responsibility of God's people to help the poor. "Gleaning," the practice of allowing people to gather leftover crops from fields farmers had harvested, was one of the provisions established by the Israelites to provide food for the poor: "When you reap the harvest of your land, do not reap to the very edges of your field or gather the gleanings of your harvest. . . . Leave them for the poor and the alien" (Leviticus 19:9-10). We are instructed many times not to neglect the poor (see Job 31:16-22; Isaiah 58:7; Matthew 25:34-36; James 1:27; 2:1-7).

But the Scriptures are clear from Genesis to Revelation that more important than man's physical need is his need of God Himself. Jesus had compassion for people's physical needs, but He always made it clear that a person's spiritual need is even greater. He said, "It is written, 'Man does not live on bread alone, but on every word that comes from the mouth of God'" (Matthew 4:4). And also, "I am the bread of life. He who comes to me will never go hungry" (John 6:35). Our good deeds are meant to be a means to this end—to make the Gospel known.

My friend Linda learned this the hard way. She had returned with her family from a difficult time of missionary service in the Philippines. They moved into a new condominium, and she was thrilled to have a home of her own for a change. I watched as she decorated the rooms with her artistic skill. I had always envied her flare for making something beautiful with very little. True to form, when she was finished, that condo was beautiful. When you entered, the first thing your eye was drawn to was the large glass door leading to the enclosed patio—a garden oasis.

Linda delighted in this quiet, secluded spot. It was her little sanctuary—a place to pray and read the Scriptures. Her delight and solitude were short-lived however. A new family moved in next door. The two condominiums were divided by a common wall, as was the patio. The neighbors were not a quiet family, and the common wall was thin. Linda's lovely new home had lost its luster virtually overnight.

The new neighbors were coarse—offensive in words and actions. The adults screamed obscenities at each other and at their children. The kids were unruly and dirty. The entire exterior of their condo began to deteriorate; the lawn was overgrown with weeds, and the window screens were ratty and torn. Worst of all, the children actually urinated out the windows on occasion. Linda was at her wit's end.

She reported to me regularly about her frustration with the situation. She knew that she should "reach out" to these wretched folks, but she'd encountered a slight problem: She hated them. They were ruining her life!

Just when she thought she could endure no more, she came home to a calamitous surprise. As she opened the door to enter her home, her eyes went to the glass doors that led to the patio. Before she closed the door, she had begun to shriek, and by the time it was closed, she was in tears and screaming out in frustration. The boys next door had climbed over the adjoining patio fence and sprayed orange paint all over her beautiful patio—garden, furniture, and fence.

While she wept, she began to pray: "Lord, I hate these neighbors. I know that I am supposed to love them, but I haven't an ounce of love for them." As she prayed, she opened her Bible and began to read in Colossians 3:12-14: "Therefore, as God's chosen people, holy and dearly loved, clothe yourselves with compassion, kindness, humility, gentleness and patience. Bear with each other and forgive whatever grievances you may have against one another. Forgive as the Lord forgave you. And over all these virtues put on love. . . ."

"How do I put on love?" she cried out to the Lord. "My heart is full of hate." Gently, the Lord began to make it clear to her. "How do I put on a coat?" she asked herself. "I take a deliberate action; I lift my arm and put it in a sleeve." *Putting on love must be a little like that,* she thought. Then she asked herself, "What would I do if I did love these neighbors?" She got out a pencil and paper and started a list:

1. I would bake them cookies.
2. I would ask the woman over for coffee.
3. I would offer to baby-sit. (Impossible!)

As she continued the list, she realized that she could put on the actions of love—the good deeds—and trust that God would give her requisite feelings in time. And that is exactly what happened.

With much fear and a lot of prayer, she began systematically to do the things on her list. The day she first took over the cookies and actually met the neighbor woman was memorable. The neighbor was very touched by Linda's kindness, and Linda was touched by what she began to understand about this couple.

In the following months in repeated visits over coffee, the woman poured out her heart to Linda. Linda learned that the children were not their own. They had taken them in when relatives had abandoned them. Although the adults were barely educated themselves, they were doing the very best they could to help these homeless children. Linda began to see them in a different light. Living next to them had not grown easier, and occasionally baby-sitting for them stretched her to the limit. But as she began to be a light for the Gospel, something was happening to Linda.

About a year later, Linda called me. She was crying. Only this time she wasn't crying because of something the neighbors had done, but rather because they were moving, and Linda was truly sad. She realized that God had used her to help this family, but she knew that God had greatly used them to sanctify her. Obedience to God's Word had transformed her heart full of hatred to one of love.

There are people all around us who need the Gospel demonstrated to them through good deeds that are done out of hearts changed by that Gospel. It isn't enough to give to people in need if all we do is take care of a few material needs, although these needs are not unimportant. Our friends, coworkers, and neighbors (even the difficult ones) need the Bread of Life, the Lord Jesus Christ. What good works has He planned for you to do in this regard?

For My Sake

What happened to my friend Linda illustrates the point that when we submit to God's Word regarding good deeds, something worthwhile happens to us. God has called us to be a people who do good even in the face of adversity. The sanctification that takes place in our hearts is simply a by-product of our obedience to God's plan.

Peter speaks to this issue repeatedly: "But if you suffer for doing good and you endure it, this is commendable before God" (1 Peter 2:20), and "Who is going to harm you if you are eager to do good? But even if you should suffer for what is right, you are blessed" (1 Peter 3:13-14).

Look for the very important little phrase "He sat down" here in context in Hebrews 10:11-12: "Day after day every priest stands and performs his religious duties; again and again he offers the same sacrifices, which can never take away sins. But when this priest [Jesus] had offered for all time one sacrifice for sins, he sat down at the right hand of God."

Jesus didn't sit down until His work was finished. God is at work in us and through us—through good deeds—sometimes in the face of adversity. Now is not the time to "sit down." It is a time to work: "As long as it is day, we must do the work of him who sent me. Night is coming, when no one can work" (John 9:4).

For God's Glory

Finally Peter tells us that we should "live such good lives among the pagans that, though they accuse you of doing wrong, they may see your good deeds and glorify God on the day he visits us" (1 Peter 2:12). Have you ever heard unbelievers give their excuse for avoiding church: "There are too many hypocrites in the church!" That's because all too often our deeds don't glorify God.

Doing good deeds apart from the motivation of a heart changed by the Gospel invariably brings slander to God's name rather than glory. Linda could have slipped a gospel tract in her neighbor's mailbox every day, but if the good news wasn't clothed in good deeds motivated by love and gratitude, her action probably would not in the end have brought glory to God.

EQUIPPED

God has given us all we need to be equipped to accomplish the good deeds He has planned for us to do. First, He has given us His Spirit to empower us: "Now to him who is able to do immeasurably more than all we ask or imagine, according to his power that is at work within us, to him be glory in the church and in Christ Jesus throughout all generations for ever and ever! Amen" (Ephesians 3:20-21).

Second, He has given us His Body, the church. "It was he who gave some to be apostles, some to be prophets, some to be evangelists, and some to be pastors and teachers, to prepare God's people for works of service" (Ephesians 4:11-12).

Third, He has given us His Word: "All Scripture is God-breathed and is useful for teaching, rebuking, correcting and training in righteousness, so that the man of God may be thoroughly equipped for every good work" (2 Timothy 3:16-17).

Good deeds are important to God. He created us and recreated us and equipped us with everything we need to do works for His glory. The day is coming when we will "sit down" from our labors here on earth. Until that day comes, we must discipline ourselves to follow His plan for our work, allowing His spirit to empower us, His church to lead us, and His Word to teach us so that we speak truth and our labor is not in vain. "Therefore, my dear brothers, stand firm. Let nothing move you. Always give yourselves fully to the work of the Lord, because you know that your labor in the Lord is not in vain" (1 Corinthians 15:58).

ENCOURAGEMENT

Finally there is a wonderful admonition in Hebrews 10:24-25 that is given to early Christians to persevere through their struggles: "And let us consider how we may spur one another on toward love and good deeds. Let us not give up meeting together, as some are in the habit of doing, but let us encourage one another—and all the more as you see the Day approaching."

In the midst of their difficulties the first-century Christians were looking for "the Day" when their struggles and their labors would be over. And the author of Hebrews surprisingly encourages them to press on in "love and good deeds." Amazing! Our tendency is to feel sorry for people when they are discouraged in their work. But Paul doesn't offer platitudes of sympathy; instead he becomes their cheerleader: "Press on! Keep at it! Don't give up!" The reason to press on, keep at it, and not give up? Paul knew that "the Day" is coming.

"The Day" is drawing near! In 1810 the soon-to-be wife of Adoniram Judson penned these words: "If nothing in providence appears to prevent, I must spend my days in a heathen land. I am a creature of God, and he has an undoubted right to do with me as seems good in his sight. . . . He has my heart in his hands. . . . I care not where I perform his work, nor how hard it be. Behold the handmaid of the Lord; be it unto me according to thy word."[12]

Thirty-six years later, Adoniram, having buried Ann in Burmese soil, spoke these words to a gathering of American Christians before his return to Burma:

> Great is our privilege, precious our opportunity, to co-operate with the Savior in the blessed work of enlarging and establishing His kingdom throughout the world. . . .
>
> Let us not, then, regret the loss of those who have gone before us and are waiting to welcome us home, nor shrink from the summons that must call us thither. Let us only resolve to follow them who, through faith and patience, inherit the promises. Let us so employ the remnant of life, and so pass away, that our successors will say of us, as we of our predecessors, "Blessed are the dead that die in the Lord. They rest from their labours, and their works do follow them."[13]

"That Day" is drawing near! Today is our day to work. How I pray that our generation will not be caught unawares when "the Day" comes. I pray that our works will follow us. Let us fill our days with good deeds, for this is God's will in the Gospel.

RENEW YOUR MIND

According to Ephesians 2:10, what was the purpose or point of our initial creation and our re-creation as believers in Christ?

What was Tabitha's reputation (Acts 9:36)? Do you know Christian women who have a similar reputation for good works? How do they inspire you?

Timothy talks about being clothed "with good deeds" (1 Timothy 2:9-10). How can your good deeds eclipse the impact of your outward appearance? Which type of "apparel" do you spend the most time and attention on?

Whatever you have—monetary wealth, social position, extraordinary talents—should be committed to good deeds, according to 1 Timothy 6:17-19. What's in your pantry or closet that could be shared? What time does your calendar afford that could be given? Take stock of your assets and get creative in applying them toward good deeds.

How can you lavish your kindness on fellow members of the family of God (see Galatians 6:7-10)? Why is it so important to God for us to exercise our commitment to good deeds within the church? And the world beyond the church?

15

Discipline of Witness

Submission's Commission

For we cannot help speaking about
what we have seen and heard.

Acts 4:20

We moved to Wheaton from Southern California in September 1979. The College Church parsonage had stood empty for two years. Every day we noticed church members driving past peering through our windows. They weren't being overly curious. They were happy—happy finally to have a pastor and family in the house. But the young couple who lived across the street in a huge old Victorian house were not so pleased. They were cutting-edge yuppies who'd recently moved with their two young children to the suburbs from their renovated brownstone in a desirable area of the city (Chicago). They'd traded a life of fine restaurants, museums, theaters, symphonies, and intelligent and stimulating conversations for suburbia where the new neighbor was the recently hired pastor at the evangelical church down the street—four kids, a dog, a cat, and a bird!

From our perspective, Deby and Jamie kept to themselves, showed little interest in socializing, and appeared to have no needs whatsoever. But Deby was inwardly struggling with many things, and when I asked her to visit our Wednesday morning Bible study, she agreed to come.

(This family's testimony is included in the back of this book.) Kent and I prayed for Deby and Jamie regularly. Now and then Deby posed a question after Bible study, but she seemed outwardly reserved about Christianity. She has since told me that they were watching our family with skeptical curiosity.

One day we got a call that made us pray with more fervor than usual. Members of our church were hosting an evangelistic dinner in Chicago for businessmen and their wives. Our neighbors had been invited and had agreed to go. The morning after the dinner, as I was turning into my driveway, I saw Deby outside with her two-year-old daughter. I prayed, "Lord, if You want me to talk to her, please have her speak to me." I couldn't know, of course, that Deby had been praying that I would come over and talk with her. As God would have it, she called out to me, and I joined her in the front garden.

Under deep conviction of sin and choked with emotion, Deby had been thinking all night about the things she'd heard the previous evening and now had many questions. We agreed that when Elizabeth went down for her nap, I would join her for coffee. Later in her kitchen, Deby asked me to explain the details of the Gospel. When she read 1 Peter 2:24, personalizing it with her own name, she broke into tears: "He himself bore Deby's sins in his body on the tree, so that Deby might die to sins and live for righteousness; by his wounds Deby has been healed." Her eyes were opened, and she saw clearly the significance of Christ's death on behalf of her sin. She believed!

EVERYDAY JOYS

Our family's most enduring spiritual joys have come through everyday personal witness to people like Deby and like Susie, our daughter Holly's kindergarten teacher. Susie promised Holly weekly she would come to church—and finally came—and returned again and again, becoming our good friend and finding Christ. Then twenty years later, Holly's son, showing concern for his playmate, shouted from the top of the jungle gym: "Hey, Mom, Joey doesn't know Jesus."

There was our neighbor, John, the industrial arts teacher, the nicest man on the block, who after several years of friendship with us became a Christian and then a deacon in our church.

Another particularly treasured memory is of our letter carrier, Damon, an ex-marine, and his young wife, Bobbie. Our daily greetings evolved into a friendship that culminated in Bobbie coming to Christ through a women's Bible study and Damon doing the same at a men's retreat.

My husband is a pastor, but we've discovered over the years that the greatest joys in ministry haven't come in extraordinary church events, but in the normal avenues of everyday person-to-person witness—the things any Christian can do regardless of gifts or calling.

When Christians look to Scripture for an example of a strong witness, they often think of Andrew—an average man who shared Christ in patently ordinary ways. The Gospels tell us that Andrew was in on the ground floor of Jesus' ministry. When he met Jesus, he was already a follower of the prophetic cause of John the Baptist (John 1:35ff.), which indicates he was a spiritually sensitive man who realized that the days were evil, a man who had been baptized in repentance for sin and was awaiting the Messiah. He also had the distinction of being the brother of Simon Peter, the soon-to-be leader of the apostolic band (John 1:40).

But Andrew's initial claim to fame was that he, along with John, was the first of the twelve disciples to follow Jesus. The early church recognized this and gave him the honored title "Protokletos," which means "First-called."[1]

Yet despite this enviable beginning, Andrew never achieved prominence among the disciples. He missed out on the great experiences shared by the inner circle of Peter, James, and John—the Transfiguration, the healing of Jairus's daughter, Jesus' sorrow in Gethsemane. He wasn't much of a leader. He preached no sermons deemed worth recording. He wrote no epistles and performed no recorded miracles. A background figure, he appears to have had none of the bold audacity of his brother Peter. His one grand distinction? He excelled in bringing others to Christ.

Andrew's humble distinction has endeared him to whole cultures. Today he is the patron saint of three diverse nations.[2] Traditions allege that Andrew traveled to minister in what is now part of modern Russia, that he was martyred on an X-shaped cross in Greece, and that an eighth-century monk brought some of Andrew's bones as relics to Scotland.

Did Andrew actually go to Greece or Russia or Scotland? No one knows. These three countries claim him because of Andrew's winsome character as it is recorded in God's Word. He was a great-hearted man of average abilities who loved to introduce others to Christ. His evangelistic heart is a wonderful model for what ought to be the ordinary experience of average Christians like you and me.

AVERAGE ANDREW'S EXTRAORDINARY HEART

A Knowledgeable Heart

Andrew may have been average so far as abilities are concerned, but he possessed an extraordinary knowledge of Christ. Andrew met Christ personally. It happened as Andrew and another disciple were standing beside John the Baptist when Jesus passed by. The Baptist cried out, "Look, the Lamb of God!" (John 1:35). Andrew and the other disciple followed Jesus and spent the rest of that day in conversation with Him (vv. 39-40). Though unrecorded, that conversation was a spiritual watershed for Andrew. Andrew heard Jesus speak words that were the truest he had ever heard, and his heart was set on fire.

Andrew's extraordinary heart was magnetized by Christ. He was so drawn to the Savior that he was sure that if others could just once meet Jesus, that would be enough. "The first thing Andrew did," the Scriptures tell us, "was to find his brother Simon and tell him, 'We have found the Messiah'" (John 1:41).

Andrew had the right idea! The Christ of Scripture is so winsome, so radically different, so utterly unlike other religious stereotypes, that when He is truly seen, He draws even the most resistant people to Himself.

The immediate response of Andrew's heart to Jesus was, "Everybody needs to know this Christ!" Ever have that feeling? A young woman in our church named Susan has. When she was recently converted, she aggressively and systematically went after the members of her family. Her father, who was dying of cancer, confessed Christ as Savior. Soon after that her husband was saved. Then her brother began meeting with one of the pastors for a weekly Bible study to investigate the claims of Christ. She can't help but proclaim, "Jesus Christ is Lord!" after all she has learned about Him.

I was converted as a child through the ministry of Child Evangelism

Fellowship. Jesus Christ was my everything. When I was a teenager, God's call through Romans 12:1-2 to "offer your bodies as living sacrifices, holy and pleasing to God—this is your spiritual act of worship" compelled me to give my life for the Gospel. I recall a high school English assignment requiring each student to write in one class period about the person in history he would most want to meet and why. Many of the students groaned, but I knew immediately whom I would choose—the apostle Paul. He expressed so well my feelings of commitment to Jesus Christ and His Gospel: "I eagerly expect and hope that I will in no way be ashamed, but will have sufficient courage so that now as always Christ will be exalted in my body, whether by life or by death. For to me, to live is Christ and to die is gain" (Philippians 1:20-21). Like Andrew, I had experienced the primary motivation and qualification for sharing Him—knowing Jesus.

It's a profound truth: The more immediate and personal your knowledge of Christ, the more natural it is to share Him with others. This is why those who have just met Christ are often so verbal and successful in leading others to Him despite not having learned all the theological arguments for faith.

Do you want a heart like Andrew's? If you know Christ, you have the essential heart qualification to share Him—even if you don't have all the answers. The key to ongoing effectiveness is a perpetual freshness in your growing knowledge of Christ through God's Word.

Learn about Christ!

A Selfless Heart

Andrew had a remarkably unselfish heart, as the Gospel of John shows: "Andrew, Simon Peter's brother, was one of the two who heard what John had said and who had followed Jesus. The first thing Andrew did was to find his brother Simon and tell him, 'We have found the Messiah' (that is, the Christ). And he brought him to Jesus. Jesus looked at him and said, 'You are Simon son of John. You will be called Cephas' (which, when translated, is Peter)" (John 1:40-42).

From this point on, in this Gospel and all the others, Andrew was commonly identified as "Simon Peter's brother" and not the other way around (see Matthew 10:2-4; Luke 6:14-16; John 6:8). Everyone knew the big, gregarious fisherman Peter. He naturally drew people to himself, but Andrew faded into the wallpaper—especially when big brother was around. Don't you think Andrew could see this coming? After all, he'd spent his whole life with his brother. He knew there would only be one seat for him once he brought Peter to Christ—the backseat. But Andrew didn't stumble here. He was unencumbered by self and introduced Peter to Christ anyway, and Peter became a major player.

The true evangelist's heart is a selfless heart. Who cares who gets the credit? Andrew's heart was ordinary perhaps, but it was extraordinary in its selflessness.

An Optimistic Heart

Andrew was optimistic about what would happen when problems were brought to Christ. While Philip expressed dismay at the possibility of feeding the 5,000, it was Andrew who suggested to Jesus using the lad's five loaves and two fishes (John 6:5-9). Andrew may have appeared foolish, but he knew Christ can mightily use all that is given to Him. The result was stupendous—the all-time picnic of the ages! After this, Andrew's optimism knew no bounds.

Our attitude makes all the difference in bringing people to Christ. So often women fail to see how God wants to use them. If you do not have obvious opportunities open to you for evangelism, such as children who connect you with neighbors and school moms or relationships that evolve with career opportunities, consider hospitality!

My friend JoAnn Cairns writes in her book *Welcome Stranger, Welcome Friend*: "Twentieth-century culture and language have distorted the meaning of the New Testament Greek word normally translated 'hospitality.' *Philoxenos* literally means 'love of strangers.' In today's society hospitality has become synonymous with entertainment or fellowship. The biblical meaning, however, focuses on the stranger—the person unknown to the host—and his needs."[3] A reason many women give for not opening their homes in Christian hospitality is their insecurity about their homes in one way or another. For more wisdom on this subject, see "Domestic Gospel Women" in the back of this book.

Andrew saw the value of a small lunch. Have you ever considered what fixing and sharing a simple meal could mean for the Gospel?

A Big Heart

John 12:20-22 preserves a vignette that showcases just how big Andrew's heart was: "Now there were some Greeks among those who went up to worship at the Feast. They came to Philip, who was from Bethsaida in Galilee, with a request. 'Sir,' they said, 'we would like to see Jesus.' Philip went to tell Andrew; Andrew and Philip in turn told Jesus."

These Greeks were, of course, Gentiles and therefore accursed in traditional Jewish thought. Philip was unsure what to do with their request, so he approached Andrew. Andrew, without hesitation, went straight to Jesus. Andrew has the great distinction of being the first disciple to understand that Jesus is the answer for everyone and to apply the universality of Jesus' ministry. No wonder he is the patron saint of Greeks and Russians and Scots.

Is there anyone you think is beyond the Gospel's power to save? The cultural gap is so wide or the rebellion so deep that you feel certain they are hopeless? Don't you believe it! Our church has a ministry to international students studying in America, young people far away from their native homes. Families can sign up to host total strangers in their home for an evening or Sunday afternoon meal. The opportunities for telling the Gospel to strangers are enormous. People will enter your home for a meal that might never cross your path any other way—Muslims, Buddhists, agnostics, atheists, you name it. Jesus Christ—Prophet, Priest, and King— is the answer to their hearts' needs. It only takes a big, optimistic heart to reach out to them—someone who will say, "I might not have all the answers, but I could fix a meal!" Hospitality for the sake of the Gospel!

Andrew was right—the Gospel is for everyone, and anyone can pass it along.

EXTRAORDINARY ENCOURAGEMENT

Andrew was an average person. He wasn't well-educated like Dr. Luke. He didn't possess the intellect of the apostle Paul. He had nothing of the force of personality and oratorical gifts of his celebrated brother. But in his own way he helped shape the Christian world—no doubt to his own eternal surprise.

Isn't that encouraging? Ordinary Andrew's extraordinary heart is a heart we gospel women can all imitate—a knowledgeable heart, a self-less heart, an optimistic heart, and a BIG heart. It's a heart any ordinary Christian can have if she wants it, as she yields to the work of the Spirit. Average Andrew's heart not only challenges but hallows everyday, ordinary, average life. The greatest joys are not in the extraordinary events of ministry, but in the normal avenues of everyday witness—in bringing others to Christ.

"GOSPELING"

Turning the Gospel into a verb is exactly what evangelism is all about. Evangelism is about telling people the Gospel. Those who study different forms of evangelism have discovered that statistically Andrew's relational evangelism is the most effective way to go. When church growth is surveyed, the pollsters indicate that a few people come to church because of a special need or to hear a certain preacher, and that others are drawn by a church program or respond to a formal visit from someone at the church. Some are reached by Sunday school and a few others come to faith through crusades or television preaching. But 75 to 90 percent—that's a whopping number—come through the influence of friends or relatives![4] Clearly, the personal, ordinary-Andrew approach is the most important aspect of evangelism, far outweighing institutional approaches.

The biblical lists of spiritual gifts indicate that a small percentage of believers will have a special gift for evangelism—such as preaching or aggressive "on the street," door-to-door witnessing. But biblical commands indicate that 100 percent of believers can do relational evangelism![5] While all forms of evangelism are important to the church, by far the most important is Andrew's each-one-reach-one style. "Gospeling"—one person telling another person about the Christ.

DISCIPLINE OF WITNESS

The simple method for telling the Gospel, "Two Ways to Live" in chapter 2, is meant to help men and women who want to bring their lives more fully under Christ's headship by prayerfully working at being Andrews—practicing the discipline of witness.

The Value of Relationships[6]

Women were created for relationship! But it's important for us to see that it's our sovereign God who is ordering all of life, including our many relationships. Our friendships and even our casual encounters are not just social accidents. God put us in our particular families, neighborhoods, and workplaces for a reason: He has put us next to people he wants us to influence for Christ.

Susie, our daughter's kindergarten teacher, was not a relational accident. Neither was Damon, our letter carrier, or Jamie and Deby, our neighbors and dear friends. Every person we encounter is an eternal soul of immense value—a person we should see in the same way that God sees him or her. Here's what C. S. Lewis, the great Oxford don, wrote so memorably:

> Remember that the dullest and most uninteresting person you talk to may one day be a creature which, if you saw it now, you would be strongly tempted to worship, or else a horror and a corruption such as you now meet, if at all, only in a nightmare. All day long we are, in some degree, helping each other to one or other of these destinations. It is in the light of these overwhelming possibilities, it is with the awe and the circumspection proper to them, that we should conduct all our dealings with one another, all friendships, all loves, all play, all politics. There are no ordinary people. You have never talked to a mere mortal. Nations, cultures, arts, civilization—these are mortal, and their life is to ours as the life of a gnat. But it is immortals whom we joke with, work with, marry, snub, and exploit—immortal horrors or everlasting splendors.[7]

Identifying Relationships

We all have a complex network of relationships. We have our family and church family. We have geographical contacts based on where we live. We have vocational contacts—the people with whom we work. And we have recreational contacts—originating where we play. We can make these natural contact areas a place for witness. We can use them to brainstorm a list of prospects for the Gospel and begin to pray for them.

Investing in Relationships

As we pray, we can also invest our time, talent, and treasure in relationships.

Become personally involved in the lives of others. Plan to spend significant time with those you'd like to reach, and then make sure your plan is represented on your kitchen calendar or in your day planner.

Invite your friends out for lunch or dinner or to your home for coffee.

Do things together. Attend plays, sporting events, art exhibits. Go shopping.

Share special days—birthdays, graduations, holidays, weddings, births. Visit, call, or write a note.

Join a service club—such as the PTA, a book club, your town's festival committee, or a library board.

Take a class through your park district, or join an interest club (gardening, cooking, quilting).

Volunteer in your local school or hospital or other charitable organization.

Open your home to the neighborhood. Be the most hospitable home on the block to children and adults.

I know from experience that some seasons of our lives are more conducive to evangelism than others. When we had children in our home, they opened doors for us we never could have opened on our own. If you have a young family, don't take for granted that the same opportunities will be yours forever. Do something now about the kids' teachers or their soccer coach. How about your son's Muslim buddy? Invite the family over for dinner—today.

Older women, whose opportunities out in the world have narrowed, can become creative. What about the woman who cuts your hair or the person who bags your groceries or takes in your clothes at the dry cleaners? What about the neighbor kid who mows your lawn or washes your car? What about the librarians at your local library? Service people tend to become invisible unless we are careful to notice them. All of these are people in need of Christ—look at them!

A month ago while visiting Philadelphia, I met Sinclair Ferguson, pastor of St. George's Tron Church in Glasgow, Scotland. He told me the story of his conversion. He was led to the Lord by a gentleman who had years before worked in a large law firm. Every day while working there, his friend passed by a room where typists were busy at work. One typist in particular drew his attention. She always seemed to be much more intent on her work than the other employees, and her speed at typing was phenomenal. Curious, he asked a fellow employee if he had noticed this woman also. His friend answered, "Oh, her! Well, yes, she's a Christian." The answer intrigued him, so he inquired of the woman herself. "Yes, I am a Christian, and everything I do must be for the Lord and His glory." This was the beginning of a friendship that resulted in the young man's conversion. Years later the young convert was responsible for leading Sinclair Ferguson to Christ!

Never underestimate the results your witness for the Lord may have for someone's future. God is always pleased to do so much with the little we give Him. And it is *never* too late to develop the discipline of witness—this is God's will for us in the Gospel.

RENEW YOUR MIND

Analyze the example of Andrew and his witness for Christ in Matthew 10; Luke 6; John 1, 6, 12. What made his witness so effective? Why did he witness? What was his message? Now compare his experience in this area with your own. Be honest.

Why do the people you know need to hear the message of John the Baptist: "Look, the Lamb of God!" (John 1:36)?

"If you know Christ, you . . . have the essential heart qualification to share Him—even if you do not have all the answers." Do you agree with this statement? Does not having all the answers make you hesitant to speak up for Christ? How can you overcome this?

With what individuals has God given you a relationship so you can be a witness by your life or word? List them. And pray for these people daily for the next month. Be alert for opportunities to share Christ with them.

What is "lifestyle evangelism"? Do you use this kind of personal outreach? Why or why not?

If you are like many Christians, the people you find most difficult to witness to are family members or relatives. Why is this? How can you build bridges of communication to them?

"We must invest our time, talent, and treasure in relationships." Should we do this only so we can win others to Christ? What other reasons should we have? Practically, how can we invest in relationships?

16

DISCIPLINE OF GIVING

Submission's Generosity

It is more blessed to give than to receive.

ACTS 20:35

Have you heard of the Beardstown Ladies? They were a group of elderly women who dreamed up a scheme to make big bucks fast on the stock market—and thousands of greedy souls snapped up their best-selling book. These days even little, old gray-haired ladies are money hungry.

Imelda Marcos's love of possessions came to light when someone took a peek in her closet and saw her collection of thousands of shoes. Squandering money at the expense of the poor was her specialty.

But there are many high-profile women whom people admire in part for their wealth and financial success. Is there anyone to compare with the fashionable Princess Diana? Martha Stewart has become a billionaire doing her "good things" in the home and garden. How about Mary Kay, queen of cosmetics, pink Cadillac and all? Or the incomparable talk-show icon Oprah Winfrey? We are a nation run amok in materialism.

Most of us, of course, don't aspire to be masters of finance or to live the lifestyles of the rich and famous. But at the same time, we are culti-vating some level of wealth, often without realizing the pitfalls: a grow-ing delusion that this world is everything, that someday we'll be content, that we ought to give our family everything "more and better," that our relationships will be enhanced by money and things, that wealth will make us better people. Do riches have a hidden grip on your heart? Materialism has taken its subtle toll on many unwitting Christian women.

As a poor, young pastor's wife, I was constantly trying to come up with creative ways to give my children the best I could. Sometimes my ideas crossed the line from industriousness to greed. I once dreamed up a product that I hoped would compete with the Pet Rock. While hanging up my coat one day, I figured that if someone could sell rocks, perhaps I could sell the common coat hanger for a BIG profit. It was during the seventies when the expression "hang loose" was in everyone's vocabulary. I created the stress-reducing Hang Loose Hanger. It came with a fabricated history (like the Pet Rock) and instructions for use that promised help for uptight people: "Just the thing for the high-powered, tense man in your life." I actually convinced many good friends to help finance production. Thank the Lord, I came to my senses before my name became forever associated with this ridiculous idea. Money had become *very* important to me.

Today Christians are increasingly prosperous. So how can we escape the power of materialism? The answer certainly isn't to step out of the world of business or join a commune. Christ firmly admonished believers against isolation. God's Word pointedly offers the cure for materialism—the grace of giving. The apostle Paul instructs the Corinthian church regarding giving by pointing to another group, the Macedonians, and their beautiful example: "We want you to know about the grace [of giving] that God has given the Macedonian churches" (2 Corinthians 8:1).

GIVING IN THE OLD TESTAMENT

Many think that Christians are supposed to give 10 percent back to the Lord, that 10 percent was the Old Testament ideal. Ten percent is a woeful misconception. There were multiple mandatory giving requirements in Israel that came to considerably more than that.

The Lord's Tithe

The foundational tithe, called "the Lord's tithe," went to support the priest's ministry: "A tithe of everything from the land, whether grain from the soil or fruit from the trees, belongs to the Lord; it is holy to the Lord" (Numbers 18:26-29). A tithe (10 percent) of the people's produce and animals was given to the Levites. This wasn't optional. Anyone who didn't pay it was robbing God (Malachi 3:8).

The Festival Tithe

After that initial 10 percent, there was the festival tithe. When Israel conquered the Promised Land, this tithe (another 10 percent) took effect to pay for the annual celebration (Deuteronomy 12:10, 11, 17-18). While the purpose of the Lord's tithe was to perpetuate ministry, the festival tithe was to build religious celebration and mutual community in God's people. Together, these tithes comprised a substantial economic bite—a mandatory 20 percent.

The Poor Tithe

Deuteronomy 14:28-29 commands a third tithe to provide for the social welfare of those who couldn't provide for themselves. This tithe was also 10 percent, but it was collected every three years. That comes to 3.3 percent per annum. That brings the Israelite's tithe total to over 23 percent per year.

Then Leviticus 19:9-10 commands even more—that the people should refrain from harvesting the corners of their fields or picking all the grapes from their vineyards so that the poor could glean. There were also occasional taxes, such as to pay for materials used in temple offerings (Nehemiah 10:32-33). Bottom line? God's people were required to give a minimum of 25 percent each year.

Grace Giving

Here's where requirements are left behind, and nonrequired offerings begin. Beyond that mandatory 25 percent were firstfruits offerings, given out of love for God (Numbers 18:11-13). Israelites would bring the firstfruits of their crops or livestock to the Lord before they'd even finished harvesting. They gave the best to God, trusting He would bring in the rest. It was faith giving and totally voluntary.

There were also freewill offerings, like the one God called for when He commanded Moses to build the tabernacle: "You are to receive the offering for me from each man whose heart prompts him to give" (Exodus 25:2). No amounts were specified, only that the offering be voluntary and from the heart. In this case the people's response was so great that Moses had to tell them to stop giving (Exodus 26:2-7).

As a pastor's wife, I am familiar with the complaints of those who begrudge giving the traditional 10 percent of their income to the church. To many, the amount is unthinkable—"Imagine giving away such an outrageous amount!" The giving described for Old Testament Israel would quiet these complaints, I'm most certain.

Giving from a heart overflowing with God's grace, whether the giving be mandatory or voluntary, has always been the ideal for God's people—before and after the coming of Christ. When a heart overflows in grace giving, a substantial amount of income goes to God.[1]

GRACE GIVING IN THE NEW TESTAMENT

Paul holds high the example of the impoverished Macedonians and their abundant giving: "We want you to know about the grace that God has given the Macedonian churches. Out of the most severe trial, their overflowing joy and their extreme poverty welled up in rich generosity" (2 Corinthians 8:1-2).

Today we fancy ourselves poor if we have to think twice before going out to dinner. The "American way" today is the credit card—buying things you do not need with money you do not have—to impress people you do not like!

But those Macedonians were really poor—dirt poor, under "the most severe trial" (v. 2). The surrounding culture rejected them and kept squeezing them harder and harder because of their devotion to Christ. Their situation was impossible—grinding poverty and severe trials. But out of it came incredible grace, and their poverty and trials were mixed with overflowing joy that "welled up in rich generosity." That's the grace of giving. Catherine Marshall's mother perfectly demonstrated this for us, as we saw in the chapter on good deeds.

Paul tells us that the poor Macedonians considered giving a privilege: "I testify that they gave as much as they were able, and even beyond their ability. Entirely on their own, they urgently pleaded with us for the privilege of sharing in this service to the saints" (vv. 3-4). They begged for the chance to give!

The grace of giving has nothing to do with being well off. It isn't dictated by ability. It is a willingness to give. It is joyously enthusiastic and pleads for the opportunity to give more.

The Macedonians' remarkable giving was the result of their first giving themselves to God: "They gave themselves first to the Lord and then to us in keeping with God's will" (v. 5). It's simple. When all you have is given to God, giving to others becomes the natural reflex of your soul.

The Macedonians did things the right way: They gave their hearts to God, and they gave themselves to their fellow believers, which in turn resulted in their giving what they had to the work of Christ. This is where grace giving begins—in giving ourselves completely to God.

The Influence of Grace Giving

Paul hoped that the Corinthians would follow the example of the Macedonians: "But just as you excel in everything—in faith, in speech, in knowledge, in complete earnestness and in your love for us—see that you also excel in this grace of giving" (v. 7).

The Corinthians were a gifted group, but Paul knew that despite all their good qualities, they would never become all they could and should be until they learned the grace of giving. He knew there is no way to grow into spiritual maturity without committing one's giving to the Lord. *God can have our money and not have our hearts, but He cannot have our hearts without having all our money.* Jesus said, "For where your treasure is, there your heart will be also" (Matthew 6:21).

Jesus talked to His followers more often about money than about heaven and hell, sexual immorality, or violence. After the rich young ruler turned away sorrowing because Jesus told him to sell all, Jesus told His disciples, "It is easier for a camel to go through the eye of a needle than for a rich man to enter the kingdom of God" (Mark 10:25). His point? That it's impossible for a man who trusts in riches to get into heaven. He added a final line: "With man this [being saved, v. 26] is impossible, but not with God; all things are possible with God" (v. 27).

Jesus consistently presents wealth (when we depend on it rather than on God) as a spiritual handicap. At the end of the Sermon on the Mount, He recommended: "Do not store up for yourselves treasures on earth, where moth and rust destroy, and where thieves break in and steal. But store up for yourselves treasures in heaven, where moth and rust do not destroy, and where thieves do not break in and steal" (Matthew 6:19-20). Later he warned, "No one can serve two masters. Either he will hate the one and love the other, or he will be devoted to the one and despise the other. You cannot serve both God and Money" (Matthew 6:24).

To a man grabbing for an inheritance, Christ shouted, "Watch out! Be on your guard against all kinds of greed; a man's life does not consist in the abundance of his possessions" (Luke 12:15). Then he related the story of the rich man who built bigger barns, only to die that very night. Jesus ended His parable with a solemn pronouncement: "This is how it will be with anyone who stores up things for himself but is not rich toward God" (v. 21). This is a good word to today's wealthy Christian women. Getting ready to redecorate the house for the third time? Do you find yourself secretly resenting the check your husband wrote to the church? Watch out!

The "rich toward God" are those who give not only themselves, but also their riches—thus laying up their treasures in heaven. The key to liberation from the power of materialism is not avoiding culture, but the grace of giving. Believe—really believe—that storing up riches in heaven will pay richer dividends in the end. Even this may sound self-centered, but it is actually believing that the invisible is more important than the visible.

Grace giving gives till it hurts. It affects your lifestyle. When you begin grace giving, there are things you cannot have and things you must pass up. Givers for God disarm the power of money. They invite God's grace to flow through them.

If you have reached a sticking point in your spiritual development, consider your giving as a possible hindrance. If you are attending church regularly, enjoying the fellowship of other Christians, even reading your Bible and praying regularly, the problem may be that you are not giving—that God still doesn't have that part of your heart.

The apostle caps his point with this astonishing illustration: "For you know the grace of our Lord Jesus Christ, that though he was rich, yet for your sakes he became poor, so that you through his poverty might become rich" (2 Corinthians 8:9). Though Jesus could put His finger on every star, He emptied Himself and became a poor earthly servant for us. That is heaven's "stewardship" program—and our pattern! The ultimate example of giving—"the grace of our Lord Jesus Christ"—produces the grace of giving in our lives. It's simply because of Jesus.

THE DISCIPLINE OF GIVING

We've talked about so many ways God's good work in our lives demands discipline—and in this matter of grace giving, there must be discipline as well.

Mental Discipline

We need a thoroughly biblical understanding of giving. First, we need to keep in mind that giving is not a meritorious work that enhances our position before God. We're not earning brownie points! Giving will not make you better than other Christians.

Second, understand that while giving will not gain favor with God, it does bring blessing. Jesus said, "Give, and it will be given to you. A good measure, pressed down, shaken together and running over, will be poured into your lap. For with the measure you use, it will be measured to you" (Luke 6:38). Correspondingly, Paul wrote: "Remember this: Whoever sows sparingly will also reap sparingly, and whoever sows generously will also reap generously" (2 Corinthians 9:6).

These blessings are essentially spiritual. I once heard of a woman who had a car accident as she was leaving the church parking lot. It was later suggested to her that if she had given the money she had considered giving while at church, God might have spared her the accident. The suggestion was that God will get His money one way or another and that had she given, God may even have blessed her with a new car. This kind of talk slanders God and distorts Scripture. Giving motivated by a heart totally given to God does produce blessing in our lives. But which would you rather have—a spiritual blessing or a bigger bank account? inner contentment or a new minivan? The way you spend your money and the way you give really does reveal what is in your heart.

Third, keep in mind that the giving that pleases God is generous and sacrificial. The Macedonians gave out of their deep poverty. Remember Jesus' comment about the poor widow who gave her fraction of a penny: "This poor widow has put more into the treasury than all the others" (Mark 12:43).

Fourth, understand that what you give is to be determined between you and God. Don't ever decide this casually or flippantly, but give the matter serious prayer. Ask God what He wants you to give.

Volitional Discipline

Once you've got the mental disciplines of giving firmly in mind, you're ready for the act of giving. Giving your money should be accompanied by offering yourself to the Lord, like those Macedonians who "gave themselves first to the Lord." This should be done silently, not so someone will see your pious act of worship. Giving yourself to God *is* worship (Romans 12:1).

Second, in light of the great giving requirements imposed on God's ancient people, consider that first 10 percent a minimum—a starting point in your giving.

Third, make your giving regular. Paul advised this same Corinthian congregation: "On the first day of every week, each one of you should set aside a sum of money in keeping with his income, saving it up, so that when I come no collections will have to be made" (1 Corinthians 16:2). Paul knew that systematic giving would help the people meet their obligations and most emergencies.

Fourth, begin now. The natural tendency is to put giving off until you feel able to give. Such thinking keeps many from ever giving. There's an old story about the preacher who came to see a farmer and asked, "If you had $200, would you give $100 to the Lord?"

"I would," answered the farmer.

"If you had two cows, would you give one to the Lord?"

"Sure."

"If you had two pigs, would you give one of them to the Lord?"

The farmer said, "Now that isn't fair! You know I have two pigs."

Giving should be regular, but it should also be responsive to need, spontaneous, like that of the Macedonians and Mary of Bethany who, in anointing Jesus, so lavishly poured out her resources.

Finally, your giving should be joyous—for "God loves a cheerful giver" (2 Corinthians 9:7). The word used here suggests a joy that leaps over all restraints.

Has money become too important to you? The act of giving is blessed. Remember that Jesus said, "It is more blessed to give than to receive" (Acts 20:35). May we gospel women be faithful and disciplined in giving ourselves and all we have to God!

RENEW YOUR MIND

What does the phrase "grace giving" mean to you? What does grace have to do with giving? When you give to the church or various Christian ministries, do you generally do so out of obligation or willingness?

How much of your income do you believe God wants you to give to Him?

What does Malachi 3:8ff. say to you about giving to God? Are you generally obeying or disobeying this passage?

Should you give only when you have it to spare, so to speak—during times when God has "blessed" you? Compare 2 Corinthians 8:1-2.

What does Matthew 6:19-21, 24 mean for your life? What are some specific ways you can apply these verses?

What example is found in 2 Corinthians 8:9? What does this verse say to you?

What principles stand out on the topic of giving in 2 Corinthians 8:1-9? List as many as you can, and then assess your life by them.

GRACE

17

GRACE OF DISCIPLINE

But by the grace of God I am what I am, and his grace
to me was not without effect. No, I worked harder
than all of them—yet not I, but the grace of God
that was with me.

1 CORINTHIANS 15:10

Remember way back at the beginning of this book when we talked about the word *discipline*? In "discipline yourself for the purpose of godliness" (1 Timothy 4:7 NASB), the word means training. This is a clear call for a spiritual workout.

This same word *discipline* suggests a conscious divestment of encumbrances and then a determined investment of all our energies. The disciplined godly woman rids herself of associations, habits, and attitudes that impede godliness. Then she invests her energy in the pursuit of godliness.

It shouldn't surprise us that vigorous spiritual discipline is essential to godliness. After all, discipline is universally acknowledged to be necessary for accomplishing anything worthwhile in this life. I often am present when my grandchildren are practicing their instruments—repeating the scales again and again. They work on technique—holding the bow properly on cello and violin or keeping fingers properly rounded as they play the keys of the piano. They must be disciplined in their practice if they are ever going to play the masterpieces of Bach and Mozart.

While athletes or musicians may begin their training with some innate athletic or musical advantages, none of us can claim an innate spiritual advantage—we are all equally sinful. None of us is born righteous; none of us naturally seeks God or is reflexively good. We need an abundance of God's grace and help to discipline our lives.

So we set out to submit every area of life, living in submission to God's will in prayer, worship, mind, contentment, propriety, perseverance, church, singleness, marriage, nurturing, good deeds, witness, and giving. That's an intimidating to-do list, even for women who are accustomed to doing sixteen things at once!

RESPONDING TO THE CHALLENGE

This challenging list may make you want to stay in bed and pull the covers over your head. But "do nothing" passivity is paralyzing; it will only make you feel worse.

Self-sufficient legalism is an equally deadly response to the challenge. Under a legalistic framework, you could create an unending list of "do's" and don'ts." Legalism reduces spirituality to obeying the rules: "If you do these six, sixteen, or sixty-six things, you'll be godly!" Christianity is far more than a checklist! Being "in Christ" is a relationship!

God save us from self-righteous judgmentalism. We so easily judge others by stricter standards than we use on ourselves.

Remember there is a universe of difference between the motivations of legalism and discipline! Legalism says, "I will do this thing to gain merit with God," while discipline says, "I will do this because I love God and want to please him." Legalism is man-centered; discipline is God-centered.

WISDOM FOR DISCIPLINE

When I imagine my daughters and granddaughters sitting across the kitchen table from me discussing the disciplines of godly women, I imagine them asking, "How? How do we go about it? Tell us how to be disciplined without being legalistic!" Here are the suggestions I have to offer.

Prioritize

Begin by reviewing the disciplines we've covered in this book and divide them into two lists—one list for areas in which you're doing pretty well already and one list for areas in which you need help. Get the help of a spouse or trusted friend to help you be objective.

Next, number your areas of need in order of importance. For example: 1) Contentment, 2) Marriage, 3) Prayer, 4) Witness, 5) Giving, and 6) Mind.

Then go back to the chapter on contentment, and choose one to three suggestions for submitting your longings to God that you think will help you improve. Don't overcommit. Set out to succeed in a few changes at a time. If contentment is your number-one area of need right now, you might glean from that chapter encouragement to study the attributes of God from Scripture and to analyze your longings to see if they are godly or ungodly ones. Those two suggestions would be an excellent first self-assignment.

Be Realistic

Take a second look at that prioritized list with honest realism. If you commit to these things, are they within your reach, with God's help? If, say, you've determined to discipline your mind by reading the Old Testament once and the New Testament twice in the month of January, think again! Give yourself a more realistic goal, such as reading the New Testament in the next six months. Your commitments push you beyond your comfort zone, but they still must be manageable. Better to increase your commitments as you master them successfully than to bite off way more than you can chew. A bit of success will encourage you on to bigger and better things!

Pray

Before you settle on your commitments, consider them for a week or two and pray over them. Seek the Holy Spirit's guidance for other ways of personal discipline not covered in this book.

Be Accountable

Ask your spouse or a close friend to hold you accountable for your disciplines. Make sure you regularly confer and pray with your accountability partner—even if it has to be over the phone. Be honest about your successes and failures. Be willing to take advice and make adjustments.

If You Stumble . . .

There are going to be times when you struggle over these commitments or even fail outright at keeping them. When this happens, wounded pride or embarrassment can make you want to run back to bed and pull those covers up again. Nobody likes to keep doing things at which they fail. But realize that failure is a part of succeeding, as long as you admit your failures and get right back to your commitments again. It is often "three baby steps forward" and then "one giant step backward." But don't give up!

Remember, you are not under law but under grace. God is not counting your failures against you, and you're not building a treasury of merit with your successes. You are simply trying to bring some discipline to your spiritual life because you know it is what your heavenly Father wants for you. He understands our failures better than we understand our own children's.

GRACE OF DISCIPLINE

The gospel woman's greatest wisdom and impetus comes from her understanding of grace. Everything in this life comes from God's grace—grace alone!

Salvation is by grace alone. We were dead in our transgressions and sins, but "God, who is rich in mercy, made us alive with Christ even when we were dead in transgressions—it is by grace you have been saved" (Ephesians 2:4-5). We are saved by God's grace, His unmerited favor—not by anything we have done. Even the smallest percentage of works debases saving grace, as Paul made so clear: "And if by grace, then it is no longer by works; if it were, grace would no longer be grace" (Romans 11:6). Grace alone!

Christian life is also lived by grace alone. I love James's encouragement to every believer: "But he gives us more grace" (4:6). This is not saving grace, but grace to live our lives as we ought to live in this fallen world—literally, "greater grace." There is always more grace.

An artist once submitted a painting of Niagara Falls to an exhibition, but neglected to give it a title. The gallery, faced with a need to supply one, came up with these words: *More to Follow*. Old Niagara Falls, spilling over billions of gallons per year for thousands of years, has more than met the needs of those below and is a fit emblem for the floods of grace God showers on us. There is always more to follow! The apostle John referred to this reality, saying, "For of his fullness we have all received, and grace upon grace" (John 1:16 NASB). "For daily need there is daily grace; for sudden need, sudden grace; for overwhelming need, overwhelming grace," says John Blanchard.[1]

Begin today to cultivate the disciplines of godly womanhood, and remember it is a matter of God's grace from beginning to end. Consider Paul's words: "But by the grace of God I am what I am, and his grace to me was not without effect. No, I worked harder than all of them—yet not I, but the grace of God that was with me" (1 Corinthians 15:10). See? There is no contradiction between grace and hard work. In fact, grace encourages us to keep at it!

Sisters, as we attempt to do God's will, He always gives more grace.

> *When we have exhausted our store of endurance,*
> *When our strength has failed ere the day is half done;*
> *When we reach the end of our hoarded resources,*
> *Our Father's full giving is only begun.*
>
> *His love has no limits, His grace has no measure,*
> *His power has no boundary known unto men;*
> *For out of His infinite riches in Jesus,*
> *He giveth, and giveth, and giveth again.*
>
> —ANNIE JOHNSON FLINT

RESOURCES

HYMNS FOR YOUR
DEVOTIONAL TIME

The following hymns are particularly suitable for singing to the Lord because they have wonderful texts and are, for the most part, in the first person singular. This selection is culled from *Hymns for the Living Church*, edited by Don Hustad and published by Hope Publishing (Carol Stream, IL), 1981.

148	"When I Survey the Wondrous Cross"	Isaac Watts
149	"Rock of Ages, Cleft for Me"	Augustus M. Toplady
156	"Alas! And Did My Savior Bleed?"	Isaac Watts
159	"Jesus Lives and So Shall I"	Christian F. Gellert
187	"Breathe on Me, Breath of God"	Edwin Hatch
194	"Holy Spirit, Light Divine"	Andrew Reed
203	"I Love Thy Kingdom, Lord"	Timothy Dwight
220	"Break Thou the Bread of Life"	Mary A. Lathbury
229	"O the Deep, Deep Love of Jesus"	S. Trevor Francis
242	"Not What These Hands Have Done"	Horatius Bonar
246	"Jesus, Lover of My Soul"	Charles Wesley
248	"And Can It Be That I Should Gain?"	Charles Wesley
260	"Just As I Am, Without One Plea"	Charlotte Elliott
288	"Amazing Grace! How Sweet the Sound"	John Newton
308	"My Hope Is in the Lord"	Norman J. Clayton
344	"Be Thou My Vision"	Irish Hymn
349	"May the Mind of Christ My Savior"	Kate B. Wilkinson
359	"More Love to Thee, O Christ"	Elizabeth P. Prentiss
360	"Speak, Lord, in the Stillness"	E. May Grimes
384	"All for Jesus! All for Jesus! "	Mary D. James
401	"When Peace Like a River Attendeth"	Horatio G. Spafford
438	"Teach Me to Pray, Lord"	Albert S. Reitz
448	"Guide Me, O Thou Great Jehovah"	William Williams
571	"Thanks to God for My Redeemer"	August L. Storm

Praise Psalms for Your Devotional Time

Psalm 8

Psalm 9:1, 2

Psalm 16:7-11

Psalm 18:1-3

Psalm 19

Psalm 23

Psalm 24

Psalm 29

Psalm 33

Psalm 34

Psalm 40:1-5

Psalm 46

Psalm 47

Psalm 63:1-7

Psalm 65

Psalm 66:1-8

Psalm 67

Psalm 68:4-6, 32-35

Psalm 72:18, 19

Psalm 84

Psalm 89:1, 2

Psalm 91

Psalm 92:1-5

Psalm 93

Psalm 95:1-7

Psalm 96

Psalm 97

Psalm 98

Psalm 99

Psalm 100

Psalm 103

Psalm 104

Psalm 105:1-6

Psalm 108:1-6

Psalm 111

Psalm 113

Psalm 115

Psalm 116

Psalm 117

Psalm 118

Psalm 126

Psalm 134

Psalm 135

Psalm 136

Psalm 138

Psalm 144:1-10

M'Cheyne's Calendar for Daily Readings

Arranged by Robert Murray M'Cheyne

A concise course whereby one can read through the whole Bible once a year— the Psalms and the New Testament twice.

This calendar with minor adjustments is published by Good News Publishers as an aid to systematic Bible reading and is available in quantities (minimum order 25 copies). Call 1-800-877-TRACTS1 for current pricing, or visit the web site: www.goodnewspublishers.org.

1. This reading schedule gives the day of the month, as well as chapters to be read in the family, and portions to be read in secret.
2. The head of the family should previously read over the chapter indicated for the family worship and mark two or three of the most prominent verses, upon which he may dwell, giving a few explanatory thoughts, and asking several simple questions.
3. The portions read, both for family and private reading, would be greatly illuminated if they were preceded by a moment's silent prayer: "Open Thou mine eyes, that I may behold wondrous things out of Thy law" [Psalm 119:18].
4. Let the conversation at the family meals frequently turn upon the chapter read; thus every meal will be a sacrament, being sanctified by the Word and prayer.
5. Let our private reading precede the dawning of the day. Let God's voice be the first we hear in the morning. Mark two or three of the richest verses and pray over every word and line of them.
6. Above all, use the Word as a lamp to your feet and a light to your path— your guide in perplexity, your armor in temptation, your food in times of faintness.

JANUARY

This is my beloved Son, in whom I am
well pleased; hear ye him.

FAMILY			SECRET		
DAY	BOOK AND CHAPTER		DAY	BOOK AND CHAPTER	
☐ 1	Genesis 1	Matthew 1	☐ 1	Ezra 1	Acts 1
☐ 2	Genesis 2	Matthew 2	☐ 2	Ezra 2	Acts 2
☐ 3	Genesis 3	Matthew 3	☐ 3	Ezra 3	Acts 3
☐ 4	Genesis 4	Matthew 4	☐ 4	Ezra 4	Acts 4
☐ 5	Genesis 5	Matthew 5	☐ 5	Ezra 5	Acts 5
☐ 6	Genesis 6	Matthew 6	☐ 6	Ezra 6	Acts 6
☐ 7	Genesis 7	Matthew 7	☐ 7	Ezra 7	Acts 7
☐ 8	Genesis 8	Matthew 8	☐ 8	Ezra 8	Acts 8
☐ 9	Genesis 9, 10	Matthew 9	☐ 9	Ezra 9	Acts 9
☐ 10	Genesis 11	Matthew 10	☐ 10	Ezra 10	Acts 10
☐ 11	Genesis 12	Matthew 11	☐ 11	Nehemiah 1	Acts 11
☐ 12	Genesis 13	Matthew 12	☐ 12	Nehemiah 2	Acts 12
☐ 13	Genesis 14	Matthew 13	☐ 13	Nehemiah 3	Acts 13
☐ 14	Genesis 15	Matthew 14	☐ 14	Nehemiah 4	Acts 14
☐ 15	Genesis 16	Matthew 15	☐ 15	Nehemiah 5	Acts 15
☐ 16	Genesis 17	Matthew 16	☐ 16	Nehemiah 6	Acts 16
☐ 17	Genesis 18	Matthew 17	☐ 17	Nehemiah 7	Acts 17
☐ 18	Genesis 19	Matthew 18	☐ 18	Nehemiah 8	Acts 18
☐ 19	Genesis 20	Matthew 19	☐ 19	Nehemiah 9	Acts 19
☐ 20	Genesis 21	Matthew 20	☐ 20	Nehemiah 10	Acts 20
☐ 21	Genesis 22	Matthew 21	☐ 21	Nehemiah 11	Acts 21
☐ 22	Genesis 23	Matthew 22	☐ 22	Nehemiah 12	Acts 22
☐ 23	Genesis 24	Matthew 23	☐ 23	Nehemiah 13	Acts 23
☐ 24	Genesis 25	Matthew 24	☐ 24	Esther 1	Acts 24
☐ 25	Genesis 26	Matthew 25	☐ 25	Esther 2	Acts 25
☐ 26	Genesis 27	Matthew 26	☐ 26	Esther 3	Acts 26
☐ 27	Genesis 28	Matthew 27	☐ 27	Esther 4	Acts 27
☐ 28	Genesis 29	Matthew 28	☐ 28	Esther 5	Acts 28
☐ 29	Genesis 30	Mark 1	☐ 29	Esther 6	Romans 1
☐ 30	Genesis 31	Mark 2	☐ 30	Esther 7	Romans 2
☐ 31	Genesis 32	Mark 3	☐ 31	Esther 8	Romans 3

FEBRUARY

I have esteemed the words of his mouth
more than my necessary food.

FAMILY			SECRET		
DAY	**BOOK AND CHAPTER**		**DAY**	**BOOK AND CHAPTER**	
☐ 1	Genesis 33	Mark 4	☐ 1	Esther 9, 10	Romans 4
☐ 2	Genesis 34	Mark 5	☐ 2	Job 1	Romans 5
☐ 3	Genesis 35, 36	Mark 6	☐ 3	Job 2	Romans 6
☐ 4	Genesis 37	Mark 7	☐ 4	Job 3	Romans 7
☐ 5	Genesis 38	Mark 8	☐ 5	Job 4	Romans 8
☐ 6	Genesis 39	Mark 9	☐ 6	Job 5	Romans 9
☐ 7	Genesis 40	Mark 10	☐ 7	Job 6	Romans 10
☐ 8	Genesis 41	Mark 11	☐ 8	Job 7	Romans 11
☐ 9	Genesis 42	Mark 12	☐ 9	Job 8	Romans 12
☐ 10	Genesis 43	Mark 13	☐ 10	Job 9	Romans 13
☐ 11	Genesis 44	Mark 14	☐ 11	Job 10	Romans 14
☐ 12	Genesis 45	Mark 15	☐ 12	Job 11	Romans 15
☐ 13	Genesis 46	Mark 16	☐ 13	Job 12	Romans 16
☐ 14	Genesis 47	Luke 1:1-38	☐ 14	Job 13	1 Cor 1
☐ 15	Genesis 48	Luke 1:39-80	☐ 15	Job 14	1 Cor 2
☐ 16	Genesis 49	Luke 2	☐ 16	Job 15	1 Cor 3
☐ 17	Genesis 50	Luke 3	☐ 17	Job 16, 17	1 Cor 4
☐ 18	Exodus 1	Luke 4	☐ 18	Job 18	1 Cor 5
☐ 19	Exodus 2	Luke 5	☐ 19	Job 19	1 Cor 6
☐ 20	Exodus 3	Luke 6	☐ 20	Job 20	1 Cor 7
☐ 21	Exodus 4	Luke 7	☐ 21	Job 21	1 Cor 8
☐ 22	Exodus 5	Luke 8	☐ 22	Job 22	1 Cor 9
☐ 23	Exodus 6	Luke 9	☐ 23	Job 23	1 Cor 10
☐ 24	Exodus 7	Luke 10	☐ 24	Job 24	1 Cor 11
☐ 25	Exodus 8	Luke 11	☐ 25	Job 25, 26	1 Cor 12
☐ 26	Exodus 9	Luke 12	☐ 26	Job 27	1 Cor 13
☐ 27	Exodus 10	Luke 13	☐ 27	Job 28	1 Cor 14
☐ 28	Exodus 11, 12:1-21	Luke 14	☐ 28	Job 29	1 Cor 15

MARCH

*Mary kept all these things,
and pondered them in her heart.*

FAMILY			SECRET		
DAY	**BOOK AND CHAPTER**		**DAY**	**BOOK AND CHAPTER**	
☐ 1	Exodus 12:22-51	Luke 15	☐ 1	Job 30	1 Cor 16
☐ 2	Exodus 13	Luke 16	☐ 2	Job 31	2 Cor 1
☐ 3	Exodus 14	Luke 17	☐ 3	Job 32	2 Cor 2
☐ 4	Exodus 15	Luke 18	☐ 4	Job 33	2 Cor 3
☐ 5	Exodus 16	Luke 19	☐ 5	Job 34	2 Cor 4
☐ 6	Exodus 17	Luke 20	☐ 6	Job 35	2 Cor 5
☐ 7	Exodus 18	Luke 21	☐ 7	Job 36	2 Cor 6
☐ 8	Exodus 19	Luke 22	☐ 8	Job 37	2 Cor 7
☐ 9	Exodus 20	Luke 23	☐ 9	Job 38	2 Cor 8
☐ 10	Exodus 21	Luke 24	☐ 10	Job 39	2 Cor 9
☐ 11	Exodus 22	John 1	☐ 11	Job 40	2 Cor 10
☐ 12	Exodus 23	John 2	☐ 12	Job 41	2 Cor 11
☐ 13	Exodus 24	John 3	☐ 13	Job 42	2 Cor 12
☐ 14	Exodus 25	John 4	☐ 14	Proverbs 1	2 Cor 13
☐ 15	Exodus 26	John 5	☐ 15	Proverbs 2	Galatians 1
☐ 16	Exodus 27	John 6	☐ 16	Proverbs 3	Galatians 2
☐ 17	Exodus 28	John 7	☐ 17	Proverbs 4	Galatians 3
☐ 18	Exodus 29	John 8	☐ 18	Proverbs 5	Galatians 4
☐ 19	Exodus 30	John 9	☐ 19	Proverbs 6	Galatians 5
☐ 20	Exodus 31	John 10	☐ 20	Proverbs 7	Galatians 6
☐ 21	Exodus 32	John 11	☐ 21	Proverbs 8	Ephesians 1
☐ 22	Exodus 33	John 12	☐ 22	Proverbs 9	Ephesians 2
☐ 23	Exodus 34	John 13	☐ 23	Proverbs 10	Ephesians 3
☐ 24	Exodus 35	John 14	☐ 24	Proverbs 11	Ephesians 4
☐ 25	Exodus 36	John 15	☐ 25	Proverbs 12	Ephesians 5
☐ 26	Exodus 37	John 16	☐ 26	Proverbs 13	Ephesians 6
☐ 27	Exodus 38	John 17	☐ 27	Proverbs 14	Philippians 1
☐ 28	Exodus 39	John 18	☐ 28	Proverbs 15	Philippians 2
☐ 29	Exodus 40	John 19	☐ 29	Proverbs 16	Philippians 3
☐ 30	Leviticus 1	John 20	☐ 30	Proverbs 17	Philippians 4
☐ 31	Leviticus 2, 3	John 21	☐ 31	Proverbs 18	Colossians 1

APRIL

O send out thy light and thy truth;
let them lead me.

FAMILY				SECRET			
DAY		**BOOK AND CHAPTER**		**DAY**		**BOOK AND CHAPTER**	
☐	1	Leviticus 4	Psalms 1, 2	☐	1	Proverbs 19	Colossians 2
☐	2	Leviticus 5	Psalms 3, 4	☐	2	Proverbs 20	Colossians 3
☐	3	Leviticus 6	Psalms 5, 6	☐	3	Proverbs 21	Colossians 4
☐	4	Leviticus 7	Psalms 7, 8	☐	4	Proverbs 22	1 Thess 1
☐	5	Leviticus 8	Psalms 9	☐	5	Proverbs 23	1 Thess 2
☐	6	Leviticus 9	Psalms 10	☐	6	Proverbs 24	1 Thess 3
☐	7	Leviticus 10	Psalms 11, 12	☐	7	Proverbs 25	1 Thess 4
☐	8	Leviticus 11, 12	Psalms 13, 14	☐	8	Proverbs 26	1 Thess 5
☐	9	Leviticus 13	Psalms 15, 16	☐	9	Proverbs 27	2 Thess 1
☐	10	Leviticus 14	Psalms 17	☐	10	Proverbs 28	2 Thess 2
☐	11	Leviticus 15	Psalms 18	☐	11	Proverbs 29	2 Thess 3
☐	12	Leviticus 16	Psalms 19	☐	12	Proverbs 30	1 Timothy 1
☐	13	Leviticus 17	Psalms 20, 21	☐	13	Proverbs 31	1 Timothy 2
☐	14	Leviticus 18	Psalms 22	☐	14	Eccles 1	1 Timothy 3
☐	15	Leviticus 19	Psalms 23, 24	☐	15	Eccles 2	1 Timothy 4
☐	16	Leviticus 20	Psalms 25	☐	16	Eccles 3	1 Timothy 5
☐	17	Leviticus 21	Psalms 26, 27	☐	17	Eccles 4	1 Timothy 6
☐	18	Leviticus 22	Psalms 28, 29	☐	18	Eccles 5	2 Timothy 1
☐	19	Leviticus 23	Psalms 30	☐	19	Eccles 6	2 Timothy 2
☐	20	Leviticus 24	Psalms 31	☐	20	Eccles 7	2 Timothy 3
☐	21	Leviticus 25	Psalms 32	☐	21	Eccles 8	2 Timothy 4
☐	22	Leviticus 26	Psalms 33	☐	22	Eccles 9	Titus 1
☐	23	Leviticus 27	Psalms 34	☐	23	Eccles 10	Titus 2
☐	24	Numbers 1	Psalms 35	☐	24	Eccles 11	Titus 3
☐	25	Numbers 2	Psalms 36	☐	25	Eccles 12	Philemon 1
☐	26	Numbers 3	Psalms 37	☐	26	Song 1	Hebrews 1
☐	27	Numbers 4	Psalms 38	☐	27	Song 2	Hebrews 2
☐	28	Numbers 5	Psalms 39	☐	28	Song 3	Hebrews 3
☐	29	Numbers 6	Psalms 40, 41	☐	29	Song 4	Hebrews 4
☐	30	Numbers 7	Psalms 42, 43	☐	30	Song 5	Hebrews 5

MAY

From a child thou hast known the holy Scriptures.

FAMILY			SECRET		
DAY	**BOOK AND CHAPTER**		**DAY**	**BOOK AND CHAPTER**	
☐ 1	Numbers 8	Psalms 44	☐ 1	Song 6	Hebrews 6
☐ 2	Numbers 9	Psalms 45	☐ 2	Song 7	Hebrews 7
☐ 3	Numbers 10	Psalms 46, 47	☐ 3	Song 8	Hebrews 8
☐ 4	Numbers 11	Psalms 48	☐ 4	Isaiah 1	Hebrews 9
☐ 5	Numbers 12, 13	Psalms 49	☐ 5	Isaiah 2	Hebrews 10
☐ 6	Numbers 14	Psalms 50	☐ 6	Isaiah 3, 4	Hebrews 11
☐ 7	Numbers 15	Psalms 51	☐ 7	Isaiah 5	Hebrews 12
☐ 8	Numbers 16	Psalms 52-54	☐ 8	Isaiah 6	Hebrews 13
☐ 9	Numbers 17, 18	Psalms 55	☐ 9	Isaiah 7	James 1
☐ 10	Numbers 19	Psalms 56, 57	☐ 10	Isaiah 8, 9:1-7	James 2
☐ 11	Numbers 20	Psalms 58, 59	☐ 11	Isaiah 9:8-21–10:4	James 3
☐ 12	Numbers 21	Psalms 60, 61	☐ 12	Isaiah 10:5-34	James 4
☐ 13	Numbers 22	Psalms 62, 63	☐ 13	Isaiah 11, 12	James 5
☐ 14	Numbers 23	Psalms 64, 65	☐ 14	Isaiah 13	1 Peter 1
☐ 15	Numbers 24	Psalms 66, 67	☐ 15	Isaiah 14	1 Peter 2
☐ 16	Numbers 25	Psalms 68	☐ 16	Isaiah 15	1 Peter 3
☐ 17	Numbers 26	Psalms 69	☐ 17	Isaiah 16	1 Peter 4
☐ 18	Numbers 27	Psalms 70, 71	☐ 18	Isaiah 17, 18	1 Peter 5
☐ 19	Numbers 28	Psalms 72	☐ 19	Isaiah 19, 20	2 Peter 1
☐ 20	Numbers 29	Psalms 73	☐ 20	Isaiah 21	2 Peter 2
☐ 21	Numbers 30	Psalms 74	☐ 21	Isaiah 22	2 Peter 3
☐ 22	Numbers 31	Psalms 75, 76	☐ 22	Isaiah 23	1 John 1
☐ 23	Numbers 32	Psalms 77	☐ 23	Isaiah 24	1 John 2
☐ 24	Numbers 33	Psalms 78:1-37	☐ 24	Isaiah 25	1 John 3
☐ 25	Numbers 34	Psalms 78:38-72	☐ 25	Isaiah 26	1 John 4
☐ 26	Numbers 35	Psalms 79	☐ 26	Isaiah 27	1 John 5
☐ 27	Numbers 36	Psalms 80	☐ 27	Isaiah 28	2 John 1
☐ 28	Deut 1	Psalms 81, 82	☐ 28	Isaiah 29	3 John 1
☐ 29	Deut 2	Psalms 83, 84	☐ 29	Isaiah 30	Jude 1
☐ 30	Deut 3	Psalms 85	☐ 30	Isaiah 31	Rev 1
☐ 31	Deut 4	Psalms 86, 87	☐ 31	Isaiah 32	Rev 2

JUNE

Blessed is he that readeth and they that hear.

FAMILY			SECRET		
DAY	BOOK AND CHAPTER		DAY	BOOK AND CHAPTER	
1	Deut 5	Psalms 88	1	Isaiah 33	Rev 3
2	Deut 6	Psalms 89	2	Isaiah 34	Rev 4
3	Deut 7	Psalms 90	3	Isaiah 35	Rev 5
4	Deut 8	Psalms 91	4	Isaiah 36	Rev 6
5	Deut 9	Psalms 92, 93	5	Isaiah 37	Rev 7
6	Deut 10	Psalms 94	6	Isaiah 38	Rev 8
7	Deut 11	Psalms 95, 96	7	Isaiah 39	Rev 9
8	Deut 12	Psalms 97, 98	8	Isaiah 40	Rev 10
9	Deut 13, 14	Psalms 99-101	9	Isaiah 41	Rev 11
10	Deut 15	Psalms 102	10	Isaiah 42	Rev 12
11	Deut 16	Psalms 103	11	Isaiah 43	Rev 13
12	Deut 17	Psalms 104	12	Isaiah 44	Rev 14
13	Deut 18	Psalms 105	13	Isaiah 45	Rev 15
14	Deut 19	Psalms 106	14	Isaiah 46	Rev 16
15	Deut 20	Psalms 107	15	Isaiah 47	Rev 17
16	Deut 21	Psalms 108, 109	16	Isaiah 48	Rev 18
17	Deut 22	Psalms 110, 111	17	Isaiah 49	Rev 19
18	Deut 23	Psalms 112, 113	18	Isaiah 50	Rev 20
19	Deut 24	Psalms 114, 115	19	Isaiah 51	Rev 21
20	Deut 25	Psalms 116	20	Isaiah 52	Rev 22
21	Deut 26	Psalms 117, 118	21	Isaiah 53	Matthew 1
22	Deut 27, 28:1-19	Psalms 119:1-24	22	Isaiah 54	Matthew 2
23	Deut 28:20-68	Psalms 119:25-48	23	Isaiah 55	Matthew 3
24	Deut 29	Psalms 119:49-72	24	Isaiah 56	Matthew 4
25	Deut 30	Psalms 119:73-96	25	Isaiah 57	Matthew 5
26	Deut 31	Psalms 119:97-120	26	Isaiah 58	Matthew 6
27	Deut 32	Psalms 119:121-144	27	Isaiah 59	Matthew 7
28	Deut 33, 34	Psalms 119:145-176	28	Isaiah 60	Matthew 8
29	Joshua 1	Psalms 120-122	29	Isaiah 61	Matthew 9
30	Joshua 2	Psalms 123-125	30	Isaiah 62	Matthew 10

JULY

They received the word with all readiness of mind,
and searched the Scriptures daily.

FAMILY			SECRET		
DAY	BOOK AND CHAPTER		DAY	BOOK AND CHAPTER	
☐ 1	Joshua 3	Psalms 126-128	☐ 1	Isaiah 63	Matthew 11
☐ 2	Joshua 4	Psalms 129-131	☐ 2	Isaiah 64	Matthew 12
☐ 3	Joshua 5, 6:1-5	Psalms 132-134	☐ 3	Isaiah 65	Matthew 13
☐ 4	Joshua 6:6-27	Psalms 135, 136	☐ 4	Isaiah 66	Matthew 14
☐ 5	Joshua 7	Psalms 137, 138	☐ 5	Jeremiah 1	Matthew 15
☐ 6	Joshua 8	Psalms 139	☐ 6	Jeremiah 2	Matthew 16
☐ 7	Joshua 9	Psalms 140, 141	☐ 7	Jeremiah 3	Matthew 17
☐ 8	Joshua 10	Psalms 142, 143	☐ 8	Jeremiah 4	Matthew 18
☐ 9	Joshua 11	Psalms 144	☐ 9	Jeremiah 5	Matthew 19
☐ 10	Joshua 12, 13	Psalms 145	☐ 10	Jeremiah 6	Matthew 20
☐ 11	Joshua 14, 15	Psalms 146, 147	☐ 11	Jeremiah 7	Matthew 21
☐ 12	Joshua 16, 17	Psalms 148	☐ 12	Jeremiah 8	Matthew 22
☐ 13	Joshua 18, 19	Psalms 149, 150	☐ 13	Jeremiah 9	Matthew 23
☐ 14	Joshua 20, 21	Acts 1	☐ 14	Jeremiah 10	Matthew 24
☐ 15	Joshua 22	Acts 2	☐ 15	Jeremiah 11	Matthew 25
☐ 16	Joshua 23	Acts 3	☐ 16	Jeremiah 12	Matthew 26
☐ 17	Joshua 24	Acts 4	☐ 17	Jeremiah 13	Matthew 27
☐ 18	Judges 1	Acts 5	☐ 18	Jeremiah 14	Matthew 28
☐ 19	Judges 2	Acts 6	☐ 19	Jeremiah 15	Mark 1
☐ 20	Judges 3	Acts 7	☐ 20	Jeremiah 16	Mark 2
☐ 21	Judges 4	Acts 8	☐ 21	Jeremiah 17	Mark 3
☐ 22	Judges 5	Acts 9	☐ 22	Jeremiah 18	Mark 4
☐ 23	Judges 6	Acts 10	☐ 23	Jeremiah 19	Mark 5
☐ 24	Judges 7	Acts 11	☐ 24	Jeremiah 20	Mark 6
☐ 25	Judges 8	Acts 12	☐ 25	Jeremiah 21	Mark 7
☐ 26	Judges 9	Acts 13	☐ 26	Jeremiah 22	Mark 8
☐ 27	Judges 10, 11:1-11	Acts 14	☐ 27	Jeremiah 23	Mark 9
☐ 28	Judges 11:12-40	Acts 15	☐ 28	Jeremiah 24	Mark 10
☐ 29	Judges 12	Acts 16	☐ 29	Jeremiah 25	Mark 11
☐ 30	Judges 13	Acts 17	☐ 30	Jeremiah 26	Mark 12
☐ 31	Judges 14	Acts 18	☐ 31	Jeremiah 27	Mark 13

AUGUST

Speak, Lord; for thy servant heareth.

FAMILY			SECRET		
DAY	**BOOK AND CHAPTER**		**DAY**	**BOOK AND CHAPTER**	
☐ 1	Judges 15	Acts 19	☐ 1	Jeremiah 28	Mark 14
☐ 2	Judges 16	Acts 20	☐ 2	Jeremiah 29	Mark 15
☐ 3	Judges 17	Acts 21	☐ 3	Jeremiah 30, 31	Mark 16
☐ 4	Judges 18	Acts 22	☐ 4	Jeremiah 32	Psalms 1, 2
☐ 5	Judges 19	Acts 23	☐ 5	Jeremiah 33	Psalms 3, 4
☐ 6	Judges 20	Acts 24	☐ 6	Jeremiah 34	Psalms 5, 6
☐ 7	Judges 21	Acts 25	☐ 7	Jeremiah 35	Psalms 7, 8
☐ 8	Ruth 1	Acts 26	☐ 8	Jeremiah 36, 45	Psalms 9
☐ 9	Ruth 2	Acts 27	☐ 9	Jeremiah 37	Psalms 10
☐ 10	Ruth 3, 4	Acts 28	☐ 10	Jeremiah 38	Psalms 11, 12
☐ 11	1 Samuel 1	Romans 1	☐ 11	Jeremiah 39	Psalms 13, 14
☐ 12	1 Samuel 2	Romans 2	☐ 12	Jeremiah 40	Psalms 15, 16
☐ 13	1 Samuel 3	Romans 3	☐ 13	Jeremiah 41	Psalms 17
☐ 14	1 Samuel 4	Romans 4	☐ 14	Jeremiah 42	Psalms 18
☐ 15	1 Samuel 5, 6	Romans 5	☐ 15	Jeremiah 43	Psalms 19
☐ 16	1 Samuel 7, 8	Romans 6	☐ 16	Jeremiah 44	Psalms 20, 21
☐ 17	1 Samuel 9	Romans 7	☐ 17	Jeremiah 46	Psalms 22
☐ 18	1 Samuel 10	Romans 8	☐ 18	Jeremiah 47	Psalms 23, 24
☐ 19	1 Samuel 11	Romans 9	☐ 19	Jeremiah 48	Psalms 25
☐ 20	1 Samuel 12	Romans 10	☐ 20	Jeremiah 49	Psalms 26, 27
☐ 21	1 Samuel 13	Romans 11	☐ 21	Jeremiah 50	Psalms 28, 29
☐ 22	1 Samuel 14	Romans 12	☐ 22	Jeremiah 51	Psalms 30
☐ 23	1 Samuel 15	Romans 13	☐ 23	Jeremiah 52	Psalms 31
☐ 24	1 Samuel 16	Romans 14	☐ 24	Lamen 1	Psalms 32
☐ 25	1 Samuel 17	Romans 15	☐ 25	Lamen 2	Psalms 33
☐ 26	1 Samuel 18	Romans 16	☐ 26	Lamen 3	Psalms 34
☐ 27	1 Samuel 19	1 Cor 1	☐ 27	Lamen 4	Psalms 35
☐ 28	1 Samuel 20	1 Cor 2	☐ 28	Lamen 5	Psalms 36
☐ 29	1 Samuel 21, 22	1 Cor 3	☐ 29	Ezekiel 1	Psalms 37
☐ 30	1 Samuel 23	1 Cor 4	☐ 30	Ezekiel 2	Psalms 38
☐ 31	1 Samuel 24	1 Cor 5	☐ 31	Ezekiel 3	Psalms 39

SEPTEMBER

The law of the Lord is perfect,
converting the soul.

		FAMILY				SECRET	
	DAY	BOOK AND CHAPTER			DAY	BOOK AND CHAPTER	
☐	1	1 Samuel 25	1 Cor 6	☐	1	Ezekiel 4	Psalms 40, 41
☐	2	1 Samuel 26	1 Cor 7	☐	2	Ezekiel 5	Psalms 42, 43
☐	3	1 Samuel 27	1 Cor 8	☐	3	Ezekiel 6	Psalms 44
☐	4	1 Samuel 28	1 Cor 9	☐	4	Ezekiel 7	Psalms 45
☐	5	1 Samuel 29, 30	1 Cor 10	☐	5	Ezekiel 8	Psalms 46, 47
☐	6	1 Samuel 31	1 Cor 11	☐	6	Ezekiel 9	Psalms 48
☐	7	2 Samuel 1	1 Cor 12	☐	7	Ezekiel 10	Psalms 49
☐	8	2 Samuel 2	1 Cor 13	☐	8	Ezekiel 11	Psalms 50
☐	9	2 Samuel 3	1 Cor 14	☐	9	Ezekiel 12	Psalms 51
☐	10	2 Samuel 4, 5	1 Cor 15	☐	10	Ezekiel 13	Psalms 52-54
☐	11	2 Samuel 6	1 Cor 16	☐	11	Ezekiel 14	Psalms 55
☐	12	2 Samuel 7	2 Cor 1	☐	12	Ezekiel 15	Psalms 56, 57
☐	13	2 Samuel 8, 9	2 Cor 2	☐	13	Ezekiel 16	Psalms 58, 59
☐	14	2 Samuel 10	2 Cor 3	☐	14	Ezekiel 17	Psalms 60, 61
☐	15	2 Samuel 11	2 Cor 4	☐	15	Ezekiel 18	Psalms 62, 63
☐	16	2 Samuel 12	2 Cor 5	☐	16	Ezekiel 19	Psalms 64, 65
☐	17	2 Samuel 13	2 Cor 6	☐	17	Ezekiel 20	Psalms 66, 67
☐	18	2 Samuel 14	2 Cor 7	☐	18	Ezekiel 21	Psalms 68
☐	19	2 Samuel 15	2 Cor 8	☐	19	Ezekiel 22	Psalms 69
☐	20	2 Samuel 16	2 Cor 9	☐	20	Ezekiel 23	Psalms 70, 71
☐	21	2 Samuel 17	2 Cor 10	☐	21	Ezekiel 24	Psalms 72
☐	22	2 Samuel 18	2 Cor 11	☐	22	Ezekiel 25	Psalms 73
☐	23	2 Samuel 19	2 Cor 12	☐	23	Ezekiel 26	Psalms 74
☐	24	2 Samuel 20	2 Cor 13	☐	24	Ezekiel 27	Psalms 75, 76
☐	25	2 Samuel 21	Galatians 1	☐	25	Ezekiel 28	Psalms 77
☐	26	2 Samuel 22	Galatians 2	☐	26	Ezekiel 29	Psalms 78:1-37
☐	27	2 Samuel 23	Galatians 3	☐	27	Ezekiel 30	Psalms 78:38-72
☐	28	2 Samuel 24	Galatians 4	☐	28	Ezekiel 31	Psalms 79
☐	29	1 Kings 1	Galatians 5	☐	29	Ezekiel 32	Psalms 80
☐	30	1 Kings 2	Galatians 6	☐	30	Ezekiel 33	Psalms 81, 82

OCTOBER

O how I love thy law!
it is my meditation all the day.

FAMILY			SECRET		
DAY	BOOK AND CHAPTER		DAY	BOOK AND CHAPTER	
☐ 1	1 Kings 3	Ephesians 1	☐ 1	Ezekiel 34	Psalms 83, 84
☐ 2	1 Kings 4, 5	Ephesians 2	☐ 2	Ezekiel 35	Psalms 85
☐ 3	1 Kings 6	Ephesians 3	☐ 3	Ezekiel 36	Psalms 86
☐ 4	1 Kings 7	Ephesians 4	☐ 4	Ezekiel 37	Psalms 87, 88
☐ 5	1 Kings 8	Ephesians 5	☐ 5	Ezekiel 38	Psalms 89
☐ 6	1 Kings 9	Ephesians 6	☐ 6	Ezekiel 39	Psalms 90
☐ 7	1 Kings 10	Phil 1	☐ 7	Ezekiel 40	Psalms 91
☐ 8	1 Kings 11	Phil 2	☐ 8	Ezekiel 41	Psalms 92, 93
☐ 9	1 Kings 12	Phil 3	☐ 9	Ezekiel 42	Psalms 94
☐ 10	1 Kings 13	Phil 4	☐ 10	Ezekiel 43	Psalms 95, 96
☐ 11	1 Kings 14	Coloss 1	☐ 11	Ezekiel 44	Psalms 97, 98
☐ 12	1 Kings 15	Coloss 2	☐ 12	Ezekiel 45	Psalms 99-101
☐ 13	1 Kings 16	Coloss 3	☐ 13	Ezekiel 46	Psalms 102
☐ 14	1 Kings 17	Coloss 4	☐ 14	Ezekiel 47	Psalms 103
☐ 15	1 Kings 18	1 Thess 1	☐ 15	Ezekiel 48	Psalms 104
☐ 16	1 Kings 19	1 Thess 2	☐ 16	Daniel 1	Psalms 105
☐ 17	1 Kings 20	1 Thess 3	☐ 17	Daniel 2	Psalms 106
☐ 18	1 Kings 21	1 Thess 4	☐ 18	Daniel 3	Psalms 107
☐ 19	1 Kings 22	1 Thess 5	☐ 19	Daniel 4	Psalms 108, 109
☐ 20	2 Kings 1	2 Thess 1	☐ 20	Daniel 5	Psalms 110, 111
☐ 21	2 Kings 2	2 Thess 2	☐ 21	Daniel 6	Psalms 112, 113
☐ 22	2 Kings 3	2 Thess 3	☐ 22	Daniel 7	Psalms 114, 115
☐ 23	2 Kings 4	1 Timothy 1	☐ 23	Daniel 8	Psalms 116
☐ 24	2 Kings 5	1 Timothy 2	☐ 24	Daniel 9	Psalms 117, 118
☐ 25	2 Kings 6	1 Timothy 3	☐ 25	Daniel 10	Psalms 119:1-24
☐ 26	2 Kings 7	1 Timothy 4	☐ 26	Daniel 11	Psalms 119:25-48
☐ 27	2 Kings 8	1 Timothy 5	☐ 27	Daniel 12	Psalms 119:49-72
☐ 28	2 Kings 9	1 Timothy 6	☐ 28	Hosea 1	Psalms 119:73-96
☐ 29	2 Kings 10	2 Timothy 1	☐ 29	Hosea 2	Psalms 119:97-120
☐ 30	2 Kings 11, 12	2 Timothy 2	☐ 30	Hosea 3, 4	Psalms 119:121-144
☐ 31	2 Kings 13	2 Timothy 3	☐ 31	Hosea 5, 6	Psalms 119:145-176

NOVEMBER

*As new-born babes, desire the sincere milk of
the word, that ye may grow thereby.*

		FAMILY				SECRET	
	DAY	**BOOK AND CHAPTER**			**DAY**	**BOOK AND CHAPTER**	
☐	1	2 Kings 14	2 Timothy 4	☐	1	Hosea 7	Psalms 120-122
☐	2	2 Kings 15	Titus 1	☐	2	Hosea 8	Psalms 123-125
☐	3	2 Kings 16	Titus 2	☐	3	Hosea 9	Psalms 126-128
☐	4	2 Kings 17	Titus 3	☐	4	Hosea 10	Psalms 129-131
☐	5	2 Kings 18	Philemon 1	☐	5	Hosea 11	Psalms 132-134
☐	6	2 Kings 19	Hebrews 1	☐	6	Hosea 12	Psalms 135, 136
☐	7	2 Kings 20	Hebrews 2	☐	7	Hosea 13	Psalms 137, 138
☐	8	2 Kings 21	Hebrews 3	☐	8	Hosea 14	Psalms 139
☐	9	2 Kings 22	Hebrews 4	☐	9	Joel 1	Psalms 140, 141
☐	10	2 Kings 23	Hebrews 5	☐	10	Joel 2	Psalms 142
☐	11	2 Kings 24	Hebrews 6	☐	11	Joel 3	Psalms 143
☐	12	2 Kings 25	Hebrews 7	☐	12	Amos 1	Psalms 144
☐	13	1 Chr 1, 2	Hebrews 8	☐	13	Amos 2	Psalms 145
☐	14	1 Chr 3, 4	Hebrews 9	☐	14	Amos 3	Psalms 146, 147
☐	15	1 Chr 5, 6	Hebrews 10	☐	15	Amos 4	Psalms 148-150
☐	16	1 Chr 7, 8	Hebrews 11	☐	16	Amos 5	Luke 1:1-38
☐	17	1 Chr 9, 10	Hebrews 12	☐	17	Amos 6	Luke 1:39-80
☐	18	1 Chr 11, 12	Hebrews 13	☐	18	Amos 7	Luke 2
☐	19	1 Chr 13, 14	James 1	☐	19	Amos 8	Luke 3
☐	20	1 Chr 15	James 2	☐	20	Amos 9	Luke 4
☐	21	1 Chr 16	James 3	☐	21	Obadiah 1	Luke 5
☐	22	1 Chr 17	James 4	☐	22	Jonah 1	Luke 6
☐	23	1 Chr 18	James 5	☐	23	Jonah 2	Luke 7
☐	24	1 Chr 19, 20	1 Peter 1	☐	24	Jonah 3	Luke 8
☐	25	1 Chr 21	1 Peter 2	☐	25	Jonah 4	Luke 9
☐	26	1 Chr 22	1 Peter 3	☐	26	Micah 1	Luke 10
☐	27	1 Chr 23	1 Peter 4	☐	27	Micah 2	Luke 11
☐	28	1 Chr 24, 25	1 Peter 5	☐	28	Micah 3	Luke 12
☐	29	1 Chr 26, 27	2 Peter 1	☐	29	Micah 4	Luke 13
☐	30	1 Chr 28	2 Peter 2	☐	30	Micah 5	Luke 14

DECEMBER

The law of his God is in his heart;
none of his steps shall slide.

FAMILY			SECRET		
DAY	BOOK AND CHAPTER		DAY	BOOK AND CHAPTER	
☐ 1	1 Chr 29	2 Peter 3	☐ 1	Micah 6	Luke 15
☐ 2	2 Chr 1	1 John 1	☐ 2	Micah 7	Luke 16
☐ 3	2 Chr 2	1 John 2	☐ 3	Nahum 1	Luke 17
☐ 4	2 Chr 3, 4	1 John 3	☐ 4	Nahum 2	Luke 18
☐ 5	2 Chr 5, 6:1-11	1 John 4	☐ 5	Nahum 3	Luke 19
☐ 6	2 Chr 6:12-42	1 John 5	☐ 6	Habakkuk 1	Luke 20
☐ 7	2 Chr 7	2 John 1	☐ 7	Habakkuk 2	Luke 21
☐ 8	2 Chr 8	3 John 1	☐ 8	Habakkuk 3	Luke 22
☐ 9	2 Chr 9	Jude 1	☐ 9	Zephaniah 1	Luke 23
☐ 10	2 Chr 10	Rev 1	☐ 10	Zephaniah 2	Luke 24
☐ 11	2 Chr 11, 12	Rev 2	☐ 11	Zephaniah 3	John 1
☐ 12	2 Chr 13	Rev 3	☐ 12	Haggai 1	John 2
☐ 13	2 Chr 14, 15	Rev 4	☐ 13	Haggai 2	John 3
☐ 14	2 Chr 16	Rev 5	☐ 14	Zech 1	John 4
☐ 15	2 Chr 17	Rev 6	☐ 15	Zech 2	John 5
☐ 16	2 Chr 18	Rev 7	☐ 16	Zech 3	John 6
☐ 17	2 Chr 19, 20	Rev 8	☐ 17	Zech 4	John 7
☐ 18	2 Chr 21	Rev 9	☐ 18	Zech 5	John 8
☐ 19	2 Chr 22, 23	Rev 10	☐ 19	Zech 6	John 9
☐ 20	2 Chr 24	Rev 11	☐ 20	Zech 7	John 10
☐ 21	2 Chr 25	Rev 12	☐ 21	Zech 8	John 11
☐ 22	2 Chr 26	Rev 13	☐ 22	Zech 9	John 12
☐ 23	2 Chr 27, 28	Rev 14	☐ 23	Zech 10	John 13
☐ 24	2 Chr 29	Rev 15	☐ 24	Zech 11	John 14
☐ 25	2 Chr 30	Rev 16	☐ 25	Zech 12, 13:1	John 15
☐ 26	2 Chr 31	Rev 17	☐ 26	Zech 13:2-9	John 16
☐ 27	2 Chr 32	Rev 18	☐ 27	Zech 14	John 17
☐ 28	2 Chr 33	Rev 19	☐ 28	Malachi 1	John 18
☐ 29	2 Chr 34	Rev 20	☐ 29	Malachi 2	John 19
☐ 30	2 Chr 35	Rev 21	☐ 30	Malachi 3	John 20
☐ 31	2 Chr 36	Rev 22	☐ 31	Malachi 4	John 21

RECOMMENDED READING LIST

This reading list of especially loved books comes from the recommendations of many godly Christian women. The selections are divided into fiction and nonfiction and subdivided as novels, missionary biographies, classic devotional or theological studies, and helps. Some are no longer in print but are still available in libraries or through a book search on the internet (your local bookseller will help you if necessary). If you still cannot locate a book, begin frequenting used book stores. Hunting for old books can be great fun!

NONFICTION

Classic Devotional and Theological Studies

Abolition of Man, The, by C. S. Lewis

According to Plan by Graeme Goldsworthy

Affliction by Edith Schaeffer

Anything by Amy Carmichael

Basic Christianity by John Stott

By the Power of the Holy Spirit by David Howard

Christian Mind, The, by Harry Blamires

Cost of Discipleship, The, by Dietrich Bonhoeffer

Decision-Making and The Will of God by Gary Friesen

Desiring God by John Piper

Dictionary of Biblical Imagery, The, edited by Leland Ryken

Expository Thoughts on The Gospels by Bishop John Ryle

Five Evangelical Leaders from the 18th Century by Bishop John Ryle

God Who Is There, The, by Francis Schaeffer

God's Smuggler by Brother Andrew

God's Way of Peace by Horatius Bonar

Gospel and Wisdom by Graeme Goldsworthy

Grace Grows Best in Winter by Margaret Clarkson
Growing in Christ by J. I. Packer
Guidance and the Voice of God by Phillip D. Jensen and Tony Payne
Heart of the Universe, The, by Peter Jensen
Hinds Feet on High Places by Hannah Hurnard
Holiness by Bishop John Ryle
How Should We Then Live? by Francis Schaeffer
If by Amy Carmichael
Journals of Jim Elliot, The, by Elisabeth Elliot
Know and Tell the Gospel by John Chapman
Knowing God by J. I. Packer
Knowledge of the Holy, The, by A. W. Tozer
Letters Along the Way by D. A. Carson and John Woodbridge
Life of Trust, A, by George Muller
Marriage to a Difficult Man by Elisabeth D. Dodds
Mere Christianity by C. S. Lewis
Mind of the Maker by Dorothy Sayers
For the Love of God, Vol. 1 and 2, by D. A. Carson
My Utmost for His Highest by Oswald Chambers
Nave's Topical Bible by Orville J. Nave
Out of My Mind by Joseph Bayly
Practice of Godliness by Jerry Bridges
Prayer by O. Hallesby
Pursuit of God, The, by A. W. Tozer
Pursuit of Holiness by Jerry Bridges
Rare Jewel of Christian Contentment, The, by Jeremiah Burroughs
Recovering Biblical Manhood and Womanhood, edited by Wayne Grudem
    and John Piper
Romans by Martyn Lloyd-Jones
Sermon on the Mount, The, by Martyn Lloyd-Jones
Shadow of the Almighty, The, by Elisabeth Elliot
Sit, Watch, Stand by Watchman Nee

Spiritual Depression by Martyn Lloyd-Jones
Spiritual Secrets by Hudson Taylor
Streams in the Desert by Mrs. Charles Cowman
Systematic Theology by Wayne Grudem
These Strange Ashes by Elisabeth Elliot
Unfolding Mystery, The, by Edmund P. Clowney
Vine's Expository Dictionary by W. E. Vine
Weight of Glory, The, by C. S. Lewis
What the Bible Is All About by Henrietta Mears

Authors from Church History
Augustine
John Bunyan
John Calvin
Jonathan Edwards
Martin Luther
Blaise Pascal
Charles Spurgeon
John Wesley

Biographies
Acres of Hope by Patty Englin
Borden of Yale by Mrs. Howard Taylor
Bruchko by Bruce Olson
By Searching by Isobel Kuhn
Chance to Die, A, by Elisabeth Elliot
Early Years, The, by Mrs. Howard Taylor
Family Nobody Wanted, The, by Helen Doss
George Whitefield and the Great Awakening by John Pollock
God's Smuggler by Brother Andrew
Green Leaf in Drought Time by Isobel Kuhn
Growth of a Soul, The, by Mrs. Howard Taylor

Hiding Place, The, by Corrie ten Boom
Joni by Joni Eareckson
Life of Jonathan Goforth, The, by Mrs. Rosalind Goforth
My Heart in His Hand by Sharon James
Shadow of the Broad Brim, The, by Richard Ellsworth Day
Small Woman, The, by Alan Burgess
Through Gates of Splendor by Elisabeth Elliot
To the Golden Shore: The Life of Adoniram Judson by Courtney Anderson
Triumph of John and Betty Stam, The, by Geraldine Howard Taylor
William Booth by David Bennet
William Carey: Missionary Pioneer and Statesman by F. Deaville Walker

Other Nonfiction

Commonsense Parenting by Kent and Barbara Hughes
Creative, Confident Children by Maxine Hancock
Dare to Discipline by James Dobson
Disappointment with God by Philip Yancey
Essence of Feminism, The, by Kirsten Birkett
Feminist Gospel, The, by Mary Kassian
For the Children's Sake by Susan Schaeffer Macaulay
For the Family's Sake by Susan Schaeffer Macaulay
Hidden Art of Homemaking, The, by Edith Schaeffer
Honey for a Child's Heart by Gladys Hunt
Let Me Be a Woman by Elisabeth Elliot
Women, Creation, and the Fall by Mary Kassian
Midwife's Tale, A, by Laurel Thatcher Ulrich
Out of the Saltshaker by Rebecca Pippert
Parents in Pain by John White
Passion and Purity by Elisabeth Elliot
Return to Modesty, A, by Wendy Shalit
Step Further, A, by Joni Eareckson & Steve Estes
What's So Amazing About Grace? by Philip Yancey

FICTION

All Creatures Great and Small by James Herriot

All Things Bright and Beautiful by James Herriot

All Things Wise and Wonderful by James Herriot

Anna Karenina by Leo Tolstoy

Anne of Green Gables series by L. M. Montgomery

Brothers Karamozov, The, by Fyodor Dostoyevsky

Cancer Ward by Alexander Solzhenitsyn

Chosen, The, by Chaim Potok

Christy by Catherine Marshall

Chronicles of Narnia, The, by C. S. Lewis

Cry, the Beloved Country by Alan Paton

Davita's Harp by Chaim Potok

Descent into Hell by Charles Williams

Emma by Jane Austen

Episode of Sparrows and Most Others, An, by Rumer Godden

Everything That Rises Must Converge by Flannery O'Connor

Father Brown Omnibus by G. K. Chesterton

Great Expectations by Charles Dickens

Idiot, The, by Fyodor Dostoyevsky

Into the Whirlwind by Eugenia Semenovna Ginzburg

King Lear by William Shakespeare

Lord God Made Them All, The, by James Herriot

Man Who Was Thursday, The, by G. K. Chesterton

Martin Chuzzlewit by Charles Dickens

My Name Is Asher Lev by Chaim Potok

Mysteries of Agatha Christie by Agatha Christie

Nicholas and Alexandra by Robert Massie

Power and the Glory, The, by Graham Greene

Pride and Prejudice by Jane Austen

Scarlet Letter, The, by Nathaniel Hawthorne

Secret Garden, The, by Frances Hodgson Burnett

Sense and Sensibility by Jane Austen

Samurai's Garden, The, by Gail Tsukiyama

Till We Have Faces by C. S. Lewis

To Kill a Mockingbird by Harper Lee

Too Late the Phalarope by Alan Paton

Trinity by Leon Uris

Uncle Tom's Cabin by Harriet Beecher Stowe

Violent Bear It Away, The, by Flannery O'Connor

Viper's Tangle by Francois Mauriac

Winnie the Pooh by A. A. Milne

WHAT I DO WITH THE HARD THINGS IN MY LIFE

Written for the Gospel Women Study at College Church by Mary Duvel

1. Immerse myself in the Word of God. His divine power has given me everything I need for life and godliness through the knowledge of Him (2 Peter 1:3).
2. Realize:
   a. He is in sovereign control of all that concerns me, His child. Everything is sifted through His fingers first.
   b. God has given each of us our own race to run. We are to keep our eyes fixed on him and stay in our own lane, not comparing our lives or the life of someone we love to the lives of others (1 Corinthians 7:17; Hebrews 12:1-2).
   c. God does not give us grace for someone else's race.
   d. God does not ask us to understand His ways, but He asks us to trust Him implicitly. He sees the whole, eternal picture.
   e. My lack of faith does not nullify His faithfulness (Romans 3:3).
   f. I am not the point—He is. It is not about me getting out of suffocating pain; it is about His Son being revealed in me, about God's image being released in me. (This idea is from *Finding God* by Larry Crabb.)
3. Yield to the instrument of refinement He has chosen in my life. God cannot fulfill His purpose in me when I am kicking and screaming.
4. Confess that I don't know how to yield, that I am helpless and angry. God is big enough to take it.
5. Confirm that I am willing to be taught in the midst of this pain and difficulty.

244 RESOURCES

6. Ask in the disappointment, loss, isolation, and pain that the Holy Spirit will teach me through the Word to trust God and understand who God is in all His mercy and love.

7. Seek to walk in obedience through the storm and not waste my energy fretting.

8. Know that the secret is Christ in me, not me in a different set of circumstances. (This thought is from *Keep a Quiet Heart* by Elisabeth Elliot.)

9. Remain hopeful that through all of life's changes, we are secure in the knowledge that we will see His face and be fully satisfied (Psalm 17:15).

10. Press on to take hold of that for which Christ took hold of us (Philippians 3:12; Acts 20:24)!

ADDITIONAL SCRIPTURES ON GOOD DEEDS

Ephesians 2:9-10

Deuteronomy 12:28

Psalm 36:3

Psalm 37:3, 27

Psalm 43:14

Jeremiah 4:22

Jeremiah 13:23

Matthew 5:16

Luke 6:26, 35

Acts 9:36

Acts 10:38

Romans 2:7

Romans 7:18, 21

2 Corinthians 9:8

Galatians 6:9-10

Ephesians 2:10

Ephesians 4:12-13

Colossians 3:1, 23

1 Timothy 2:10

1 Timothy 5:9-10, 25

1 Timothy 6:18

Titus 2:7, 14

Titus 3:1-2, 8

Hebrews 10:2, 24

Hebrews 13:16

James 2:14, 20, 26

James 3:13

1 Peter 2:12, 15, 20-21

1 Peter 3:8-14, 17

1 Peter 4:19

Revelation 2:2, 23

Revelation 3:2

Revelation 14:13

Revelation 19:6, 8

OPPORTUNITIES FOR GOOD DEEDS

Ministries to the handicapped
Hearing impaired
Blind
Lame
Retarded

Ministries to the sick
Nursing
Physician
Hospice care—cancer, AIDS, etc.
Community health

Ministries to the socially estranged
Emotionally impaired
Recovering alcoholics
Recovering drug-users
Escaping prostitutes
Abused children, women
Runaways, problem children
Orphans

Prison ministries
Women's prisons
Families of prisoners
Rehabilitation to society

Ministries to youth
Teaching
Sponsoring
Open houses and recreation
Outings and trips
Counseling
Academic assistance

Sports ministries
Neighborhood
Church teams

Audiovisual ministries
Composition
Design
Production
Distribution

Writing ministries
Free-lance
Curriculum development
Fiction
Nonfiction
Editing
Institutional communications
Journalistic skills for publications

Teaching ministries
Sunday school: children, youth,
students, women
Grade school
High school
College

Music ministries
Composition
Training
Performance
Voice
Choir
Instrumentalist

Evangelistic ministries
Personal witnessing
Parachurch groups
Home Bible studies
Outreach to children
Visitation teams
Counseling at meetings
Telephone counseling

Therapeutic counseling
  Independent
  Church-based
  Institutional

Radio and television ministries
  Technical assistance
  Writing
  Announcing
  Producing

Theater and drama ministries
  Acting
  Directing
  Writing
  Scheduling

Social ministries
  Literacy
  Pro-life
  Pro-decency
  Housing
  Safety
  Beautification
  Drug rehabilitation

Pastoral care assistance
  Visitation
  Newcomer welcoming and
    assistance
  Hospitality
  Food and clothing and
    transportation

Prayer ministries
  Praying
  Mobilizing for prayer events
  Helping with small groups of
    prayer
  Coordinating prayer chains
  Promoting prayer days and weeks
    and vigils

Missions
  All of the above across cultures

Support ministries
  Countless "secular" jobs that
    undergird other ministries

The awesome significance of
  motherhood
Making a home as a full-time wife

James and Deby Fellowes's
Witness to Their Faith

James: My wife, Deby, and I are glad to give witness to the change that came into our lives when we accepted Jesus Christ as Lord and Savior. We are grateful to those who stood tall in their faith and were instrumental in our decision for Christ.

During our courtship and early years of marriage, we never attended church, nor do I recall ever discussing God or what we believed. We were too busy with our careers and each other.

I had been born into a churchgoing family. My parents were and are marvelous examples of the Christian ideal. They are generous, loving, gracious, compassionate, kind, and humble. But, as good as their example was, in my youth I never really understood Jesus' life, death, or resurrection. I figured I was a Christian because I went to church and tried to be a good person just like my mom and dad.

Deborah: Like Jamie, I grew up going to church. My mother was a Sunday school teacher for many years, and she made sure my brother and I attended every Sunday. It was in church, I believe, that the three of us found comfort and strength to deal with difficult family problems.

In the midst of a time of uncertainty and insecurity during my junior high years, I remember having a keen interest in spiritual matters. I felt a strong desire to go to church, but could find no answers. I recall a stained-glass window in our church depicting an angel kneeling with its wing outstretched. How I yearned to crawl under that wing for security, protection, and peace.

When I fell in love with Jamie, it seemed like I could find all these things I was searching for in him and our relationship. We had each other, and I turned my back on God. We lived for the moment and for ourselves.

James: On December 23, 1975, at 2:00 in the afternoon, our first child, Jennifer, was born. Seeing childbirth firsthand in the delivery room was more than this new father could handle. I cried uncontrollably, overcome with the emotions of joy, awe, and thankfulness. This magnificent moment of birth tugged the spiritual cords within me.

In the hours and days afterward, I thought a lot about God and the creation of a baby. *Only God can create a baby*, I thought. I wanted to know God. I had seen His great and powerful work.

The next Sunday we searched for a neighborhood church in the Lincoln Park area of Chicago where we lived, and we finally found one we liked. I really enjoyed this new dimension in my life. I began to learn about Christianity as an adult. I liked the people and being part of the church community. In time I became an usher, an elder, the chairman of the board of elders.

Deborah: While Jamie was finding a new dimension and fulfillment in his life, I became resentful of this new interest. He now had more meetings to attend and obligations to fill that did not include me. Knowing how much this church meant to Jamie, however, I became somewhat involved along with him.

On a spiritual level, I was needy. Singing hymns alone would bring me to the brink of tears. I wanted to know what to believe in. I was searching for meaning in my life, but I was looking in the wrong places. Material possessions and worldly success were far too important to me. These were attainable goals since Jamie's responsibility and stature were growing in his family's business. In spite of our material success, though, I felt an emptiness in my life.

Both Jamie's and my background made us leery of evangelical churches. When we moved to Wheaton [Illinois] in 1979, we looked for a house far removed from the Wheaton College campus. However, the house of our dreams happened to be one block from the area we were trying to avoid.

Five months after we moved in, the new pastor of College Church—Kent Hughes—and his family moved in across the street from us. I became friends with his wife, Barbara. She invited me to come to a Bible study at their church on Wednesday mornings, and I decided I would give it a try. From the moment I walked into that room, I sensed a difference in this group. The women seemed to care sincerely about each other. There was not the superficiality I had encountered at so many other social and business groups. Before long the Bible study became a highlight of my week. I admired these women's strength of character, something I sensed was lacking in myself. I began to recognize that these women were different because of the teachings of the Scripture. They were committed to displaying through their lives what the Bible taught—acting upon what they had learned. They trusted Christ to rule their lives instead of themselves. That was so contrary to the way we were living our lives.

It was during this time that Jamie and I received an invitation to a dinner being held at a country club by a business acquaintance of Jamie's. It was to feature a testimony by a business executive and his wife on what their relationship with Christ has meant in their lives. Out of respect for our friend, we went. Here I heard what I had been hearing at Bible study but by a business executive's wife, someone who had been struggling with many of the things that I was struggling with. I could definitely identify with her. I realized that Revelation 3:20 was speaking to me: "Here I am! I stand at the door and knock. If anyone hears my voice and opens the door, I will come in and eat with him, and he with me."

That night was one of the most stressful for me. In a moment of anxiety I prayed that my friend Barbara would come speak to me the next day. And she did. After explaining to her the previous evening's events, she could sense the struggle I was having. She offered to lead me through the Scriptures and explain Jesus' claims. Through her leading, I took a step of faith and surrendered my life to Christ. I knew my commitment would make a big change in our marriage, but I knew this was what I had to do.

James: I went to the same dinner, of course. At the end of the testimony, we were given cards to fill out. I checked the box "don't call me." I distrusted the "born-again" types. I thought they were self-righteous and often a lot worse than the rest of us. Besides that, I had been chairman of the board of elders and served our church in other ways. Was that not religious enough?

It made me sick that my susceptible wife had been drawn into this "born-again" business. Maybe it would die away.

Soon a division between Deby and me began to open. She read the Bible all the time. If not that, she was reading Chuck Swindoll, C. S. Lewis, or Kent Hughes, our neighbor. She spent all her time in Bible studies and prayer groups. She accepted party invitations, and they were boring. I felt out of it, and I didn't want "in." In many ways we began to grow apart.

Deborah: Actually what I had feared would happen did happen. Jamie could not understand how my priorities could change overnight. Where did he now fit in the scheme of things? Although our relationship was as important to me as it had always been, a new relationship was deepening within me—one with Christ. My desire to follow, serve, and obey Christ had become first in my life. With that decision I wanted to spend my time differently. Lifestyle preferences changed. The division in our marriage opened wider. I simply had to trust Christ.

James: I was trying to be understanding and patient, but I often found myself resentful and angry. I felt lonely in my own house. If God is good, how could He be the center of a heretofore successful, happy marriage? I was very confused.

I had my own views about God based on I know not what. I figured I had a reasonable shot at heaven because I was a pretty good person. God graded on a curve, no doubt—hopefully a generous one. Deby refuted my arguments based on Scripture. She spoke of salvation through faith and God's grace.

In the interest of family unity, I decided to go to a Sunday evening service with Deby. My experience was rather similar to Deby's the first time she visited the women's Bible study. I sensed something different from other church experiences I'd had. I decided to go back the next Sunday. I sensed the presence of Christ in a new and deeper way.

Maybe there was some good in all this, I thought, difficult as it might be to admit. For all that I resented our new lifestyle, Deby had changed positively in many ways. For openers she was at peace with our relationship. I was the one in emotional stress. She definitely was a stronger, more independent person. She was less argumentative and more forgiving. Irony of ironies, she was somehow more romantic through this period of tension.

I decided I might read some of her books that were lying around— *In His Steps* by Charles Sheldon, *Mere Christianity* by C. S. Lewis, *Loving God* by Chuck Colson. Kent Hughes and I read *Basic Christianity* by John Stott together. We began to talk about faith. On a difficult business trip to San Francisco I read the Gospel of John from a Gideon Bible in the motel desk drawer. The power of Scripture was beginning to take hold for the first time in my life.

Deborah: Jamie had changed. It was not an overnight experience as it had been with me, but I sensed a gradual open and sensitive spirit to know the Lord. Our relationship grew in a way it never had before—on a spiritual level. We began to trust God for our daily decisions. We realized that God was sovereign and in control of our lives. We became happier and closer than we ever had been before. Looking back over the years, we could see how God had gently yet firmly pulled us to Himself, and in the process drew us closer to each other. God had done what He promised in Ezekiel 11:19-20: "I will give them an undivided heart and put a new spirit in them; I will remove from them their heart of stone and give them a heart of flesh. Then they will follow my decrees and be careful to keep my laws. They will be my people, and I will be their God."

James: There had been an emptiness to my life, despite a great marriage, kids, and all the nice things we could afford. How do you define an emptiness or void? It's hard. Most of the time we suppress it or feebly attempt to fill it with something superficial.

As I began to understand the claims of Christ and why He had come to earth and died for me, I looked at my life. It was embarrassing when I reflected upon God's riches in my life and compared it to the selfishness and downright wickedness of my heart. I was ashamed.

I journeyed frequently to the foot of the cross and begged forgiveness. I prayed in detail, sickening as it was. The more I read and listened, the better I understood where I had gone wrong. More importantly, I discovered how to get on track. Through God's forgiveness and grace I began to feel free and alive in a new way.

In those early days God seemed to fill me with a new power and a totally new sense of self-worth. As I trusted in Him, things seemed to work out better. Trying to please Him instead of myself somehow took the pressure off and made me feel better about my life.

Jesus Christ made all the difference in our lives. We are a living testimony to His power. Through countless trials, struggles, and everyday events He has guided our path. He has blessed us beyond our hopes. We are grateful to the many who prayed for, nurtured, and discipled us.

Because I am a businessman by profession, a healthy skepticism comes naturally. My own conversion was slow and deliberate, unlike Deby's. But I discovered the Way, the Truth, and the Life—the Lord Jesus Christ. I've learned where to put my trust. God is faithful. He loves you, and He loves me. Trust in Him.

Domestic Gospel Women

Written for the Gospel Women study of
College Church by Sue Bowen

All aspects of our domesticity must be rooted in the Gospel!

Do not let your hearts be troubled. Trust in God; trust also in me. In my Father's house are many rooms; . . . I am going there to prepare a place for you. (John 14:1-2)

Hopefully, our eyes will be constantly turning toward our heavenly home. But does this mean our earthly homes and the domestic concerns that are part of daily living are unimportant? Do our homes reflect, in some part, the beauty, comfort, and peace of our future heavenly home? Perhaps we have forgotten the importance of creating a haven (an orderly, God-centered home) from the world's chaos. We are all responsible for making our homes and church a pleasant refuge that will draw its members and visitors toward God: A place where people will see our love for Christ and the family of God. For all women, whether young or old, married or single, this attitude will cause us to evaluate the home we are a part of and its impact on those in its inner circle, as well as on visitors. It requires all women to think of the whole family of God. We are called to be sacrificially caring for God's people.

The heavenly home of the Bible is depicted as a beautiful, exciting place and a place of refuge.

The wise woman builds her house, but with her own hands the foolish one tears hers down. (Proverbs 14:1)

This verse applies to more than simply the physical home. It refers also to the network of relationships within a woman's domain. In the practical, everyday affairs of my domestic life, am I reflecting a godly character (orderly, serene, just, and loving)? In my home and in the family of God, am I building up my relationships or tearing them down?

Proverbs 31:10-31 beautifully describes an industrious, prepared, noble, hard-working, domestic woman whose life work revolves around making provision for her household so that she has no fear for them (v. 21). Again, this provision probably is for spiritual as well as for physical needs. J. I. Packer, in his book *The Quest for Godliness*, writes:

> Puritan teachers thought humane family life, in which Christian love and joy would find full and free expression, could not be achieved till the ordered pattern they envisaged—the regular authority-structure and daily routine—had been firmly established. Their passion to please God expressed itself in an ardor for order; their vision of the good and godly life was of a planned, well-thought-out flow of activities in which all obligations were recognized and met, and time was found for everything that mattered: for personal devotion, for family worship, for household tasks, for wage-earning employment, for intimacy with spouse and children, for Sabbath rest, and whatever else one's calling or callings required.

The goal of a well-ordered household is a worthy one. It promotes a more balanced, healthy, and productive way of living that better prepares us for whatever God brings our way. Order also reflects God's nature; He is a God of order. Just look at His creation!

One day we will account for the way we have spent our energy and effort in our domestic life. Did we do it all unto Him to bring Him glory? Is our motivation to please, serve, and obey Him in this seemingly mundane area of our lives?

CHALLENGES

Without Christ as our reason and reference point, it is impossible to make sense of the seemingly mundane aspects of our domestic pursuits and to know how daily to balance the many demands in this area. Our efforts may be temporarily rewarding, but only for their fleeting effects. If we do everything as unto Christ, even the smallest, most tedious job has meaning.

Putting household matters, skills, and efforts in proper perspective is a formidable task. They are not to become the focus of our lives or an end in themselves. Yet we should not minimize the domestic tasks and the benefits creative homemaking can bring. The desire to "keep it simple" may sometimes mask a laziness that neglects our obligation to use our gifts and talents to make moments special and beautiful to honor others and show our love and devotion. Biblical domesticity requires discipline, love, stamina, and discernment in the use of our time, talents, and gifts.

Different seasons of a woman's life and changing circumstances may require a temporary shift in emphasis in certain aspects of domestic life (temporary disruptions: moving, babies, sickness, divorce, job stresses). We must guard against judging other women without knowing their circumstances and watch for ways to encourage each other in our domestic responsibilities.

In our materialistic culture, there are women working outside the home to escape from the sheer hard work and challenge of creating a well-ordered home life. Yet the stay-at-home mother may pride herself on putting family and home first, only to fill her time with activities that, in fact, put family and home second—such as hobbies, clubs, shopping, and idleness.

If we fail to put God first, if we fail to seek simply to obey and trust His direction in every aspect of our lives, we may appear to others to be accomplished in our domestic life. Yet our efforts in these areas will be our only reward.

Notes

Discipline for Godliness

1 John Wesley, quoted in *Garden of Prayer* (Santa Ana, Calif.: Vision House, 1976), p. 45.

Discipline of the Gospel

1 John Chapman, *Know and Tell the Gospel* (Sydney, Australia: Hodder and Stoughton, 1990), p. 19.

2 Ibid., p. 20.

3 William Tyndale, *Doctrinal Treatises* (Cambridge: Parker Society, 1849), p. 8.

4 "Two Ways to Live: A Brief Look at the Message of Christianity," a pamphlet published by St. Matthias Press, P.O. Box 665, London, England, SW20 8RU. Reprinted by permission.

Discipline of Submission

1 Betty Friedan, as quoted by Mary A. Kassian in *The Feminist Gospel* (Wheaton, Ill.: Crossway Books, 1992), p. 15.

2 Kirsten Birkett, *The Essence of Feminism* (Sydney, Australia: Matthias Media, 2000), p. 121.

3 Jeremiah Burroughs, *Rare Jewel of Christian Contentment* (Carlisle, Pa: Banner of Truth Trust, 1648, reprinted 1998), p. 33.

4 Peter Jensen, *At the Heart of the Universe* (Wheaton, Ill.: Crossway Books, 1997), p. 87.

5 John Wesley, quoted in *Garden of Prayer* (Santa Ana, Calif.: Vision House, 1976), p. 51.

6 Mary A. Kassian, *Women, Creation, and the Fall* (Wheaton, Ill.: Crossway Books, 1990), p. 33.

7 Robert Coles, "Discipline" in *Family Weekly*, March 27, 1983, pp. 4-5.

Discipline of Prayer

1 E. Stanley Jones, *A Song of Ascents* (Nashville: Abingdon, 1979), p. 383.

2 Annie Dillard, *Pilgrim at Tinker Creek* (New York: Bantam, 1978), p. 35.

3 J. I. Packer, *Knowing God* (Downers Grove, Ill.: InterVarsity Press, 1973).

4 Brother Lawrence, *The Practice of the Presence of God* (New York: Revell, 1958), pp. 30-31.

5 John Wesley, *Works*, VIII (Grand Rapids, Mich.: Zondervan, 1959), p. 343.

6 H. G. Haile, *Luther: An Experiment in Biography* (Garden City, N.Y.: Doubleday, 1980), p. 56.

7 Augustine, *Confessions*, 9:33.

8 Marilee Melvin, "A Cherished Life of Prayer," College Church Fellowship, February 2001, p. 6.

9 Elisabeth Elliot, *Notes on Prayer* (Wheaton, Ill.: Good News Publishers, 1982), writes: "People who ski, I suppose, are people who happen to like skiing, who have time for skiing, who can afford to ski, and who are good at skiing—something you do if you can afford the trouble, something you do if you are good at it."

DISCIPLINE OF WORSHIP

1 Annie Dillard, *Teaching a Stone to Talk* (New York: Harper & Row, 1982), pp. 40-41.

2 A. W. Tozer, *The Pursuit of God* (Camp Hill, Pa.: Christian Publications, 1993), p. 87.

3 John Stott, *Guard the Truth* (Downers Grove, Ill.: InterVarsity Press, 1966). Page 121 quotes Justin Martyr, *First Apology*, trans. A. W. F. Blunt, Cambridge Patristic Texts, Vol. 1.

DISCIPLINE OF MIND

1 Harry Blamires, *Recovering the Christian Mind* (Downers Grove, Ill.: InterVarsity Press, 1988), p. 9.

2 Bob DeMoss, *TV: The Great Escape* (Wheaton, Ill.: Crossway Books, 2001), pp. 67-68.

3 Ibid., p. 27.

4 J. I. Packer, *Knowing God* (London: InterVarsity Press, 1973), p. 182.

DISCIPLINE OF CONTENTMENT

1 *The American Heritage College Dictionary*, 3rd ed.

2 Jeremiah Burroughs, *The Rare Jewel of Christian Contentment* (Carlisle, Pa: Banner of Truth Trust, 1648, reprinted 1998), p. 19.

3 D. Martyn Lloyd-Jones, *Spiritual Depression: Its Causes and Cure* (Grand Rapids, Mich.: Eerdmans, 1963, 1974), p. 278.

4 Phillip Jensen, *Guidance and the Voice of God* (Sydney, Australia: Matthias Media, 1997), p. 55.

5 Burroughs, *Rare Jewel*, p. 109.

6 Margaret Clarkson, *Grace Grows Best in Winter* (Grand Rapids, Mich.: Zondervan, 1972), p. 199.

7 Lloyd-Jones, *Spiritual Depression,* pp. 280-81.

8 Marie Ebner von Eschenbach, *Aphorism,* quoted in *The Quotable Woman,* Vol. 1 (Los Angeles, Calif.: Pinnacle Books, 1977), p. 140.

9 Douglas Jones and Douglas Wilson, *Angels in the Architecture: A Protestant Vision for Middle Earth* (Moscow, Idaho: Canon Press, 1998), p. 69.

10 J. I. Packer, *Knowing God* (Downers Grove, Ill.: InterVarsity Press, 1973), p. 147.

11 "How to Read and Study the Bible," College Church, Wheaton, Ill. The six questions for personal study originated with Dick Lucas, former pastor of St. Helen's Church, London.

12 Ibid., p. 27.

DISCIPLINE OF PROPRIETY

1 Bob DeMoss, *TV: The Great Escape* (Wheaton, Ill.: Crossway Books, 2001), p. 97.

2 Elisabeth Elliot, "Can Christian Higher Education Cope with Femininity?" Essay presented at 46th National Convention of National Association of Evangelicals, Orlando, March 10, 1988.

3 Quoted in Wendy Shalit, *A Return to Modesty* (New York: Simon and Schuster, 1999), pp. 163-64.

4 *Merriam Webster's Collegiate Dictionary,* 10th ed., 1993, p. 194.

5 Shalit, *Return to Modesty,* pp. 172-73.

DISCIPLINE OF PERSEVERANCE

1 Michael A. Lev, "Couple Held on to God in Tragedy," *Chicago Tribune,* November 17, 1994, pp. 1, 18.

2 *Merriam-Webster's Collegiate Dictionary,* 10th ed., 1993.

3 Leland Ryken, James C. Wilhoit, Tremper Longman III, eds., *Dictionary of Biblical Imagery* (Downers Grove, Ill.: InterVarsity Press, 1998), p. 636.

4 Jeremiah Burroughs, *The Rare Jewel of Christian Contentment* (Carlisle, Pa: Banner of Truth Trust, 1648, reprinted 1998), p. 30.

DISCIPLINE OF THE CHURCH

1 John Armstrong, *Viewpoint: A Publication of Reformation & Revival Ministries,* Vol. 5, No. 2, March-April 2001, p. 1.

2 Robert L. Saucy, *The Church in God's Program* (Chicago: Moody Press, 1972), p. 17.

3 Ibid., p. 8.

4 Leland Ryken, James C. Wilhoit, Tremper Longman III, eds., *Dictionary of Biblical Imagery* (Downers Grove, Ill.: InterVarsity Press, 1998), p. 148.

5   J. I. Packer, *God's Words: Studies of the Key Bible Themes* (Grand Rapids: Baker Books, 1998), p. 191.

6   Ibid., p. 193.

7   Ryken, Wilhoit, Longman, *Dictionary of Biblical Imagery*, p. 148.

8   Ibid.

9   John Piper, *The Pleasures of God* (Sisters, Ore.: Multnomah, 1992), pp. 123-125.

10 Adapted from R. Kent Hughes and Bryan Chapell, *1 & 2 Timothy and Titus* (Wheaton, Ill.: Crossway Books, 2000), pp. 69-71.

11 Douglas Moo, "What Does It Mean Not to Teach or Have Authority Over Men? 1 Timothy 2:11-15," John Piper and Wayne Grudem, eds., *Recovering Biblical Manhood and Womanhood* (Wheaton, Ill.: Crossway Books, 1991), p. 186.

12 John R. W. Stott, *Decisive Issues Facing Christians Today* (Old Tappan, N.J.: Revell, 1990), pp. 269-270.

13 Michael G. Maudlin, "John Stott Speaks Out," *Christianity Today,* Vol. 37, No. 2, February 8, 1993, p. 38.

14 Phillip Jensen, *To the Householder* (Sydney, Australia: Matthias Press, 1996), p. 47.

15 Peter Bolt, "I Don't Like It," *The Briefing*, 159/60, June 10, 1995, p. 4.

DISCIPLINE OF SINGLENESS

1   *Merriam Webster's Collegiate Dictionary*, 10th ed., 1993, p. 360.

2   John Piper and Wayne Grudem, eds., *Recovering Biblical Manhood and Womanhood* (Wheaton, Ill.: Crossway Books, 1991), p. xxiv.

3   Albert Hsu, "Singleness: A Biblical Perspective," *Discipleship Journal*, issue 108, 1998, p. 30.

4   Phillip Jensen, *Pure Sex* (Sydney, Australia: St. Matthias Press, 1998), p. 97.

5   Ada Lum, *Single and Human,* cited in *Recovering Biblical Manhood and Womanhood* (Wheaton, Ill.: Crossway Books, 1991), pp. 44-45.

DISCIPLINE OF MARRIAGE

1   Lance Morrow, "The Hazards of Homemade Vows," *Time*, June 27, 1983, p.78.

2   Philip D. Jensen and Tony Payne, *Beyond Eden* (Sydney, Australia: St. Matthias Press, 1990), p. 33.

3   Wendy Shalit, *A Return to Modesty* (New York: Simon & Schuster, 1999), pp. 139-40.

4   Kirsten Birkett, "Reopening a Window," *The Briefing*, 159/60, June 20, 1995, p. 2.

5   Jensen and Payne, *Beyond Eden*, p. 19.

6   Claire Smith, "Two Commands to Women," *The Briefing*, 159/60, June 20, 1995, p. 16.

7 Wayne Grudem, *Systematic Theology* (Downers Grove, Ill., InterVarsity Press, 1994), pp. 249-50.

8 Barbara Brotman, "Matter of Roles," (WomanNews), *Chicago Tribune*, October 11, 2000, p. 2.

9 Colin Brown, *The New International Dictionary of New Testament Theology*, Vol. 2 (Grand Rapids: Zondervan, 1979), pp. 256-57.

10 William Barclay, *A New Testament Wordbook* (New York: Harper & Brothers, n.d.), p. 103.

11 Ibid., p. 104.

12 James Johnston, from a sermon delivered in College Church, Wheaton, Ill., September 13, 1998.

DISCIPLINE OF NURTURING

1 Charles Krauthammer, "Motherhood Missed," *The Washington Post*, May 12, 2000, p. A47.

2 Susan Hunt, *By Design* (Wheaton, Ill.: Crossway Books, 1998), p. 136.

3 Elisabeth Elliot, *Let Me Be a Woman* (Carol Stream, Ill.: Tyndale, 1976), p. 53.

4 *Merriam-Webster's Collegiate Dictionary*, 10th ed., 1993, p. 799.

5 Ibid., p. 799.

6 Thomas R. Schreiner, "An Interpretation of 1 Timothy 2:4-15: A Dialogue with Scholarship," Andreas J. Kostenberger, Thomas R. Schreiner, and H. Scott Baldwin, eds., *Women in the Church* (Grand Rapids, Mich.: Baker, 1995), p. 151.

7 Barbara Dafoe Whitehead, "The Girls of Gen-X," *The American Enterprise*, January/February 1998, pp. 54-55.

8 This is the account of Steve and Lois Krogh in a letter to me.

DISCIPLINE OF GOOD DEEDS

1 Barbara Dafoe Whitehead, "The Girls of Gen-X," *The American Enterprise*, January/February 1998, p. 55.

2 F. F. Bruce, *The Epistle to the Ephesians* (London: Pickering & Inglis, 1973), p. 52.

3 Ibid.

4 Ethel May Baldwin and David V. Benson, *Henrietta Mears and How She Did It!* (Glendale, Calif.: Gospel Light, 1966), p. 77.

5 Ibid., introductory comments by Dr. Wilbur M. Smith.

6. Elizabeth Catherwood, "Selina Hastings, Countess of Huntingdon: An English Deborah" (London: The Evangelical Library Annual Lecture, 1991).

7 Ibid., p. 19.

8 Ibid., p. 24.

9 Catherine Marshall, *Meeting God at Every Turn* (Lincoln, Va.: Chosen Books, 1980), pp. 19-20.

10 Ibid., p. 20.

11 Ibid., p. 21.

12 Sharon James, *My Heart in His Hand* (Durham, England: Evangelical Press, 1998), cover, p. 39.

13 Ibid., p. 220.

DISCIPLINE OF WITNESS

1 William Barclay, *The Master's Man* (Nashville: Abingdon, 1978), p. 41.

2 Ibid., pp. 44-46.

3 JoAnn Cairns, *Welcome Stranger, Welcome Friend* (Springfield, Mo.: Gospel Publishing House, 1988), p. 19.

4 Win Arn, *The Master's Plan for Making Disciples* (Monrovia, Calif.: Church Growth Press, 1982), p. 43.

5 "Heart for the Harvest Seminar Notebook and Study Guide" (Lutherville, Md.: Search Ministries), p. 3.

6 Ibid., p. 9.

7 C. S. Lewis, *The Weight of Glory and Other Addresses* (Grand Rapids, Mich.: Eerdmans, 1965), pp. 14-15.

DISCIPLINE OF GIVING

1 See John F. MacArthur, Jr., *Giving: God's Way* (Wheaton, Ill.: Tyndale, 1979), pp. 60-73, where the author succinctly delineates the three mandatory tithes and two types of voluntary giving in the Old Testament.

GRACE OF DISCIPLINE

1 John Blanchard, *Truth for Life* (West Sussex, England: H. E. Walter Ltd., 1982), p. 239.

GENERAL INDEX

Scripture Index